Visceral Screens

For Duncan and Isobel

Visceral Screens

Mediation and Matter
in Horror Cinema

Allan Cameron

EDINBURGH
University Press

Edinburgh University Press is one of the leading university presses in the UK. We publish academic books and journals in our selected subject areas across the humanities and social sciences, combining cutting-edge scholarship with high editorial and production values to produce academic works of lasting importance. For more information visit our website: edinburghuniversitypress.com

Edinburgh University Press Ltd
The Tun – Holyrood Road
12(2f) Jackson's Entry
Edinburgh EH8 8PJ

First published in hardback by Edinburgh University Press 2021

Typeset in Monotype Ehrhardt by
Servis Filmsetting Ltd, Stockport, Cheshire,
and printed and bound by CPI Group (UK) Ltd,
Croydon, CR0 4YY

A CIP record for this book is available from the British Library

ISBN 978 1 4744 1919 2 (hardback)
ISBN 978 1 3995 1124 7 (paperback)
ISBN 978 1 4744 1920 8 (webready PDF)
ISBN 978 1 4744 1921 5 (epub)

Contents

Illustrations

Figures

Acknowledgments

This book has been a long time in the making, and I'm grateful to all who have helped nudge it forward in ways both large and small.

First of all, I appreciate the insights, encouragement and support I've received from colleagues and students at the University of Auckland, particularly Misha Kavka, Neal Curtis, Nabeel Zuberi, Jennifer Frost, Jenny Stümer, Jennifer Kirby, Larry May and Emily Holland (whose deep engagement with horror cinema sparked many useful conversations).

The project has also been enriched by productive exchanges with conference co-panellists, research collaborators and scholarly friends. Special thanks to fellow travellers Marc Olivier, Saige Walton, Sean Cubitt, Angela Ndalianis, Kevin Fisher, Martine Beugnet and Kriss Ravetto-Biagioli.

For insightful feedback on earlier versions of specific chapters, I'm indebted to Vivian Sobchack, Kyle Kontour and Irene Lee, as well as Carol Vernallis, who continues to be a source of intellectual inspiration and energy.

Particular gratitude is due to Richard Misek, who has contributed to this project at numerous points along the way as a careful reader, incisive critic and invaluable friend.

And for their love, forbearance and support, endless thanks to my partner Bridget and my children Duncan and Isobel.

An earlier version of Chapter 2 appeared as 'Zombie Media: Transmission, Reproduction, and the Digital Dead', in *Cinema Journal*, 2012, 52; 1: 66–89.

An earlier version of Chapter 5 appeared as 'Colour, Embodiment and Dread in *High Tension* and *A Tale of Two Sisters*', in *Horror Studies*, 2012, 3; 1: 87–103.

Introduction

Bodies are horror cinema's raw material. Not only do horror films aim to excite a visceral response in their viewers; they also, more than any genre, make textual play out of the bodies of their characters, submitting them to mutations and transfigurations that run the gamut from the gory to the ghostly. Human beings are framed not only as active subjects but also as the stuff of media: *matter* on which actions and forces imprint themselves. From the spectacular incarnations of the vampire and the zombie to the aestheticised fragmentation of *giallo* and 'sensory horror', horror films often treat the physical figure as a kind of media artefact, dramatically *dis*-figuring it with distortions, interruptions, glitches and misalignments. Bodies take on the properties of media, as media themselves become 'embodied'. Horror thus renders the materiality of the body not simply as viscera, flesh and blood but also as light, vibration and surface. There is, I argue, a *mediatic imaginary* that recurs throughout various types of horror, running from the shadowy figures of silent cinema to their morphing counterparts in the digital era. These figures – projected, refracted, reflected, reprocessed – link the fate of media to the fate of bodies. Accordingly, this book explores how horror films have framed bodies *as* and *through* media.

The question of meaning is central to this metaphorical exchange, since horror frequently pushes both bodies and media to the limits of their expressive capacity. Here, the key point is not merely that such films articulate anxieties regarding specific media technologies. Rather, in this context, media technologies serve to disclose something about the body, showing how it can oscillate between subjecthood and objecthood, form and formlessness, sense and non-sense. As I will go on to argue, horror cinema parallels Jean-Luc Nancy's conceptualisation of the body as a discursive boundary, as a frontier where signification finds its limit.[1] The body is neither matter nor discourse, Nancy argues, but the point at which they meet. Horror cinema, by engaging with bodies and media as mutual metaphors, produces a reflection on this material-discursive body. It is not simply that horror threatens the mortal body, but that it renders it as a *medium* opening into alien spaces and sensations. Conducting their own anatomies of the screen, cutting into the matter of cinema, horror films revel in the breakdown of forms, patterns and figures, undermining both order and meaning.

Image-Bodies

In a photographic darkroom, an image rises out of its chemical bath: the figure of a priest, a faint but unmistakable line projecting diagonally upwards from his body. This image, with its signature blemish, carries a chilling message. Captured before the priest's death but processed subsequently, it prefigures the church steeple, struck by lightning, that will topple over and fatally skewer him. This photographic omen, one among several in *The Omen* (Richard Donner, 1976), signifies the malign power of Damien Thorne, a young boy adopted into a wealthy family who will ultimately be identified as the Devil's son. Similarly ominous prefigurations and grisly fates await others who have displeased Damien or thwarted his plans. The photographer, noticing the uncanny detail in the priest's photograph, next turns his attention to two similar images, one older and one more recent. In the first, a line traces upwards from the neck of Damien's young nanny, foreshadowing her imminent death by hanging. The final image shows the photographer himself, who, having inadvertently snapped himself in a mirror, is unnerved to see a jagged line extending across his throat. Given the premonitory pattern linking photographic flaws to mortal consequences, character and audience alike are left to wonder about his fate. The film ultimately provides an answer, as a freak accident sees an unsecured sheet of glass slip from the back of a truck and decapitate him. Although this character is not the film's protagonist, his forensic investigation serves an important role, driving forward the mystery narrative and crystallising the film's themes of fate and fatality.

What is ominous about the photographs is not simply their technological uncanniness. *The Omen*'s photographic subplot is not about the threat of media *per se*, but about what media threaten to reveal. As per Martin Heidegger's argument, technology is not, in itself, humanity's alien other. Instead, technology can be seen as a kind of 'bringing-forth', which works to reveal some fundamental 'truth'.[2] Here, what is revealed or brought forth in the photographer's darkroom is a picture of mortality and contingency, expressed in the tracing of a metaphorical line between image and body. What bodies and images bear in common is a relationship to death (which is certain and unavoidable) and to the accident (which is arbitrary

Figure 0.1 The photographer's image foreshadows his own fate in *The Omen* (Richard Donner, 1976).

and unpredictable). *The Omen*'s deadly triptych of still images concentrates both of these aspects. These are therefore not simply photographs *of* the body; in their disfigured state, demonstrating the injury that will fatally afflict their human subjects, they *are* the body. This metaphorical exchange moves between two and three dimensions. The flat, two-dimensional mark on each image transforms into a tactile threat in three-dimensional space (the steeple, the rope, the sheet of glass). At the same time, each of these deadly three-dimensional objects possesses an abstract linearity that seems to refer back to the geometry of the frame and the image's planar surface. They indicate that the body in each case is already an image. Moreover, these abstract lines and edges do not simply frame the image-body: they also penetrate it. In this way, they recall Roland Barthes' argument that photographs foreshadow the deaths of their subjects (by stilling them and by promising to outlast them),[3] but also his concept of the *punctum*, the unexpected contingent detail that leaps out of the image and 'pricks' or wounds the viewer.[4] *The Omen*'s brutal dissections produce an equivalent interleaving of images and bodies, foregrounding how both are haunted by death and contingency.

The Omen looks backwards to the nineteenth-century practice of spirit photography, and forwards to subsequent horrors in which media technologies serve as the vehicle for malevolent forces; examples include *Poltergeist* (Tobe Hooper, 1982), *Videodrome* (David Cronenberg, 1983), *Ring* (Hideo Nakata, 1998), *Sinister* (Scott Derrickson, 2012) and *Host* (Rob Savage, 2020). From haunted videotapes to glitching digital interfaces, these films explore the media-body nexus via the infrastructure of production, distribution and display. A number of them portray the screen itself as a membrane through which characters, monsters and other threats can move, either through wholesale physical traversal or transformative effects. In such films, the recurrent fantasy/nightmare of entering the screen jeopardises the integrity of the body, menacing it with analogue 'snow', digital 'glitches' or other manifestations of visual disorder. In *Ring*, for example, the spirit of a murdered girl named Sadako stalks the viewers of a haunted videotape, manifesting as a televisual image that advances in a series of glitched movements before climbing through the screen to fix her victims with a deadly stare. Sadako is thus, simultaneously, a media artefact and a concrete bodily presence. The 'video-bodies' articulated in *Ring* and other media-intensive horrors possess an ambiguous material-ity which partakes of the physical world even as it appears vulnerable to virtual dissolution and fragmentation. Bodies flicker, disappear or mutate in this context, becoming monstrous or (in their loss of voice or face) meaningless.

This entwining of bodies, media and meaning is usefully illuminated by Jean-Luc Nancy's theoretical writing on the body. Nancy is not directly concerned with mediation, but his discussion of the body invokes media metaphors, both textual and visual. Firstly, Nancy sets up the body in relation to writing, a relationship characterised by mutual foreignness: '[w]riting touches upon bodies *along the absolute limit* separating the sense of the one from the skin and nerves of the other'.[5] According to Nancy, bodies can be assigned neither to the abstraction of discourse nor the concreteness of matter. Instead, 'They take place at the limit, *qua limit:* limit-external border, the fracture and intersection of anything foreign in a continuum of sense, a continuum of matter'.[6] This interrogation of matter and meaning parallels Maurice Merleau-Ponty's phenomenologi-cal framing of the body-world relationship (in which both body and world share a common materiality),[7] but Nancy's perspective insists on a funda-mental otherness. His theorisation of the body is grounded in the notion of 'exscription', which places the body outside, but at the margin of, discourse: it is '*exscribed* in advance from all writing'; the body is 'placed *outside the text* as the most *proper* movement of its text; the text *itself* being abandoned, left at its limit'.[8] The flickering, fragmented bodies of tech-horror, poised between materiality and discourse, parallel this movement of exscription. In *Ring*, Sadako's mediatic body provides a metaphorical instantiation of this writing procedure: she is a material manifestation written into being by both technological and historical processes. At the same time, the bodies of her victims, shrinking from the menace that emerges from the televisual frame as they cower at the edge of the cin-ematic one, are also circumscribed by discourse, having been informed by telephone that they have seven days to live after watching Sadako's tape.

Nancy's metaphorical engagement with bodies encompasses not only writing but also images, via his emphasis on the fundamental *exteriority* of the body. 'It's through my skin that I touch myself', he writes. 'And I touch myself from outside, I don't touch myself from inside'.[9] Nancy rejects Husserl and Merleau-Ponty's return to a primary interiority, and ideas of the 'intimacy of the body', finding it only in the body's silences, 'when I don't sense my stomach, my heart, or my viscera'. Conversely, 'when I sense my stomach or my heart, or my lung, I sense it, and if I sense it, it's from the outside'.[10] For Nancy, this exteriority means that the body is encountered as a kind of image – not an image that represents something else, but as

> the *coming to presence*, like an image coming on a movie or a TV *screen – coming from* nowhere behind the screen, *being* the spacing of this screen, existing as its extension-exposing, laying down this areality, not as an idea given *to* my own vision as a punctual subject (and still less as a mystery), but *right at* my eyes (my body), as their areality, themselves coming into this coming, spaced, spacing, themselves a screen – less 'vision' than *video*.[11]

Through this somewhat cryptic passage, Nancy is suggesting that the body's very otherness means that it presents itself to us as if on a screen, lacking depth and interiority. For Nancy, the coming to presence of this 'areal body, this video-body, this clear-screen body' is a constantly unfolding process: 'it's a coming-and-going, a rhythm of bodies being born, dying, open, closed, delighting, touched, swerving'.[12] This process, despite its grounding in organic matter, bears much in common with the creative-technical dimensions of human culture. To experience the body is already to experience something mediated, something 'mediatic'. Nancy's metaphorical video-body thus precedes any literal engagements with technologies of recording and reproduction. It is characterised not only by sensory activity, but also by the asensory, by the body's 'silences'. Viewed from this perspective, media-intensive horror films demonstrate not so much the encounter between a 'natural' body and 'alien' technologies, but rather a reflexive illumination of the body's inherent mediations.

Lamberto Bava's schlock horror *Demons* (1985) offers a particularly literal interweaving of bodies and mediation. In the film, cinema patrons find themselves locked in an old movie theatre as a horde of zombie-like 'demons' runs riot. The plot is ultimately quite simple, concentrating primarily on the characters' attempts to outrun or dispense with the demons. However, the inception of the demons, which occurs as the film-within-the-film is being screened, is based on a complex metaphor that links together image, sound and body. The film that the characters are watching is itself a horror movie, in which a group of young people exploring an ancient tomb discover a mysterious mask. After scratching himself on the mask, one of the young people is transformed into a demon and begins killing his friends. Meanwhile, Rosemary, a cinema patron who earlier scratched herself on an identical mask (displayed in the cinema lobby as a promotional gimmick), is staring at herself in the bathroom mirror, the surface of her skin beginning to bubble. Going to check on Rosemary and finding her fully transformed, her solicitous friend Carmen is rewarded with a vicious scratch to the neck before being chased around the movie theatre. Carmen ends up behind the cinema screen as the onscreen attacks escalate, her neck wound bulging grotesquely and issuing forth green liquid. At this point, two demonic manifestations appear blended: one on the screen and one behind it, one represented and one real. As Carmen's body presses against the screen, causing it to bulge, and her anguished groans mingle with noises from the film, a young woman in the audience remarks that 'those screams sound real'. 'It's the Dolby system', her companion reassures her. As a large blade is depicted tearing through the side of a tent, menacing the onscreen characters, Carmen herself bursts violently through the cinema screen. Before the shocked audience, she undergoes an abject transformation: her hands become claws, she vomits green liquid, her tongue extends obscenely, and her teeth fall out to be replaced by fangs. 'It's happening just like in the movie', someone says.

The curious gestation of the demons generates ontological questions about the screen's relation to the body. Here, the threat emerges from behind or beyond the screen rather than within it, although there are clear connections between the onscreen bodies and their offscreen counterparts. This ontological problem occupies the characters, who try unsuccessfully to stop the demons by disabling the film projector before deciding that the building itself is responsible: 'it's not the movie', declares one character, 'it's the theatre. This theatre kills'. *Demons* might thus appear to deny the ontological link between body and image, emphasising instead the infrastructure of exhibition and unhinging Nancy's metaphor in the process: the screen remains a flat surface of display, while bodies are revealed in all of their visceral depth. Yet on closer inspection, notions of depth and interiority bear little importance here. Instead, the film treats each of its various bodily mutations as an exterior manifestation, a 'coming-to-presence' that works very much like the screen image of Nancy's analogy. Carmen's emergence through the screen delivers her demonic transformation as a spectacular performance of abjection. Close-up images of bodily liquids, lacerated flesh and emerging fangs do not pull the viewer inside the body, but instead confront them with a series of outsides. Each exterior, opened up, produces only another exterior. One surface replaces another, as the body itself becomes a kind of screen on which phenomena are projected. Tracing these phenomena back to their notional origin leads to surfaces rather than depths, as in each case (onscreen and offscreen) it is a mask, the very emblem of exteriority, that triggers the curse. Rather than separating the body and the image, *Demons* suggests that the body is already an image. The flexibility of this metaphor is further underlined in the sequel *Demons 2* (Lamberto Bava, 1986), where the monsters are not cinematic but televisual, bulging forth from the cathode-ray tube (CRT) screen as pixelated, staticky shapes before resolving into fully-fledged demons. As in the first film, this initial audiovisual manifestation prefigures the coming-to-presence that will take place as one character after another is bitten and remade as a demonic image-body.

The image-body metaphor is central to the films I will discuss in subsequent chapters, although in most of these examples the metaphor is not grounded in direct representations of media technologies. Rather, I focus on the various ways in which mediation manifests itself as a thematic and formal concern across different horror subgenres. Frequently, these films involve the dissolution of the bodily figure, a process that is not simply literal (the breaking down of skin and flesh) but also profoundly *mediatic*, as the figure is absorbed into the *mise-en-scène*, fractured by editing, dissolved into luminescence or overtaken by media noise. Paralleling Nancy's theorisation of the body, these figures of horror are characterised by disjunctures and dead zones. According to Nancy, disjuncture is not external to bodily experience and meaning, but fundamental to it. The body is defined by dislocation, displaying a 'corpus of features' that are 'foreign to each other' and are 'coming together *and* being dislocated at one and the same time'.[13] As opposed to the phenomenological insistence on the sensorium, Nancy foregrounds the notion of thresholds, asking 'aren't senses separate universes? Or else the dislocation of every possible universe?'[14] The body is constituted by these separations. Accordingly, the image-bodies of horror cinema involve encounters between sense and non-sense, sensation and numbness, order and disorder. In ways that range from the overt to the oblique, these films produce disjunctive and ambiguous image-bodies, embodying an array of media metaphors. These include the flickering present-absent image-body of the vampire, the disintegrating image-body of the zombie, the composite camera-body of the found-footage film, the flattened and delineated frame-body in the Italian *giallo*, and the unstable chromatic-bodies and desynchronised sonic-bodies in various psychological thrillers.

The Meaning of Media

Horror's dissolution and remaking of bodily forms suggests the presence of contingent events and forces, introducing elements of randomness, happenstance and, ultimately, nonmeaning. Conversely, much existing analysis of the horror genre has been concerned with questions of signification, proposing interpretations (whether psychoanalytic, allegorical, or contextual) of its most prominent monsters and narrative tropes. One might even suggest that horror provokes a critical anxiety in this regard: how to anchor, explain or try to make sense of a genre that seems, to many of its critics, to lack proper justification ('why would anyone watch *those* films?') The quest for cultural/social meaning is concentrated in a number of areas, from gender,[15] to repressed political realities,[16] national traumas,[17] historical events,[18] the ontology of monsters[19] and the nature of evil.[20] Meanwhile, interpretation of media-focused horror has tended to converge on the idea that it expresses social 'anxieties' about modernity and the rise of new technologies.

For example, Fred Botting and Catherine Spooner argue that ghost effects (from nineteenth-century magic lantern shows to contemporary digital formats) often appear as the result of encounters between old and new media: 'ghosts are traces of previous media formations and prior senses of (mediated) selfhood'.[21] Similarly, in *Haunted Media*, Jeffrey Sconce traces cultural discourses of haunting in relation to the menace and fascination of electronic media, from telegraphy to radio, and television to the internet.[22] This social framing of media technologies is also evident in a number of recent anthologies, including the edited collections *Cinematic Ghosts*[23] and *The Scary Screen*, the latter of which features a range of essays on *Ring* and its American remake *The Ring* (Gore Verbinski, 2002).[24] Similarly, in their introduction to the edited collection *Digital Horror*, Linnie Blake and Xavier Aldana Reyes suggest that many recent horror films 'offer reflections on contemporary fears, especially those regarding digital technologies themselves'.[25] A number of the essays in *Digital Horror* address threatening depictions of new media technologies, whether in relation to industrial and domestic settings, [26] communication networks,[27] military imaging[28] or surveillance.[29] For Blake and Aldana Reyes, '[t]his makes for an exceptionally anxious cinema', which expresses anxieties about digital technology's mediation of violent images, its misuse as an instrument of power and its apparent threat to human identity.[30]

Although these arguments are broadly persuasive, one should not take for granted that the sole (or even primary) significance of 'mediatic' horror lies in its articulation of generalised anxieties regarding technology. For one, technology itself should be regarded not only as an object of interpretation, but also as a mechanism for generating and interrogating meaning. Indeed, Judith Halberstam has argued that gothic fiction itself functions as a 'technology of subjectivity' which positions the bodily figure of the gothic monster in relation to multiple textual meanings (including questions of race, gender and sexuality).[31] In this polysemantic space, meaning itself becomes unstable and negotiable. Accordingly, technology-focused horror films can reflect on how meaning is constituted in the relay between matter and media. In many cases, this exploration leads not simply into hermeneutic resolution, but into the violent dissolution of meaning, expressed via the mediatisation of the human figure. Pixelation and static, optical and sonic distortions, chromatic shifts and disjunctive cuts: all of these are used to destabilise the body and its capacity for sense and expression. Through such techno-corporeal deformations, horror cinema thus renders fraught the question of signification. These evocations of bodily and technical materiality recall the place of nonmeaning within Jean-Luc Nancy's theorisation of the body. Since the body is always written 'outside', argues Nancy, it is never fully circumscribed by discourse. Interpretation finds its limit as we arrive at a threshold of 'non-sense', where the body is not coterminous with the self/subject, but instead, 'infinitely other'.[32]

Exploring this sense of otherness through the metaphorical exchange between bodies and media, the psychological horror film *Cam* (Daniel Goldhaber, 2018) depicts a protagonist who loses control over her digital representation. Under the pseudonym 'Lola_Lola', a 'cam girl' named Alice livestreams erotic online video shows from her home, which become increasingly disturbing as her clients ask her to perform violent and degrading acts. However, Alice soon finds herself locked out of her user account, which is taken over by a mysterious digital doppelgänger. Investigating further, Alice discovers other online accounts that have continued running despite the deaths of the original performers, suggesting that her own life may be at risk. Ultimately, Alice plays ingeniously with the tools of mediation in order to reclaim her identity, setting up her monitor to face a mirror so that she can interact directly and visibly onscreen with the counterfeit Lola, while challenging her to undertake increasingly extreme acts. Bashing her own face on the table and breaking her nose, Alice succeeds in having herself declared the 'real' Lola by her fans. At the moment of Alice's self-inflicted violence, the fake Lola appears to glitch in response, revealing herself to be merely an image. In the process, one might suggest that Alice has managed to pry apart her real body from the flattened, mediated one.

However, the film suggests another perspective, which has to do with the body's existence at the boundary of matter and discourse and its

Figure 0.2 Alice confronts her digital counterparts in *Cam* (Daniel Goldhaber, 2018).

nonalignment with any kind of coherent 'self'. For one, the narrative is haunted by the surplus bodies of the disappeared cam girls: continuing to perform on screen, they are categorisable neither as digital artefacts nor as material figures. Moreover, Alice's own experience of the interface involves the generation of surplus bodies, from the new identity that she creates in order to challenge her doppelgänger, to the additional figures that are produced on screen by her ingenious arrangement of the mirror and the monitor. These additional figures involve both discursive and material strategies, from the adoption of a new username and manipulation of media interfaces to the execution of self-directed violence. In the process, we are made aware of the arbitrary and tenuous aspects of any articulation of identity, as Alice's performance is channelled through the cam girl website, accumulating ratings and comments from online viewers. By the end of the film, Alice has acquired a new username and a new look, as if to underline the way that both real and virtual worlds require subjects to pull together and project an image of the self. Meanwhile, the residual image-body of Lola_Lola continues to haunt the narrative, since the cause of Alice's uncanny doubling is never revealed directly. Implicit in this unresolved mystery is the idea that the body is always already other to itself. Alice's problems in *Cam* cannot be resolved by insulating the body from technology. Rather, technology serves to disclose the threat of meaninglessness that is already, in Nancy's terms, inherent to the body.

A more visceral and perplexing treatment of the media-body metaphor is demonstrated by David Cronenberg's *Videodrome* (1983). The main character, a media entrepreneur named Max Renn, takes an interest in a satellite channel featuring sadomasochistic violence, but soon begins to experience hallucinations associated with the broadcast signal, several of which involve outlandish physical exchanges between bodies and media. In one of these exchanges, Max inserts himself headfirst into a swollen television screen that bears the image of a woman's lips. In another, he experiences the insertion of a pulsating, fleshy-looking videotape into a hole of distinctly vaginal appearance that has opened up in his abdomen. Absorbed fully into this fleshly world of media representations and technologies, Max ultimately witnesses his own televised suicide, accomplished with an organically-mutated handgun following his cryptic declaration 'long live the new flesh'. After the television explodes, sending forth chunks of what appear to be human body parts, the 'real', extra-televisual Max repeats the same declaration and fatal act. Despite the film's ostensible emphasis on dematerialised signals and hallucinatory visions, scenes like this one emphasise bodily materiality. Moreover, Brian O'Blivion, the McLuhanesque figure who is involved with the development of the 'Videodrome' signal and who only ever appears as a televisual image, explains that the hallucinations are grounded in a brain tumour caused by the signal. As Caetlin Benson-Allott argues, the film refuses to treat technology independently of the human: '*Videodrome* foregrounds the flesh as the site of our interactions with technology, the material that is transformed by those exchanges'.[33] At the same time, Benson-Allott insists on a reading of the film that situates its 'meaning' in relation to technological anxieties. She focuses in particular on how the still relatively new home video format seems to threaten various boundaries within the film: psychic, domestic and even (given the film's Canadian provenance and setting) national.

However, the very interleaving of bodies and technologies in *Videodrome* also suggests other possible readings, based not on the idea of technology as an external threat but as something connected more fundamentally with human bodies and experiences. Indeed, the film plays on the ambiguous nature of these connections by actively blurring the causal connections between humans and technology, making technology appear organic and human matter artificial. As Steven Shaviro puts it, Max is 'transformed into a human video machine'.[34] Video technology in this film 'reaches directly into the unseen depths, stimulating the ganglia and the viscera, caressing and remoulding the interior volume of the body', as illustrated by the grotesque techno-organic transformations Max undergoes.[35] At the same time, Max's own body is involved in the process of remaking technology. Having inserted a handgun into his abdomen-wound, Max later retrieves it as a part-metal part-flesh extrusion connected to his hand. Moreover, the film blends images and bodies by refusing to clearly demarcate fantasy from actuality and represented figures from embodied ones. William Beard notes that a number of characters are encountered primarily as images: this is how we are first introduced to Nicki Brand, the radio host who enters into a sexual relationship with Max before once again disappearing into the world of mediation; and it accounts entirely for the presence of Brian O'Blivion. Just as 'video and actuality become impossible to tell apart', images and bodies in *Videodrome* are interchangeable.[36] As in *Demons 2*, these bodies provide an electronic 'coming to presence' that reflects on the body itself as a kind of image – one characterised by an inherent sense of otherness.

Videodrome, through this ontological commingling of images and bodies, reflects on the question of meaning. The story involves various kinds of breakdown: of narrative, as the plot becomes increasingly confused and ends abruptly with the protagonist's suicide; of the self, as Max's identity is hijacked by the Videodrome signal; and of the image-body, as it oscillates between televisual and non-televisual manifestations. When Max eventually points the flesh-gun at his head, the tearing apart of bodies and meaning reaches its ultimate expression, something that is underlined by Max's repetition of the phrase 'long live the new flesh'. Does this declaration signal Max's transformation into a post-human form? Does it signal the death of human consciousness in the face of brute materiality? Is the 'new flesh' electronic, organic or machinic? Of course, these questions are not to be resolved definitively. Rather, the undermining of meaning is precisely the point. The televisual world of images and the lived world of sensory experience are no longer separable, as the image-body metaphor collapses on itself. The body is figured as a site of raw materiality but also of discourse. The discursive address of the body incorporates not only Max's declaration but also Brian O'Blivion's stern pronouncements regarding the Videodrome signal and its bodily manifestations, and Nicki Brand's televisual exhortations for Max to enter the screen. Yet all of these pronouncements lead not towards a clear articulation of bodily meaning; rather, they become woven into the perplexing aggregation of flesh, metal and media represented in Max's final moments. To an even greater degree than *Cam*, Cronenberg's film illustrates Nancy's argument regarding the body, namely that it extends beyond discursive boundaries, including those delimiting the concept of the self, thus becoming 'infinitely other'.[37] Whereas phenomenology (with its emphasis on the shared 'flesh' of the world and the lived body) tends to privilege subjectivity, Nancy makes the objecthood of the body primary: 'corpus *is never properly me*. It's always an "object," a body objected precisely *against the claim of being a body-subject*, or a subject-in-a-body'.[38] Without denying subjective experience, he places it within an objective frame. 'Bodies are first and always other – just as others are first and always bodies'.[39] *Videodrome* works towards a similar insight, reminding us of the fundamental otherness of bodies – our own and everyone else's.

Anatomies of the Screen

In staging a metaphorical exchange between bodies and media, horror cinema blurs the boundary between subjects and objects. On the one hand, horror films speak to the senses, invoking subjective experiences of terror, pain and disgust. On the other, they invoke senselessness, understood not only as semiotic disorder but also as affective deadness. Via scenes of death, torture or transformation, horror films can pose the question of what it might feel like to be an object, to be a thing, whether by passing into a mortal state or sloughing off human consciousness. This suspension of the body between subject and object aligns with Nancy's discussion of mortality. For Nancy, death is already integral to the body; the body carries deadness and alterity within it. 'In the span of its lifetime,' he writes, 'the body is also a dead body, the body of a dead person, this dead person I am when alive. Dead or alive, neither dead nor alive, I *am* the opening, the tomb or the mouth, the one inside the other'.[40] Horror film often plays imaginatively with this in-between state, not only by representing figures of ghostliness or living death, but also by showing characters moving between activity and passivity, agency and victimhood, subjecthood and objecthood. In horror, the body is, above all, *intermediate*. This relay or hesitation has further parallels in debates regarding subject-object relations in phenomenology on the one hand, and what has been called 'speculative realism' or 'object-oriented-ontology', on the other.

In Vivian Sobchack's phenomenological account (which builds on the work of Merleau-Ponty), subjective and objective dimensions are entwined in the relationship between film and viewer. For Sobchack, the film itself has a 'body', consisting of the cinematic apparatus in its entirety – the *dispositif*, as it were. Not reducible to the human body, the film's body nonetheless parallels ours, in the sense that it is, in Sobchack's terms, 'a *subjective object*. It is an intentional instrument able to perceive and express perception, to have sense and make sense'.[41] For Sobchack, both the viewer and the film embody an intentional relationship to the world, in which perceptions are taken up by a perceiving subject. Horror, I argue, provides a fruitful (and fraught) experiential-conceptual frame for engaging with the 'semiotic phenomenology' advanced by Sobchack. In a very direct way, horror addresses questions of the subjective and objective,

of the perceptive and the expressive. Delving further into filmic materiality, Jennifer Barker has expanded upon Sobchack's work, suggesting more
specific bodily analogies between the spectator's body and the 'body' of
the film as technology and apparatus.[42] These analogies encompass skin
(embodied in cinema's concern with surfaces and textures), musculature
(in its capacity to produce empathetic or mimetic reactions) and viscera
(in its underlying technical base – which remains virtually invisible until it
malfunctions, or is made to malfunction).[43]

Yet the horror film also challenges phenomenology's insistence on
intentionality and sense. The threat of disorder and nonmeaning, of
dismemberment and disarticulation, haunt the more benign framings of
the subject–object exchange described by Sobchack and Barker. Horror
engages not only with the subject's perceptual–sensory experiences of the
world but also, repeatedly, with the narrative negation of such experiences
via depictions of mortality. The viewer is thus confronted with bodies
on the way to becoming senseless. By working to represent such mortal
phenomena via formal means, horror often plays with the disordering
or dislocation of the senses, rendering sound and image indecipherable or
incommensurable. Moreover, in witnessing scenes of extreme violence and
physical disintegration, we may recoil in horror, but we are also reminded
of the sensory threshold: the pain we don't feel, the disfigurement or
maiming that afflicts the characters but not us. Thus, whereas Sobchack
emphasises the potential for films to speak to all of our senses – and for
adjacent senses to be stimulated synaesthetically, or, in her own clever
turn of phrase, 'cinesthetically' – horror also demonstrates a delinking
or desyncing of the senses, producing a numbing effect and undermining
notions of subjective experience.

Meaning itself is implicated in this process. To understand this point,
we can return to the dual sense of 'sense' indicated by Sobchack, which
hinges both on sensation ('having sense') and interpretation ('making
sense').[44] As Sobchack puts it, phenomenological description 'demands
that we consider the embodied and enworlded subject as always already
immersed in meaning, both supported and constrained by the inherited
"fortune" of language'.[45] Meaning is thus immanent to lived bodily experience, inflected by the contingencies of existence and illness. 'I am conscious of the world', writes Merleau-Ponty, 'through the medium of my
body'.[46] In its exploration of bodies in states of disorder and death, horror
uses both narrative and formal devices to explore the body as medium,
and to test the boundaries of its capacity for having and making sense.
Jennifer Barker claims that 'If the film has a body, it must also have body
language'.[47] But the 'language' in question here appears more partial and

prone to breakdown than this statement suggests. The fragmented narratives and unmotivated violence prevalent in many horror films gesture
towards a collapse of meaning and order. In many cases, we witness deaths
that are not ascribed any particular meaning beyond their shock value
– as evoked by the term 'senseless violence'. In others, we see nonhuman agents (including inanimate objects and alien beings) taking over as
primary actors, eclipsing human meaning with asubjective matter.

Here, a useful counter perspective is suggested by the broad philosophical movement that has been referred to, variously, as speculative realism
or object-oriented ontology. As Ian Bogost summarises it, object-oriented
ontology (or OOO) 'puts *things* at the centre of being. We humans are elements, but not the sole elements, of philosophical interest.'[48] For theorists
pursuing this approach, correlationism, or the idea 'that being exists only
as a correlate between mind and world', must be emphatically rejected.[49]
Phenomenology, with its emphasis on the 'givenness' of experience and
the centrality of the human subject, is found guilty on this count. As
Steven Shaviro puts it,

> We habitually grasp the world in terms of our own preimposed concepts. We need
> to break this habit in order to get at the *strangeness* of things in the world – that is, at
> the ways that they exist without being 'posited' by us and without being 'given' to or
> 'manifested' by us. Even the things that we have made ourselves possess their own
> bizarre and independent existence.[50]

From this perspective, it would seem that horror films, with their (often
dispassionate) foregrounding of human finitude and the agency of objects,
point towards a radically external perspective on the human, from the
malevolent plants and animals of eco-horror to the fatal possibilities of
everyday objects in the *Final Destination* series (2000-2011). In such cases,
horror produces a deframing of the human species, presenting us with a
world of objects and processes that is indifferent to us. Of course, horror
films are made by and for humans, addressing us with affects and concepts
that are oriented around our own subjective concerns. Yet by pushing
at the frontiers of human bodies, situations and experiences, these films
can stage an imaginative leap beyond the bounds of the phenomenal.
Addressing themselves very directly towards embodied experience, they
nonetheless insist, to varying degrees, on the objective finitude of human
consciousness and existence.

I therefore suggest that horror cinema stages a *de facto* encounter between phenomenology and speculative realism, by overlaying
human-centred narrative concerns and affective structures with non-
anthropocentric perspectives. Indeed, horror points towards elements of

commonality between these two philosophical movements, in particular, their commitment to overcoming the rigid boundary between subjective and objective. It is at and across this boundary that horror gains its energy, rendering subjects as objects and objects as subjects. Humans are pulled both reluctantly and ecstatically beyond their subjecthood, while the world of objects takes on a heightened sense of agency. The question of mediation is central to this oscillation between the subjective and the objective. Media are an instrument of human activity, a means by which we imprint our expressions on the world of objects. Yet considering media as metaphorical bodies repositions them as the site of a fundamental passivity: to be a medium is to receive an imprint, to be the vehicle for an alien force or expression.

Writing about the 'anthropotechnical' figure of Frankenstein's monster in fiction and film, Shane Denson has suggested a similar kind of composite view. He proposes reconciling Sobchack's 'notion that film has a lived body' with the 'alien phenomenology' advanced by Bogost.[51] This approach involves setting the intentionality of phenomenology within a broader ontological frame, leaving space for the extra-phenomenal. 'Would it be possible', speculates Denson, '. . . to imaginatively feel our way into profoundly different, non-anthropomorphic filmic bodies and to describe their difference from our own being, that is, their specific positions between objective framings and subjective framers of material experience?'[52] Here, the intersubjectivity shared by film and spectator is shaped too by a corresponding interobjectivity, which constitutes both as objects or processes. Horror, I argue, is the genre that most directly takes up this philosophical project, overlaying our intersubjective experience of spectatorship with a reflexive articulation of the nonhuman.

As Dylan Trigg has proposed, horror invokes not only an encounter with materiality or organic life; it also 'marks the point at which language falls into an inchoate abyss, while at all times straddling the line between the body as it presents itself in the phenomenal world and the reality that not only resists description but also destroys the subject'.[53] Horror cinema, moving backwards and forwards across the frontier between subjectivity and objectivity, between the intentionality of phenomenology and the nonhuman indifference of the universe, toys with the collapse of language and meaning. This is demonstrated not only in the dispassionate eviscerations of 'body horror'. It also inflects the horror genre more generally, via its articulation of matter and form. This articulation includes the deformation of conventional narrative structures, the disintegration of bodies in zombie and vampire films, the mobilisation of nonhuman perspectives in found-footage cinema, and the use of formal elements (such as editing, colour and sound) to perform reflexive manipulations of bodies and sensory experience. All of these processes suggest the unsettling presence of the nonhuman within the human, rendering the body as a medium in which meaning itself is always provisional and uncertain.

This *intermediate* position recalls Jean-Luc Nancy's framing of the body as produced at the boundary between matter and discourse. Nancy acknowledges that our orientation is towards signification: 'we're *organised* for this'. However, our existence involves 'an infinitely finite suspending of this organisation, a fragile, fractal, exposition of its anatomy'. This anatomy is not that of the clinical dissection; rather, it is one 'of configurations, of the plasticity of what we'd have to call states of body, ways of being, bearing, breathings, paces, staggerings, sufferings, pleasures, coats, windings, brushings, masses'. These various configurations of the body do not always resolve into unities of sense. The body, instead, is defined by its tendency to come apart, to reveal the seams of matter and signification. As Nancy puts it, '[t]here is nothing to decipher in a body – except for the fact that the body's cipher is the body itself, not ciphered, just extended'.[54] Horror cinema works reflexively in this domain. It produces 'anatomies of the screen', paring apart both the human body and the cinematic *dispositif*, and interrogating their capacity for meaning-making when pushed to their existential limits. While some films deal with mediation very directly by featuring recording and broadcasting technologies as part of the story, others display a kind of indirect or latent reflexivity via the formal workings of editing, colour and sound design. The theme of mediation is thus broader than the direct consideration of media *per se*. In the subsequent chapters, I outline how the body is rendered 'mediatic', and how horror film plays across the threshold between meaning and nonmeaning, sensation and deadness, figure and ground.

In Chapter 1, I focus on the cinematic vampire's special relationship to light, reflecting on how it flickers between illumination and obscurity, presence and absence, and the transmission and dissolution of signs. Chapter 2 examines the phenomenon of 'zombie media', in which spectacular scenes of death, decay and dismemberment are accompanied by the incidental traces of mediation, including film grain, distortion, and digital pixelation, thus linking the breakdown of bodies, images, and meaning. Chapter 3 is concerned with the reflexive treatment of the frame as the phenomenological and epistemological boundary in found-footage horror, where events are 'captured' by cameras within the film's own narrative world, thus generating new articulations of the body as both a dislocated figure and an opening out into (uncertain) spaces. Chapter 4 looks at the 'matter of the cut' in Italian *giallo* films, where a concern with visual fragmentation and aestheticisation links bodies and images in a mutual grammar of violence. Chapter 5 explores how horror films have used colour's mobility and semiotic instability to both produce and undermine structures of meaning, modulating shifts between atmospheric and graphic horror, psychological anxiety and visceral embodiment. Finally, Chapter 6 examines films that dwell reflexively on sound-image relations, arguing that their experimentation with synchronisation undermines synaesthetic assumptions and invites us to think of both bodies and media as fundamentally fractured. In sum, the book posits a *mediatic imaginary* that recurs throughout various types of horror. The mediatic imaginary frames bodies and media as mutual metaphors, and then goes on to explore the back-and-forth between light and skin, noise and viscera, figure and frame, sense and non-sense.

Notes

1. Nancy, *Corpus*.
2. Heidegger, 'The question concerning technology', p. 12.
3. Barthes, *Camera Lucida: Reflections on Photography*, p. 93. As Barthes puts it, 'at the end of this first death, my own death is inscribed; between the two, nothing more than waiting'.
4. Ibid. p. 27.
5. Nancy, *Corpus*, p. 11.
6. Ibid. p. 17.
7. Merleau-Ponty, *Phenomenology of Perception*. Central to Merleau-Ponty's project is overcoming the subject-object dichotomy: should we think of the self as one or the other? He argues that we must overcome this split. 'The body is our general medium for having a world'. The senses, although separate, provide 'means of access to one and the same *world*', confirming its unity via sensory equivalence and analogy.
8. Nancy, *Corpus*, p. 11.
9. Ibid. p. 128.
10. Ibid. p. 129.
11. Ibid. p. 63–5.
12. Ibid. p. 65.
13. Ibid. p. 31.
14. Ibid. p. 31.
15. Creed, *The Monstrous-Feminine: Film, Feminism, Psychoanalysis*; Clover, *Men, Women, and Chain Saws: Gender in the Modern Horror Film*.
16. See, for example Robin Wood's chapter on American horror of the 1970s in *Hollywood from Vietnam to Reagan*. Wood reads certain key films as emblematic of the 'return of the repressed', emblematising the failings of American institutions from the nuclear family to the military-industrial complex.

17. See, for example, Lowenstein, *Shocking Representation: Historical Trauma, National Cinema, and the Modern Horror Film*; Blake, *The Wounds of Nations: Horror Cinema, Historical Trauma and National Identity*.

18. See, in particular, Hantke, ed., *American Horror Film: The Genre at the Turn of the Millennium*; Briefel and Miller, eds., *Horror after 9/11 World of Fear, Cinema of Terror*.

19. Carroll, *The Philosophy of Horror, or Paradoxes of the Heart*.

20. Freeland, *The Naked and the Undead: Evil and the Appeal of Horror*.

21. Botting and Spooner, *Monstrous Media/Spectral Subjects: Imaging Gothic from the Nineteenth Century to the Present*, p. 6.

22. Sconce, *Haunted Media: Electronic Presence from Telegraphy to Television*, pp. 8–9.

23. Leeder, ed., *Cinematic Ghosts: Haunting and Spectrality from Silent Cinema to the Digital Era*.

24. Lacefield, ed., *The Scary Screen: Media Anxiety in The Ring*.

25. Blake and Aldana Reyes, 'Introduction: horror in the digital age', p. 3.

26. Hantke, 'Network anxiety: prefiguring digital anxieties in the American horror film'.

27. Kirk, 'Networked spectrality: *In Memorium, Pulse* and beyond'.

28. Monnet, 'Night vision in the contemporary horror film'.

29. Christensen, 'Uncanny cameras and network subjects'.

30. Blake and Aldana Reyes, p. 3.

31. Halberstam, *Skin Shows: Gothic Horror and the Technology of Monsters*.

32. Nancy, *Corpus*, p. 13.

33. Benson-Allott, *Killer Tapes and Shattered Screens: Video Spectatorship from VHS to File Sharing*, p. 95.

34. Shaviro, *The Cinematic Body*, p. 138.

35. Ibid. p. 141.

36. Beard, *The Artist as Monster: The Cinema of David Cronenberg*, p. 158.

37. Nancy, *Corpus*, p. 13.

38. Ibid. p. 29.

39. Ibid. p. 29.

40. Ibid. p. 15.

41. Sobchack, *The Address of the Eye: A Phenomenology of Film Experience*, pp. 247–48.

42. Barker, *The Tactile Eye: Touch and the Cinematic Experience*.

43. Although Barker's book is not dedicated to horror *per se*, she does, in her section on skin, reflect on film's capacity to explore physical boundaries and evoke contamination, presenting the skin as a membrane of exchange between inside and outside.

44. Sobchack, *The Address of the Eye*, p. 44.

45. Ibid. p. 44.

46. Merleau-Ponty, *Phenomenology of Perception*, pp. 94–5.

47. Barker, *The Tactile Eye*, p. 69.

48. Bogost, *Alien Phenomenology, or, What It's Like to Be a Thing*, p. 6.
49. Ibid. p. 4.
50. Shaviro, *The Universe of Things: On Speculative Realism*, pp. 66–7.
51. Denson, *Postnaturalism: Frankenstein, Film, and the Anthropotechnical Interface*, p. 298.
52. Ibid. p. 298.
53. Trigg, *The Thing: A Phenomenology of Horror*, Chapter 1.
54. Nancy, *Corpus*, p. 47.

CHAPTER 1
Vampire Optics:
Projection, Diffusion, Contact

The vampire is a figure defined by light. One of horror cinema's most sharply delineated, iconographic monsters and, at the same time, a protean being that assumes multiple forms, it both avoids illumination and attracts it, inhabits shadows and also projects them, flaunts hard-lit contours and dissolves into mist. Questions of the vampire's physical and metaphysical form are often expressed in optical terms, from reflection and refraction to diffusion and dissolution. This is evident in Bram Stoker's 1897 novel *Dracula*, when Jonathan Harker, upon being introduced to the titular character, observes a 'strange optical effect': a flame is visible through Dracula's semi-transparent body.[1] In *Dracula* and other popular texts, the vampire's ability to evade detection and compress physical distances often appears as a trick of the light. These optical properties, moreover, parallel the vampire's social and technical mobility. Emerging from the penumbral past of a fantasised Eastern culture, the Dracula of Stoker's novel finds a home within the bright modern city, infiltrating London's transport systems and communication networks. He shimmers between dark and light, ancient and modern. Cinema, as a medium of illumination, has been ideally placed to take up these optical themes, articulating a kind of vampiric flickering that moves not only between light and shadow, but also visibility and invisibility, presence and absence, knowledge and concealment, information and signal.

This is not to suggest, however, that the cinematic vampire is a purely optical phantom. Indeed, its well-established taste for blood reveals a visceral, corporeal dimension. Rather, the vampire oscillates between vision and touch, the optical and the haptic. Its power is vested in spectacle as well as physical force, the look as well as the bite. The vampire can manifest as a spectral or fleshly being, or both at once. Motifs of optical fluctuation therefore serve to index its ontological instability. However, this instability poses its own challenge: any investigation of this horror subgenre must reckon with the immense variability of the vampire, its refusal to abide by consistent rules and traits. Is vampirism a spiritual condition or a disease? Are vampires fatally vulnerable to light? Will they be dispatched by garlic and crosses? Are they our enemies, our friends or our lovers? The answer in each case seems to be 'that depends'. As Nina Auerbach puts it, 'There is no such creature as 'The Vampire'; there are only vampires'.[2] My argument therefore depends on a flexible conception of the vampire, which reveals a set of aesthetic and ontological patterns that recur across the subgenre. In charting these patterns, I do not aim to construct a cohesive history of vampire cinema, or to suggest that my argument applies equally to all vampire films. Yet while recognising inconsistency as a key property of the subgenre, I argue that two significant filaments connect the earliest vampire films with the most recent.

The first of these is the emphasis on *codes*. What makes the vampire distinctive as a horror monster is the sheer concentration of signs and rules that attend it, determining what can kill the vampire and what gives it energy, how it travels and how it hunts, how it secretes itself and how it infiltrates the home. The vampiric or vampirised body may be inscribed by spiritual codes (involving crosses and holy water) or, in much contemporary cinema, by genetic codes (involving viral mutation and transmission). Vampire fiction is thus centrally concerned with signification and its relationship to the body. The second connecting filament, as I have already suggested, is to do with *light*, emphasising the optical properties of vampire bodies and environments. Here, I use the term optics in its broadest sense, to refer to the science of light, encompassing phenomena of projection, reflection, refraction and diffusion. My focus on optics is therefore not exclusively confined to light as directed at or through the human eye, but rather emphasises mediation, including all the ways in which light is channelled and controlled. Screen vampires are commonly associated with cinematographic effects: from overexposure to underexposure, desaturation to chromatic excess, and superimposition to shallow depth of field. At the same time, vampire films are overtly concerned with ocular power, as the vampire's gaze often commands spaces and bodies at a distance, exerting a force that is not simply optical but also haptic. Light (reflected, refracted, perceived and virtual) is thus central to the subgenre's articulation of meaning, mediation and embodiment.

Vampire Projections

The idea of the cinematic vampire as an optical monster is foreshadowed in the most influential literary text: Stoker's *Dracula*. Media occupy a central role within the book, from the interpolated chain of diary entries, reports and newspaper stories that together constitute the narrative, to the recording of testimony on wax cylinders and the use of a typewriter to transcribe all of these recordings and texts. Conspicuous by its omission from Dracula's list of then-modern media technologies is cinema. However, by incorporating numerous references to optical effects, Stoker's novel sets the scene for cinema's staging of mediated light. As mentioned earlier, Dracula's body initially appears to be translucent. Later in the novel, Mina Harker spies Dracula preparing to feed on her friend Lucy. At first he appears to have 'great eyes like burning flames', but this is instantly revealed to be an optical illusion: 'The red sunlight was shining on the windows of St. Mary's Church behind our seat, and as the sun dipped there was just sufficient change in the refraction and reflection to make it appear as if the light moved'.[3] As Dracula infiltrates Mina's bedroom later in the novel, she sees him as two red lights shining through thick mist. In all of these examples, the optical mediation of light produces the vampire's uncanny ontology: he is a spectral presence that can project himself into rooms like a beam of light, but also possesses physical weight and force, as evidenced by the toll he takes on his victims. Mediation here takes place not through specific technologies, but through the interaction between light and the vampire's body, as well as various features of the natural and built environment (mist, glass, fabric, and so forth).

The vampire's forceful gaze is linked to these effects – he is able to project his vision across distances and physical barriers, and to project himself into various spaces (he is extraordinarily mobile, moving across urban London with apparent ease even though no one seems to witness his transit). In this way, vampire optics involves the exertion of the vampire's power through projections of light and shadow. It is thus perhaps unsurprising that early examples of the vampire on film would unite optics and ontics.[4] F. W. Murnau's 1922 film *Nosferatu* is undoubtedly the cinematic urtext in this regard. This unauthorised adaptation of Stoker's *Dracula* introduces a number of media-specific qualities to the vampire: the sinister Count Orlok can move at inhuman speed (conveyed through undercranked footage), his horses and carriage are presented at one point via negative images, and his death by sunlight is depicted via a double exposure, his body and being fading out as dawn bursts through the window behind him. Famously, Murnau's film introduced the convention that sunlight could kill vampires, something that had not been part of vampire lore until that point.[5] Thus, in the early days of narrative cinema, vampires, light and technology are tied together. In one of the film's most memorable scenes, Orlok's shadow creeps up the wall of a stairwell and advances across the bed where the film's heroine is sleeping. As Stacey

Figure 1.1 The vampire's fatal encounter with light is depicted via double exposure in *Nosferatu* (F.W. Murnau, 1922).

Abbott argues, this can be seen as a cinematic metaphor, with the bed and nightdress together functioning as a screen onto which the vampire's shadow is projected.[6] Additionally, there is a carnal aspect to this projection, as 'Orlok's shadow has both spectral and physical form'.[7] His victim reacts violently when he clenches his shadowy fist, as if he has grasped her heart. Yet Orlok, with his pale face constituting a further screen-like surface, is not solely a figure of darkness. He embodies both light and shadow at once. It is these hesitations – between light and dark, spectral and fleshly – that distinguish the vampire from other media monsters.

As Abbott's analysis indicates, the vampire exhibits an intimate connection with the cinema as a technological apparatus. Indeed, Jeffrey Weinstock goes so far as to assert that 'vampire films are always about the cinema itself'.[8] On the one hand, he points out, the cinematic vampire is a 'celluloid entity', manifested via special effects, editing, and other cinematic techniques and technologies; on the other, cinema itself 'must be conceived of as a vampiric creation',[9] given its stilling and reanimation of bodies, as well as the centrality of darkness:

> Like a vampire, the camera 'drains the life' out of the persons and objects represented, consigning them to an uncanny limbo zone between life and death – film

creates legions of the undead that morph and transform before our eyes. Like a
vampire, film shuns the light and only manifests in darkness.[10]

Dependent on light, cinema is also, like the vampire, devised and domi-
ciled in the dark.

As Stacey Abbott points out, the cinematic treatment of vampires has
transformed over the decades following *Nosferatu*'s release. Abbott argues
that vampires have consistently reflected new advances in film technologies and techniques – from the optical effects of *Nosferatu*, to the rich
and colourful *mise-en-scène* of Hammer Studios' mid-century films, to
the sophisticated practical effects of 1980s vampire films and the digital
interventions of the *Blade* and *Underworld* franchises. In the process, and
in tandem with changing cultural contexts (such as the turn towards realistic depictions of violence in film, and the emergent 'body culture' of
the 1970s and 1980s), the vampire loses its spectral qualities, becoming
a creature of flesh and bone (or perhaps latex): 'a physical, rather than
spectral, being'.[11] Subsequently, according to Abbott, the vampire goes on
to regain some spectrality in its digital incarnations, as CGI 'releases the
vampire from the confines of the body and into the virtual'.[12] In films like
Van Helsing (Stephen Sommers, 2004), *30 Days of Night* (David Slade,
2007) and *Dracula Untold* (Gary Shore, 2014), the vampire's body undergoes new transformations: these vampires can dissolve into a flurry of bats,
or perform outlandish facial distortions. In *Blade* (Stephen Norrington,
1998) and *30 Days of Night*, vampire bodies exposed to the light do not
simply fade, flame or explode, but flake away into pixelated fragments. To
chart these ontological transitions more schematically, we might say that
vampires start out as cinematographic monsters, are subsequently defined
by the material accoutrements of *mise-en-scène* (props, performance and
prosthetics) and then finally become digital.

Illuminating as it is, Abbott's account tends to produce a rather linear
and technologically determinist narrative of vampire cinema. It also overlooks the residual power of optical metaphors, which reappear throughout
the subgenre's history. In some cases, the ongoing link with cinematic
optics is made quite explicit, as in Francis Ford Coppola's *Dracula* (1992),
which stages an encounter between Mina Harker and Count Dracula
against the backdrop of an early projection of the Lumière brothers'
films in London. As Jeffrey Weinstock points out, in this case Dracula
himself seems to coincide with the arrival of film technology.[13] *Shadow
of the Vampire* (E. Elias Merhige, 2000) extends this self-reflexive notion
by reimagining Max Schreck, the star of Murnau's *Nosferatu*, as a real
vampire. Vampire and film alike are presented as 'an uncanny creation of

shadow and light that can only survive in the dark. Each is the uncanny projection of the other'.[14] At the end of the film, the celluloid itself, overwhelmed by light, goes up in flames just like its metaphorical double.

Understanding the vampire film's ongoing invocation of optical effects, however, entails going beyond the cinematic. That is, one must avoid yoking the vampire too tightly to a linear technological history. The fleshy vampires that superseded *Nosferatu* may have been less conspicuously spectral, but have commonly been presented, nonetheless, via an expressionist aesthetic involving the play of light and shadow, with the optical interventions of gauze and fog. The aesthetics of projection, diffusion, reflection and refraction in vampire films are not exclusively to do with invoking specific film technologies, whether state-of-the-art or obsolete. Rather, the subgenre's characteristic projections of light onto fog, gauze or glass produce images of mediation that both invoke and exceed the cinematic. In this sense, the vampire is properly understood as a *paracinematic* monster, which haunts not only screens but also a host of other mediating surfaces, whether reflective, refractive or diffusive.

One such surface is, of course, the mirror. Notably, Stoker's Dracula lacks a reflection, a convention of vampire optics that reappears in numerous novels and films, including Werner Herzog's 1979 remake of *Nosferatu*, in which Isabelle Adjani stares in shock at her own lonely mirror image as Klaus Kinski's shadow and finally his body enter the frame without their accompanying reflection. Here, one might suggest that the vampire, already functioning as a kind of media image (capable of dissolution, transmission and rematerialisation) has no need for mirrors. Yet vampire films are perhaps more notable for their inconsistency around rules than their adherence to them. Many films ignore the convention regarding mirrors. Timur Bekmambetov's *Night Watch* (2004) makes creative use of the convention by inverting it: in one key scene, the vampires are *only* visible via optical mediation. The main character, a vampire hunter named Anton, fights two vampires that have become invisible. The special glasses that allow him to see them have been knocked off, so he needs to look in a mirror to see the vampires and coordinate his response. The fight thus takes place simultaneously in two worlds: a haptic world (in which the vampires are encountered through touch and kinetic movement) and an optical world (in which the vampires appear as reflections). Although *Night Watch* does not link the vampire to cinematic or televisual technologies, it nonetheless associates vampires with principles of mediation. In this context, mediation both separates and splices vision and touch, the optical and the haptic.

Vampire cinema's recurring images of projected shadows, nonreflecting mirrors and so forth are thus not solely cinematic metaphors. Rather, they capture a more generalised consciousness of mediated light. These examples all involve a projective logic, which renders both bodies and environments unstable. The body seems volatile and mutable, capable of dematerialising and rematerialising like an image, while spatial settings are transformed into zones of projection and optical permeability. Rather than a unified sensorium, the paracinematic, vampiric body points towards an interleaving of separate senses, which is always haunted with the possibility of discontinuity and disarticulation.

Vampire Time

The vampire's projective logic in relation to bodies is temporally ambiguous. On the one hand, light is associated with instantaneity, presence, communication, transmission. In *Interview with the Vampire: The Vampire Chronicles* (Neil Jordan, 1994), the vampire Louis is capable of getting up, turning off the light switch and returning to his seat with such speed that his human interlocutor cannot perceive the movement. Physical alacrity is thus aligned with electricity and the control of illumination. The cartoon TV show *Spongebob Squarepants* makes light of this convention, when Spongebob and his friends, distracted by a mysterious flickering effect, realise that Max Schreck's Orlok (in a brief cutaway of doctored footage from Murnau's film) is standing in the doorway, flipping the switch off and on.

On the other hand, the dislocation between spaces, shadows and reflections also suggests that light has somehow been diverted or delayed. In this sense, light is latency: the reflection or shadow fails to appear in the appropriate place at the appropriate time. In Carl Theodor Dreyer's *Vampyr* (1932), the protagonist witnesses a number of projected shadows moving around separately from their bodies – they resemble memory-images of past actions. For Jeffrey Weinstock, these figures 'reveal the nature of cinema itself – detached shadows that dance across the screen cast only by the camera which has drained the life out of referents, preserving their essence in an uncanny state that is not life and is not death'.[15] Francis Ford Coppola, in his 1992 version of *Dracula*, quotes Dreyer's film by dislocating Dracula's shadow from his body in one scene, and having it carry out a series of asynchronous movements. In this case, the split between Dracula and his shadow is not spatial (it still attends him) but temporal (it is out of phase with his body). The shadow plays out an anterior or future (or perhaps virtual) chain of actions. Like cinema itself, it involves the delaying and recasting of light and shade. Yet not all representations of optical latency are specifically cinematic. In *Near Dark* (Kathryn Bigelow, 1987), starlight becomes the basis for a reflective moment for Mae, the sympathetic vampire who 'turns' the protagonist towards vampirism. She muses that 'I'll still be here when the light from that star gets down here to Earth in a billion years', thus providing an optical measure of the protracted *durée* of vampires' temporal experience.

The split temporality of the vampire caught between past and present, latency and immediacy, highlights its complex relationship to modernity. For Stacey Abbott, cinematic vampires should be viewed as fundamentally modern: although they are often depicted as atavistic shadows of the past emerging from their alpine lairs, their mutability, speed and disruptive influence mark them out not as archaic throwbacks but as embodiments of modern communication, travel and media.[16] This parallels Fred Botting's account of modernity's gothic resonances: '[i]t is as if the uncanny disturbances, spectres and ghosts that once were limited as effects of gothic fictions extend, via other media, into the fabric and shadowy formation of modern life, a kind of "phantomodernity"'.[17] Vampires and other gothic tropes are thus associated with the variability and uncertainty of modern life. Stoker's novel, Botting argues, presents patriarchal tradition and morality as lines of defence against the vampire, 'in a novel full of the machines and media of urban modernity'.[18] Such arguments are broadly persuasive. However, to render the vampire solely as a symptom of modernity would be to neglect its bipartite temporal provenance. It is not simply that the vampire embodies the shock of the new; at the same time, it harbours within it the atavistic and ancient.

Vampire films often express this idea by counterposing different media formats in order to show the vampire's dislocated temporal position. Both *Only Lovers Left Alive* (Jim Jarmusch, 2013) and *A Girl Walks Home Alone at Night* (Ana Lily Amirpour, 2014) feature vampires listening to vinyl records, a gesture which marks them both as engaged with the past and up-to-date with the contemporary vinyl renaissance. This temporal variability is captured by Jeffrey Weinstock's observation that the vampire is partly defined by its relation to various technologies, from the archaic (stakes and crosses) to the modern (resistant viruses and light-based weapons).[19] Sometimes, vampires are associated with arcane objects, like the mysterious artifact in *Cronos* (Guillermo del Toro, 1993), and Eli's collection of antique puzzle toys in *Let the Right One In* (Tomas Alfredson, 2008). Such objects suggest not simply that vampires are 'modern', but that they produce a temporal disjuncture within the modern, in which present and past coincide.

This temporal split is particularly evident in the subgenre's periodic return to black-and-white images. These not only serve as a 'pure' expression of shadow and light, thus concentrating the thematic treatment of optics, but have also been used, particularly since the 1960s, to connote pastness. In George Romero's *Martin* (1977), a number of brief black-and-white sequences place the vampire protagonist inside an ornate fantasy of old-world vampirism, while the rest of the film uses dull colours to depict the banality and harshness of his present-day existence (in this world, the vampire has no special powers but is instead an introverted sociopath who uses razor blades rather than fangs to extract blood).[20] Michael Almereyda's *Nadja* (1994) also uses black and white to position the vampire between past and present. Nadja, an Eastern European émigré resident in New York City, is defined both by her vampiric heritage and her contemporary urban identity. The opening scene links her immediately with the optical, superimposing city lights over a close-up of her face as she walks through New York at night. A hooded, enigmatic figure stalking a monochrome city, she seems to occupy two spaces and times at once. In certain scenes, the footage becomes grainy and indistinct, having been filmed with the Fisher and Price 'Pixelvision', a toy camera that records low-resolution images onto standard audiotapes. These degraded images suggest both the overwhelming buzz of the modern and the arcane mystery of the ancient.

Black-and-white footage is also central to Abel Ferrara's *The Addiction* (1995), in which the vampire, a postgraduate student who has been converted to vampirism, is a thoroughly contemporary figure, but also finds herself burdened with notions of guilt linked to the collective memory of genocide (via references to the Holocaust and the My Lai Massacre). Here, the lack of colour seems to dislocate the vampire in time, folding together the past and the present. More recently, black and white has been used to evoke both modern detachment and vampiric tradition in the stylised Iranian-American film *A Girl Walks Home Alone at Night* (2013), which, like the two previous examples, features a young female vampire as protagonist. These monochromatic vampires are both present and absent, immediate and delayed, modern and ancient. They index a specific type of ontological in-betweenness. Viewed from this perspective, the vampire *flickers*. It is both spatially and temporally unstable: a body that questions the integrity and permanence of bodies.

A more explicit articulation of temporal disjuncture is offered by Guy Maddin's monochromatic *Dracula: Pages from a Virgin's Diary* (2002). Based around the Winnipeg ballet's performance of *Dracula*, this film makes extensive use of outdated technologies and techniques in its restaging of Bram Stoker's narrative. Deploying an array of optical effects, Maddin integrates the story into his own broader aesthetic project, which involves recycling aspects of early cinema, particularly Soviet montage and German expressionism. The materiality of old media is made visible in various ways, including harsh shadows, film grain, high contrast and the diffuse light associated with old film stock and lenses. In another gesture to early cinema, the footage is tinted, so that Dracula's very presence seems able to alter the film's chromatic profile. At the narrative level, the film also produces a complex relation between past and present, cleaving closely to Stoker's original story while reframing the meaning of the vampire for a new political moment. Here, Dracula is played by an actor of Chinese ethnicity, and the Crew of Light's campaign to exterminate Dracula is framed as a xenophobic crusade, unlike the righteous quest depicted in the novel. Meanwhile, the use of intertitles, grainy footage and a host of silent film tropes renders the film's temporal moment uncertain. The film is at once resolutely up to date – a twenty-first-century pastiche, charged with contemporary political resonances – and also completely out of time. Here, the vampire is not simply a beacon of modernity. He rises up from past technologies and representations. And he does so via light. At certain points, Dracula is pure silhouette, as when he appears as a bat-shadow that flits above Lucy's bed. At others, he seems charged with luminous power, appearing as the beam of the local lighthouse sweeps Lucy's window-lined bedroom with a wash of light. Fully embracing the optical aspects of the vampire, Maddin saturates the film with motifs of projection, reflection, refraction and diffusion. Here, vampire optics are a thoroughly analogue phenomenon, emerging out of the grain and fog of old media.

Vampire Codes

The flickering ambiguity of the vampire's own body (between living and dead, material and immaterial, light and shadow) parallels its ambiguous relationship to meaning. One of the most ontologically unstable of monsters, it is also hermeneutically unstable. Judith Halberstam has argued that 'monsters are meaning machines', capable of generating interpretations and embodying 'any horrible trait that the reader feeds into the narrative'.[21] This seems particularly true of the vampire. For Ken Gelder, the vampire hosts a diversity of interpretations, but revolves in particular around one key aspect – its essential queerness.[22] In Richard Dyer's account, vampires' skin marks them out as figures of excessive whiteness, associated with colonialism's deadly legacy: they haunt Western culture with its own lethal qualities.[23] Meanwhile, Halberstam notes the vampire's links with anti-Semitic imagery.[24] Dracula is therefore capable of generating multiple interpretations: he 'can be read as aristocrat, a symbol of the masses; he is predator and yet feminine, he is consumer and producer, he is parasite and host, he is homosexual and heterosexual, he is even a lesbian'.[25] Combining signifiers of racial, sexual and gendered otherness, the vampire thus represents 'otherness itself'.[26]

In the case of the vampire, skin and blood serve as magnets for interpretation. Skin, in particular, is readily textualised. As Steven Connor observes, the rending of the skin in horror shapes not only affect but also signification, producing 'a condition in which the skin is no longer primarily a membrane of separation, but a medium of connection or greatly intensified semiotic permeability, of codes, signs, images, forms, desires'.[27] For Halberstam, skin can be seen as 'a kind of metonym for the human; and its colour, its pallor, its shape mean everything within a semiotic of monstrosity'.[28] Dracula's 'too pale' skin, for example, is an index of his alienness. For Jennifer Wicke, skin in vampire fiction works like the ground of a photographic image: 'the alembic contamination of vampire blood produces the "image" of vampirism as a red mark on white skin'.[29] This emblematic image, repeated again and again in vampire cinema, of the punctured skin and/or the trickle of blood suggests this idea of the body as an image or a text to be read.

Blood, meanwhile, is freighted with religious and genetic significance, serving not only as the 'ink' that 'writes' on skin but also as a carrier of hidden codes. The significance of these codes, as Stacey Abbott notes, extends from mystical and Christian resonances in earlier examples (whether as menstrual blood, lifeblood or the Holy Communion) to 'the potential of modern genetics and the mysteries of DNA'.[30] In contemporary vampire films, vampirism tends to function like a blood-borne virus that circulates, rather than a spiritual affliction. This accords with what Weinstock terms the 'clichéd' image of altered vampire blood viewed through a microscope in films like *Rabid* (David Cronenberg, 1977) and *Blade*. Although Weinstock reads such scenes as signalling that the vampire has become 'the offspring of modern technology',[31] one could also view them as uniting blood and optics. This trope is repeated in Tony Scott's *The Hunger* (1983) and in Claire Denis' *Trouble Every Day* (2001), where the characters turn themselves into vampires by submitting themselves to scientific experiments. Here, the 'puzzle' of vampirism is hidden in the blood, and the characters struggle to assign causality and meaning to it. At the thematic level, multiple sanguinary readings are possible: blood can stand in for other substances and systems of circulation, from milk and semen to immigration and capitalism.[32] Blood, like skin, is rich with semiotic potential.

Meanwhile, popular vampire texts seem to perform their own mid-level interpretative work: no other monster seems quite as overlaid with arcane symbols and rules (crosses, garlic, the invitation to enter, the stake through the heart, the aversion to light), but these rules are constantly up for renegotiation, as vampires transform from foe to friend and back again. These different interpretations do not cancel each other out but instead cast the vampire as a polyvalent text, capable of sustaining multiple readings. In hermeneutic terms, the 'optics' of the vampire are multiperspectival, a composite of different meanings that reveals the monster's capacity to 'transform the fragments of otherness into one body'.[33] Yet this fluid quality of the vampire, its semantic receptiveness, can arguably destabilise the notion of meaning itself.

Linking the vampire to Jacques Lacan's concept of the Real, Slavoj Žižek argues that vampires are resistant to signification. Whereas the subject's entry into the symbolic order is heralded by the mirror stage (in which one recognises oneself as a social subject), the vampire, lacking a reflection, belongs outside of the Symbolic.[34] It is thus not confined by human systems of meaning. Žižek writes: '[t]he analysis that focuses on the "ideological meaning" of monsters overlooks the fact that, before signifying something, before serving as a vessel of meaning, monsters embody enjoyment qua the limit of interpretation, that is to say, *nonmeaning as such*'.[35] Here, the vampire's peculiar (nonreflective) optical qualities indicate its place outside the frame of sense and order. Halberstam dismisses Žižek's account, however, insisting on the meaningfulness of the vampire and rejecting the very notion of nonmeaning, arguing that it 'is only possible in a structural universe in which form and content can easily be separated . . . Monstrosity always unites monstrous form with monstrous meaning'.[36] Yet in the case of the vampire, the unstable relationship between form and content is a defining feature, I would argue. Many vampire tales hinge on conceptions of a bodily spirit that can be decanted and reinfused, and of the skin as a membrane and container. Slippages between body and shadow, figure and fog, human and animal suggest a notional separation of form and content, even if such a separation is not sustained. The vampire manifests as an ontological puzzle with no easy solution.

Furthermore, nonmeaning enters the frame from another angle if the vampire is considered in the light of technical mediation. For media theorist Friedrich Kittler, Bram Stoker's Dracula 'survives under technological conditions'.[37] Kittler makes note of the novel's format, which presents us with collated media fragments (news reports, sound recordings and diary entries) that are converted into a typewritten transcription by the character Mina Harker. According to Kittler, rather than merely defending against Dracula, this system of bureaucratic recording is itself a type of technical vampirism, which reduces discourse to mere information.[38] In Kittler's words, Dracula in Stoker's novel 'has become nothing more than the stochastic noise of the information channels'.[39] As Thomas Elsaesser puts it, for Kittler 'Dracula stands for the eternal repetition of mechanical inscription, which has entered the Western world with the typewriter, the gramophone/phonograph, and the cinema'.[40] The vampire emerges via communication technologies and thus represents the threat of discourse, the threat of messages reduced to information.[41] Indeed, for Kittler, in Stoker's novel, blood itself is data: when Dracula forces Mina to drink from his breast, it signals 'nothing more than a flow of information'.[42] From this perspective, the vampire's monstrosity is tied not to a specific cultural representation, but to the very threat of asignification. Although Stoker's novel lacks a direct engagement with cinema, Kittler's reading suggests a paracinematic dimension, as he isolates the moment in which Harker sees a trio of female vampires materialise as 'phantom shapes' from within a dusty beam of moonlight. Here, projected light works as a vehicle for the contingent, the random and the disordered: '[i]t is not without reason that vampires arise before Harker's eyes from motes of dust in the moonlight, in other words, as Brownian molecular movements'.[43] The metaphor here is, of course, optical: in this beam of light Harker observes a chaotic movement that represents media's tendency towards entropy and nonmeaning.

Vampire Lenses

A body made of light: in the figure of the vampire, questions of optics and materiality, and hence mediation, are concentrated. The vampire's relationship to mediation raises in turn the spectre of contingency, since media, by their nature, play host to chance occurrences, errors and interruptions. The vampire's hesitation between meaning and nonmeaning is thus replicated optically. Light is symbolically overcoded – it is associated with knowledge, with power and moral judgement, via the notion of enlightenment.[44] Yet light is also, as Sean Cubitt observes, associated with contingency. The oscillation between control and contingency, he argues, is a feature of the history of light's technological mediation:

> The effervescent superfluity of light is one of the entropic instances to which we seek to bring order . . . The genealogy of visual technologies traces a historical dialectic between the urge to control, even to fascistic excess, and the constant reemergence

of entropy in the interstices of devices designed to curtail and command the excess of light.[45]

Cubitt charts the progression in the ordering of space and light, from the 'projective geometries of Alberti and Mercator'[46] to the 'arithmatic and probabilistic' ordering of light associated with printing, telegraphy, TV and digital media.[47] Within this dialectic of chaos and control, '[t]he risk of meaninglessness haunts mediation' – the imposition of new systems of ordering and technologisation can disrupt systems of meaning.[48] The figure of the vampire encapsulates this struggle between order and excess. Vampire optics involves the focusing and channelling of light (and establishes parallel regimes of order based around ocular power), but it also involves refraction, diffusion and filtering. The vampire, I argue, embodies both aspects of projection: a geometry of the gaze, in which power and intentionality are sent forth along precise vectors; and a more diffuse logic of contact and unpredictability.

On the one hand, the projective logic of the vampire offers a geometrical spatial order constructed around a directional beam, invoking power, intentionality and knowledge. Indeed, ordered optical relations in vampire narratives are often connected with ocular power, as force is applied via the vampire's gaze. In the Hammer classic *Horror of Dracula* (Terence Fisher,

Figure 1.2 The vampire's gaze, charged with optical power, in *A Girl Walks Home Alone at Night* (Ana Lily Amirpour, 2014).

1959), deep focus aesthetics are used to map out the geometry of Dracula's power. His look acts at a distance upon his victims. Christopher Lee's dominating persona does not even require him to move in order to exert his control. At key moments, he stands still, like a dark shape cut out of the *mise-en-scène*. Meanwhile, the frequent close-ups on his eyes underline the notion that knowledge and power are channelled through his gaze. Stacey Abbott notes the way that vampire narratives, from nineteenth-century novel to twentieth-century cinema, have drawn upon longstanding super-stitions regarding the 'evil eye' and the power of the gaze. Accordingly, '[t]he close-up upon the face or eyes of vampires as they stare at their victims has become a staple convention of most vampire films, used to emphasise both their power over their victims and their desire for blood'.[49] In *A Girl Walks Home Alone at Night*, one scene in particular exemplifies the projective logic of vampire optics, as well as the centrality of the gaze. As the film's antagonist, a local small-time thug, sits in his car, he is unnerved to see the vampire reflected in his rearview mirror. Her abrupt appearance and disappearance from view makes her resemble an optical effect. The mediating role of glass is highlighted not just by the mirror but by the distinctive lens-shaped rear side window of the car. In this scene, the mediation and spatial organisation of the vampire's gaze establishes it as an expression of power. The look is as important as the bite.

On the other hand, in contrast to this emphasis on clarity and direc-tionality, the vampire's optical connotations include diffusion. As per Sean Cubitt's argument, the projection of light involves contingency. 'Projection', he writes, 'concerns the complexity of our relations with the world, the relations Kant described in terms of contingency, the subjec-tion of human will to natural laws, as opposed to the freedom in which human will transcends physics'.[50] Projection entails the scattering of light and the interaction with surfaces; it is shaped by material encounters, and is not determined solely by human will or intention. Vampire films often underline this sense of projection, moving beyond the willed extension of the gaze, and evoking uncertain relations of touch and proximity. In certain vampire films, light takes on a hazy, tactile quality, filtered (as in Stoker's novel) through fog, gauzy curtains or other elements of the *mise-en-scène*, or mediated by the materiality of the cinematic apparatus itself, through the use of shallow focus, grainy film stock or optical filters. Carl Theodor Dreyer's *Vampyr* is an early example of this: his use of gauze over the lens imbues the imagery with a ghostly, spectral quality. The char-acters and spaces of the film seem often to be receding to another plane of existence. The film's murky plot has the main character, Allan Gray, witnessing two sisters fall prey to a vampire's curse. Rather than adhering strongly to vampire lore, the film relies instead on atmospheric imagery. As mentioned earlier, in one scene Gray witnesses autonomous shadows going about their work, apparently uncoupled from physical bodies but also from a clear narrative explanation. Later in the film, Gray finds himself incarcerated in a coffin, his view mediated by a small pane of glass inset into the lid. These evocative images of projection and mediation are accompanied by the film image's marked optical diffusion. This diffusion apparently extends to the dreamlike narrative itself, as its contours become increasingly vague (in this context, it seems entirely appropriate that the film's villain is ultimately suffocated by flour).

Diffusive vampire aesthetics are not restricted to such works of elevated abstraction. They can also be found, in a much pulpier form, in Jess Franco's 1971 exploitation film *Vampyros Lesbos*. On the surface, this film would appear to be much less about light. It features none of the aesthetics of expressionist cinema: dark shadows are in short supply, and the story mainly takes place against a sunny Mediterranean backdrop, where the vampires are not at all afraid of light but, in the case of the main vampire Countess Carmody, actually go sunbathing. Uniting the aesthetics of erotica with those of vampire cinema, *Vampyros Lesbos* abounds with motifs of optical mediation, from the shimmering image of a scorpion scuttling across the bottom of a swimming pool, to recurrent shots of blood trickling down a glass door, to gauzy garments and curtains. The emphasis is on refraction, reflection and diffusion. These surfaces make light tactile and sensuous. At the same time, Franco's excessive aesthetic involves the deliberate overuse of zoom lenses: these not only produce depth of field effects by rendering some planes out of focus, but they also create a wholesale flattening and softening of the vampire's environment. The setting sun is thus rendered as a hazy pink abstraction, and objects and characters occupy an unstable plane between resolution and dissolution. Franco's extraordinary, almost experimental use of light and colour recasts the threat of vampirism as a pleasurable, erotic phenomenon, which brings bodies and spaces into tactile proximity with the assistance of optical effects.

In both their languid displays of soft light and their elliptical, half-formed narratives, *Vampyr* and *Vampyros Lesbos* provide precarious grounds for meaning. Here, vampirism is less a clearly delineated, rule-based affliction than an aesthetic phenomenon. In this context, the meaning of the vampire as part of a generic sign-system becomes unclear. Narratives and images alike are rendered hazy, dreamlike, ephemeral, arbitrary. Like the swirling motes described by Kittler, and like Cubitt's 'effervescent superfluity of light',[51] these films pursue contingency as a structural and visual principle, relinquishing clarity of signification in favour of sensation and texture.

Vampire Haptics

This casting of projections as contingent draws together vampire optics and vampire haptics. Rather than emphasising control from a distance, this perspective foregrounds touch and proximity: 'contingency' in the sense of contact, as well as the sense of coincidence and chance. Vampire optics, in this context, involve the relationship between light and skin. Roland Barthes, writing about photography, makes the link between light, the gaze, and epidermal contact: 'A sort of umbilical cord links the body of the photographed thing to my gaze: light, though impalpable, is here a carnal medium, a skin I share with anyone who has been photographed'.[52] Steven Connor argues that this perspective takes photography beyond associations with ghostly immateriality: 'Far from spectralising the world, putting it at a distance, the photograph is the modern embodiment of the contiguity between looking and grasping'.[53]

I suggest that vampire films often pick up on this connection, turning light into tactility. Light in vampire films can indeed function as a carnal medium. This is the case not only when the vampire is explicitly coded as an optical being (as in *Nosferatu*). In his *Village Voice* review of *The Lost Boys* (Joel Schumaker, 1987), David Edelstein comments that '[c]inematographer Michael Chapman . . . overlights [Kiefer] Sutherland, drowning him in harsh pools of white, and he leaves some of the images cottony, murky, deliberately out-of-focus'.[54] Applied to the vampires' faces, this aesthetic of diffusion serves also as an aesthetic of skin, linking the optical directly to the haptic. The 'cottony' texture of the image, in other words, lends it a sense of tactile intimacy. This effect can also be found in *Let the Right One In* (Tomas Alfredson, 2008), in which a young boy named Oskar befriends Eli, a vampire who appears to be of his own age. Here, the extensive use of shallow focus suggests Oskar's limited, foreshortened perspective on the world (in keeping with the fact that it is a coming of age film), but also renders light tactile. Like the snow that blankets Oskar's Stockholm neighbourhood, the film's blurry backdrops provide a soft sensory ground that presses in around the characters. The film makes much of windows as the entryway for vampires, and links them both with touch and with optical diffusion, as when Oscar, as if reaching out to Eli, raises his hand to touch the fogged-up glass of his bedroom window. Light and touch are thus mediated by glass, and by the associated figure of the vampire. Such scenes also suggest a somewhat ambiguous relationship with the notion of ocular power. Whereas vampires are often able to project themselves crisply into distant spaces and command others with their eyes, they may also in some cases manifest their influence more diffusely, as a fuzzy optical presence.

The movement between the geometry of the gaze and the contingent diffusion of light invokes the haptic on two fronts. On the one hand, the vampire, through the projected power of the gaze, is often able to act upon its victims at a distance. On the other, the contingent confusion of the defocused image suggests a tactile intimacy that overwhelms the visual, imposing the fuzzy optics of the bite. Vampire films often move between these two modes. In a key scene in *Horror of Dracula*, the crisply delineated image of Christopher Lee's vampire as beacon of knowledge and sexual intent produces an immediate effect on the young woman who is to be his next victim. After he has climbed the stairs and entered her bedroom, where she succumbs to this projected force (with a mixture of fear and desire), diffusion takes over. As he moves in for the bite, there is a brief moment, viewed from her perspective, where he appears out of focus. The geometry of the gaze thus gives way to the blur of proximity, where optics become haptics.

In this way, the push and pull of vampire optics mediates between distance and proximity. The cinematic image may appear to hold things at one remove, but it can also seize characters and viewers alike with a profound bodily force. The ambiguity of this visual regime recalls phenomenologically-oriented perspectives on vision, according to which, as Jennifer Barker puts it, 'perception always involves the coexistence of distance and proximity'.[55] Similarly, Steven Connor, drawing on Maurice Merleau-Ponty, argues that '[s]eeing is not merely a fixing and grasping, it is also a sort of reaching, touching, bringing and palpation'.[56] This oscillation between the distant and the proximate also recalls Laura Marks's distinction between 'optical visuality' and 'haptic visuality': the latter approach, which Marks identifies as particularly prominent in experimental film and video, emphasises surface and texture rather than depth and form.[57] In vampire cinema, this kind of aesthetic play with light and texture can parallel the logic of the monster itself: the vampire is at once an apparition, apt to disappear and reappear like a phantasmagorical projection, and also a body that can come close to ours and extract a painful toll. Both vampires and images are thus defined by a kind of contingent physicality. As Barker points out, the word 'contingency' captures both the chance emergence of images and their capacity to touch the viewer, two qualities that are reflected in Roland Barthes' concept of the punctum.[58] In Barthes' terms, the 'punctum' is the chance detail in a photographic image that produces an abrupt effect on the viewer: 'A photograph's *punctum* is that accident which pricks me (but also bruises me, is poignant *to* me)'.[59] The vampire film mirrors this dynamic by literalising the punctum: the vampire is a projected figure that emerges to literally puncture the skin. The observer is bitten by the image.

In this dynamic optical-haptic interplay, the conception of skin is central. Is skin a textual surface, a medium for inscription and significa- tion? Is it an interface, a medium of transmission? Or does the vampire film suggest, in the play of light and surface, something else? Steven Connor, in his book on the cultural history of skin, looks at some of the governing metaphors that have shaped our conception of it, charting a progression from skin as 'screen' or 'membrane' towards skin as 'milieu'.[60] Connor lingers at length on philosopher Michel Serres's framing of the pellicle, not as a 'surface, membrane or interface' but as 'an entire environ- ment'.[61] Serres (as translated by Connor) writes: 'Through the skin, the world and the body touch, defining their common border. Contingency means mutual touching: world and body meet and caress in the skin'.[62] Following Serres' argument, Connor declares that 'the skin is the ground for every figure'.[63] Similarly, Jennifer Barker uses the concept of skin to refer to film's tangible contact with the viewer, which occurs, as per Barthes' argument on photography, via the capacity of images to 'touch' viewers both emotionally and physically.[64] Horror films in general have a heightened engagement with this kind of contact: they tend to aim directly at producing bodily affect for spectators, and are populated with numerous scenes of pellicular engagement. Indeed, Connor notes the way that contemporary horror films often involve moments in which 'the frail containing envelope of the skin is torn, dissolved, melted and lacerated'.[65] Zombie, splatter and 'body horror' films, with their frequent rending of skin and flesh, are perhaps the best examples of this tendency.

The vampire film, however, tends to hesitate at this threshold. Although there are numerous examples of vampires undergoing gory or fiery dissolution – from Christopher Lee's incineration in *Horror of Dracula* to the bloody eviscerations in *30 Days of Night* – the skin remains, in most vampire films, as a notional boundary, an envelope as well as an environment. In films from *Nosferatu* to *Near Dark* and *Dracula* to *Twilight* (Catherine Hardwicke, 2008), the image of the punctured yet otherwise intact pellicular surface retains its signifying power. Moreover, the iconic presence of the vampire is associated with its qualities as a dis- tinct *visual figure*, standing out from the background, in many cases with the assistance of chiaroscuro lighting effects. In this instance, the skin serves as envelope: demarcating the boundaries of the figure and convey- ing a sense of semiotic coherence. Transformations of this body – whether dissolving into shadow or overexposure, bats or pixels – are commonly reversible effects. There is thus an unmaking and remaking of the figure, an oscillation between wholeness and disarticulation. Just as the vampire film pits sharpness against defocus and distance against proximity, it also suggests a movement between figure and formlessness, flesh and fog, skin as envelope and skin as environment.

Furthermore, as my earlier discussion indicates, the vampire takes on the role not only of projected image but also, in its embodiment of skin-surfaces, of a type of screen. Just as the optical bears haptic implications, via the contingent contact described by Roland Barthes, physical surfaces in the vampire film tend to become optical. As Steven Connor points out, skin in general has optical connotations: 'cosmetics, theology and aesthetic theory cohere in this quasi-conviction of the power of the skin to produce and give out its own light'.[66] Accordingly, vampire skin is often defined by lighting effects: from the excess of light on Kiefer Sutherland's skin in *The Lost Boys*, to the lights overlaying the protagonist's face in *Nadja*'s opening sequence, to the sparkling of the vampires in *Twilight* (notwithstanding exceptions like *Blacula* (William Crain, 1972) and *Blade* (Stephen Norrington, 1998), skin in vampire films is predominantly, and often excessively, white). In *Daughters of Darkness* (Harry Kümel, 1971), the vampiric Countess Bathory sports a silvery dress that, in conjunction with a star filter placed over the camera's lens, turns her into a spangled, shimmering figure of light. Observing a similar phenomenon, Martine Beugnet crystallises the cinematicity of the vampire, observing that vampire films that focus on sensation and surface unite bodies and media. For example, in Olivier Assayas's films *Irma Vep* (1996) and *Demonlover* (2002), the characters' skin-tight outfits 'cling to their bodies like a film as they slip through the window into the night; "becoming-vampire" is also "becoming-image", "becoming-film"'.[67] The vampire's skin thus serves as a materialisation of the screen-surface and/or image-surface.

Tony Scott's *The Hunger* (1983) provides an example of the vampire film's various engagements with skin as screen, threshold and milieu. The opening sequence, which takes place in a gloomy nightclub, is a veritable essay on light and surfaces. Strobing lights illuminate the blackness in abrupt bursts, revealing edges and contours fleetingly. Caged behind a wire grid, the goth band Bauhaus perform their song 'Bela Lugosi's Dead', the vocalist's pallid face contrasting with the black of his leather jacket, which he lifts and stretches into silhouetted, wing-like shapes. Meanwhile, two stylish vampires (played by Catherine Deneuve and David Bowie) overlook the scene; the deep black lenses of their sunglasses, shown in extreme close-up, mirror points of flashing illumination. In one memo-rable moment, a young woman in a leather jacket strikes a pose against a pale wall in a wash of light: she thus resembles an image projected against a screen. We are invited to compare how light interacts with different surfaces: white and black, absorptive and reflective. Bowie and Deneuve's elegant figures represent the vampire as screen-image, reflecting light with their skins and their shades. Later in the film, it becomes clear that maintaining one's skin and one's screen-image are coextensive. When Bowie's character falls ill and begins to waste away, it is the state of his skin that indexes his deterioration. Riven with folds and creases, it loses its projective, screen-like quality. Meanwhile, the film is filled with visual effects that privilege surfaces and thresholds, as if literalising Connor's notion of skin, not simply as screen or text, but also as environment. Tony Scott's deployment of music video aesthetics involves a ceaseless exploration of optical diffusion, beaming light through smoke, windows, and gauzy curtains. In *The Hunger*'s erotic imaginary, the skin touches and is touched by light; it is both physically and conceptually enmeshed in relations of projection, reflection, diffusion and touch.

In its capacity for reflecting light, the skin can be seen as producing a kind of secondary gaze. Steven Connor argues that the luminosity of skin connects it to the ocular:

> The lustre or glow of flesh implies and approximates to the eye, the moistest and most lustrous part of the outward appearance of a terrestrial creature. And perhaps the living glow or shine of the skin is fascinating partly because it has eyes for us, because it is all eyes.[68]

The skin looks back at us. Vampire films, particularly by concentrating on excessively white skin, suggest just such an idea. The power of the vampire's look is vested not only in its eyes but also its luminous skin. This pellicular 'look' is charged, moreover, with metaphysical associations: the secondhand illumination of the vampire, its capacity to project skin-light without sunlight, parallels its usurpation of godly knowledge and power. The vampire, in other words, is a celestial *body*, overlooking life and death with an authority that contends with the Almighty's. This secondary gaze also, once again, binds together looking and touching: it affords the possibility of seeing with the skin and touching with the eyes.

This notion is literalised in Mario Bava's 1960 film *Mask of Satan (Black Sunday)*. Skin and sight are concentrated in the film's play with light and shadow, rendered in sharply contrasting black and white, and also in its plot, involving issues of appearance and identity. Here, Barbara Steele plays two roles: Katia, a fresh-faced and innocent young lady of the manor, and Asa, her malevolent ancestor, a vampiric witch who returns from the dead. The vampire herself presents an uncanny concentration of light and dark and, as Silver and Ursini note, Bava makes use of 'sophisti-cated optical devices' to show her return to life.[69] Asa's execution, depicted at the start of the film, involves a mask backed with long spikes, hammered into her face. Her pale skin is therefore pocked with large holes. However, when she returns (inadvertently revived by the blood of a feckless noble-man), we see the black voids of her eye sockets gradually becoming occu-pied as two gummy eyeballs rise to the surface. On the one hand, she seems to represent a kind of anti-vision – a face filled with black holes. On the other, the appearance of the eyeballs out of darkness suggests a kind of generalised vision, located in the face's shadowy hollows *and* its pale pellicle. This pock-marked visage is thus, to mirror Connor's comment on the luminosity of skin, all eyes.

Vampire Spaces

I have argued that the vampire is connected to light through metaphors of projection, which reflect its fluctuations between meaning and nonmean-ing, control and contingency, vision and touch. It is thus defined onto-logically by the conceptual relay between optics and haptics. This unique ontology can be further understood by considering how it is connected to mediated light not only metaphorically but also metonymically, in particu-lar through the spaces it characteristically occupies. The vampire tends to project itself outwards, into its environment. It is therefore an expres-sionistic monster – not only because its most significant early cinematic exemplar, Murnau's *Nosferatu,* is a landmark work of German expression-ism, but also because the vampire's signature settings (sepulchral, penum-bral, decaying, obscure) typically suggest a kind of sinister psychological projection. Accordingly, these settings are generally shaped by light and its absence. Even in films where the vampire itself appears primarily as an embodied, physical presence rather than an optical artefact, it is com-monly associated with expressionistic lighting effects. In *The Lost Boys,* for instance, light itself takes on a heavy, almost tactile sense of presence, as clouds of blue-lit fog become architectural features. Although the vam-pires in this film are unambiguously material figures, their environment is one defined by optical mediation. Exaggerated lighting effects invest key locations such as the local amusement park and video store with equal measures of menace and appeal.

Of course, one might argue that the vampire's habitat, whether showily illuminated or shadowy, is merely a generic convention. The vampire's relationship with space, however, is dynamic and equivocal in a way quite different from that of other cinematic monsters. Firstly, vampires have an ambiguous relationship with their characteristic spaces. They generally require a home base of some sort but are not tethered to a single locale. Vampires can colonise spaces (as in Stoker's novel, where Dracula establishes a base at Carfax Abbey), or can bring their spaces with them (in the form of coffins, most notably, but also sea vessels and even automobiles). They retire and return again and again, in a relay between familiar and unfamiliar locations. Secondly, the vampire's relationship to space is defined by thresholds, most obviously windows and doorways. These thresholds are governed by specific rules. For example, there is the convention that a vampire must be invited into one's home in order to enter, and that once granted, such an invitation cannot be revoked. A symbolic utterance (the invitation itself) is thus accorded material weight. In other cases, the vampire's admission requires no such authorisation. Like light itself, the vampire can often project itself across liminal boundaries, even if they appear closed or blocked. Here, doorways and windows serve not as definitive barriers but as medial zones, registering the vampire's infiltration of the domestic space. Yet as *Nosferatu* and countless other films illustrate, the window can also threaten the vampire by allowing in the destructive force of daylight.

These architectural thresholds parallel other kinds of thresholds, in particular bodily thresholds (defined by the skin as boundary) and mediatic thresholds (defined by screens, lenses and mirrors and their capacity to admit or refuse light). In this sense, the metonymic aspects of vampire spaces are projected back into the realm of metaphor. In Kathryn Bigelow's *Near Dark*, for example, the vampires are hiding out in a motel when they become involved in a shootout with police. The police gunshots pierce holes in the walls, letting in beams of intense light. Here, the metaphors are both cinematic and pellicular. That is to say, the dark space of the room becomes a space of optical projection, like a camera obscura or a cinema, but also, in its vulnerability to penetration, serves as a metaphor for the vampires' bodies, which burn under direct sunlight.[70] Skin and environment, in an elaboration of Steven Connor's argument, become coextensive.

In horror-comedy *Fright Night* (Tom Holland, 1985), media metaphors take on a central role in framing the vampire. At the beginning of the film, the main character Charley watches old gothic movies on a TV set which sits adjacent to his bedroom window. Soon after, he gets his visual introduction to a real vampire when, using binoculars to look through the very same window, he spies one preying on a woman in a house across the street. The vampire imaginary thus enters Charley's home through the twin portals of the window and the TV screen. *Fright Night* flaunts various kinds of mediatised boundary-crossing, as Charley enlists onscreen vampire hunter Peter Vincent to help him defeat a real vampire. Vincent himself is a B-movie star who has found a second life, as it were, in the world of late-night television reruns. Meanwhile, the characters' awareness of vampire lore is all conspicuously drawn from popular media. Via the mediatic threshold of the television screen, the vampiric infiltrates Charley's world. Appropriately, the film's vampiric villain bursts through a pane of stained glass during the climactic scene. In this way, physical thresholds in vampire cinema often become ontological thresholds: an opening which normally admits only light now admits bodies.

Working in an entirely different mode, Jonathan Glazer's *Under the Skin* (2013) suggests a related perspective on vampire spaces and ontology. Although it is not conspicuously a vampire film, it is centrally concerned with light, skin and the draining of bodies. The main character is a pallid alien figure wearing bright red lipstick who drives around Glasgow, picking up men and extracting their blood and viscera via an obscure process. Entering her flat, each victim follows her into a dark, mysterious space in which light itself appears swallowed up. They step out onto a vast black floor, which resembles a hard surface, but turns out to be liquid. Descending beneath the surface, the men's bodies are abruptly eviscerated, becoming floating twists of skin. This vampiric space is defined by its curious relationship to light. Light, it seems, is absorbed or cancelled out in this overwhelming darkness, yet the floor nonetheless gleams, evoking both a skin and a media screen. Although the alien does not enact conventional vampiric behaviours, the space she occupies performs the central functions on her behalf. The floor constitutes a material, optical and ontological threshold, marking the transition between solid and liquid, light and dark, living and dead.

Architectural, physical and optical thresholds are connected via a swirl of digital imagery in Timur Bekmembatov's *Day Watch* (2006). The film's convoluted plot involves a conflict between forces of light and darkness, and a number of key characters are vampires. In one key scene, the main characters, Anton and Svetlana, must put on special sunglasses in order to pursue a vampire into a parallel ontic realm, which is shot through with the aesthetics of optical diffusion. Here, objects and spaces appear luminous and streaky. Although the vampire in the chase scene is a fleeting presence, the entire space effectively becomes vampiric, defined as it is by the reflection, refraction and digital transformation of light. Meanwhile, interaction with the vampire itself is achieved only via optical means, namely the sunglasses which make it visible, and the special flashlight which acts as a weapon to counter it. Pushing a button on the flashlight

Figure 1.3 A luminous digital swirl signifies the vampire's presence in *Day Watch* (Timur Bekmambetov, 2004).

sends forth a jolt of illumination that strikes the vampire with physical force. This interaction between the optical and the haptic is also underlined by the mediating role of glass. After donning his special sunglasses, Anton is able to project himself through a plate glass window in order to follow the vampire. However, once the vampire exits this space, Anton finds himself trapped behind the glass as Svetlana faces the threat of the vampire outside. The body thus transforms from an optical artefact which can move through glass, to a heavy material presence which lacks the same facility. In this scene, optical mobility and ontological mobility fall in and out of alignment.

These examples illustrate the diversity of vampire spaces. Although cinematic vampires archetypically occupy darkened locales, from dungeons and coffins to high-tech bunkers, examples of more generously illumined spaces are numerous, extending from the streaky luminosity of *Day Watch*'s parallel realm to the airy rooms of *Vampyros Lesbos*, in which floor-to-ceiling windows let in the Mediterranean sunshine. Such vampire spaces, whether shadowy or shining, have a metonymic relationship to the vampire. In some cases, their function is also metaphoric, to the extent that they reproduce the vampire's ontic qualities, in particular its connection to mediation. Just as the breached walls of the motel in *Near Dark* parallel sunlight's effect on vampire skin, the digitised streams of light in *Day Watch* parallel the vampire's capacity for dematerialisation. These examples present a fantastical rendering of Steven Connor's notion of skin as environment. Indeed, the vampire is commonly engaged in a dynamic exchange with its environment, folding into it, emerging from it, reshaping it. Vampire ontology is thus a question of figure and ground. The figure of the vampire – hard-edged and well-delineated or diffuse and ephemeral – may dissolve, resolve or disappear into spaces of light and shadow, reflection and refraction.

In sum, the vampire is in-between: it typically displays neither the raw materiality of the zombie nor the ethereal ghostliness of the wandering spirit. Rather, it tends to oscillate between these two poles. The ambiguous rendering of the vampire's body (whether as tangible flesh or optical artefact, brute matter or spectral cipher) reveals its 'mediatic' logic. It moves like light, across spaces and thresholds (doors, windows, national boundaries). Its arrival (like the reflection in the mirror) can seem at once perpetually delayed but also (with the action of the bite) viscerally immediate. The vampire's skin, as optical and haptic surface, evokes the ambiguous ontology of the screen, hesitating between flat materiality and luminous abstraction, between envelope and environment, containment and dissolution. Interpretations are projected onto this vampiric screen, but they tend not to be fixed or absolute. The vampire oversignifies; it is a figure of semiotic projection. Although vampires are associated with light and hence with consciousness, knowledge and the promise of meaning, this meaning is framed as a mutable, contingent effect. The vampire flickers between presence and absence, between the observation of symbolic codes and the dissolution of meaning.

Notes

1. Stoker, *Dracula*, p. 19.
2. Auerbach, *Our Vampires, Ourselves*, p. 5.
3. Stoker, *Dracula*, p. 105.
4. This tendency has roots in popular culture more generally. Tom Gunning has commented that the creation of 'optical phantoms' was not only used for entertainment in the eighteenth century, but also infiltrated literature, providing 'a convention of the Gothic novel' (Gunning, 'To scan a ghost: the ontology of mediated vision', p. 108). Gunning also points to the Greek origins of the phantasmastic, pointing out that 'the name *phantasia* (imagination) has been developed from *phaos* (light)' (p. 104).
5. Abbott, *Celluloid Vampires: Life after Death in the Modern World*, p. 58.
6. Ibid. p. 53.
7. Ibid. p. 53.
8. Weinstock, *The Vampire Film: Undead Cinema*, p. 35.
9. Ibid. p. 120.
10. Ibid. p. 182.
11. Abbott, *Celluloid Vampires*, p. 112. Here, Abbott proposes that George Romero's zombie film *Night of the Living Dead* (1968), with its parade of

decaying and mutilated figures, influenced subsequent depictions of the vampire.

12. Abbott, p. 214.
13. Weinstock, *The Vampire Film*, p. 158.
14. Ibid. p. 181.
15. Ibid. p. 176.
16. Abbott, *Celluloid Vampires*, p. 5.
17. Botting, *Gothic*, p. 149.
18. Ibid. p. 147.
19. Weinstock, *The Vampire Film*, p. 123.
20. See Silver and Ursini, *The Vampire Film: From Nosferatu to Interview with a Vampire*. Silver and Ursini comment that while the flashbacks in Martin 'may seem to romanticise 19th Century vampirism with its low-key shots of canopied bed chambers and torch-bearing mobs of pursuers' the film otherwise counters such expressionistic imagery with 'a grainy, quasi-documentary feel' (p. 171).
21. Halberstam, *Skin Shows: Gothic Horror and the Technology of Monsters*, p. 21.
22. Gelder, *Reading the Vampire*, p. 64.
23. Dyer, *White*, p. 210.
24. Halberstam, *Skin Shows*, p. 92.
25. Ibid. p. 22.
26. Ibid. p. 88.
27. Connor, *The Book of Skin*, p. 66.
28. Halberstam, *Skin Shows*, p. 7.
29. Wicke, 'Vampiric typewriting: *Dracula* and its media', p. 473.
30. Abbott, *Celluloid Vampires*, p. 200.
31. Weinstock, *The Vampire Film*, p. 129.
32. Halberstam, *Skin Shows*, p. 101.
33. Ibid. p. 90.
34. Zizek, *Enjoy Your Symptom!: Jacques Lacan in Hollywood and Out*, p. 126.
35. Ibid. p. 134.
36. Halberstam, *Skin Shows*, p. 10.
37. Kittler, 'Dracula's legacy', p. 79.
38. Jennifer Wicke, similarly, argues that '[t]he typewriter reproduces the vampire, but is also one means through which the Crew of Light contrive to defeat him'. Wicke, 'Vampiric typewriting: *Dracula* and its media', p. 476.
39. Kittler, 'Dracula's legacy', p. 79.
40. Elsaesser, 'Freud and the technical media: the enduring magic of the Wunderblock', p. 111.
41. Kittler, 'Dracula's legacy', p. 79.
42. Ibid. p. 77.
43. Ibid. p. 79.
44. As Martin Jay highlights, light and the sun as well as the sense of vision

have all served as longstanding metaphors for knowledge and truth since classical Greek philosophy and significantly influenced the ocularcentrism attributed to Western thought. Jay, *Downcast Eyes: The Denigration of Vision in Twentieth-Century French Thought*, pp. 24–5.

45. Cubitt, *The Practice of Light: A Genealogy of Visual Technologies from Prints to Pixels*, p. 3.
46. Ibid. p. 202.
47. Ibid. p. 203.
48. Ibid. p. 64.
49. Abbott, *Celluloid Vampires*, p. 94.
50. Cubitt, *The Practice of Light*, p. 167.
51. Ibid. p. 3.
52. Barthes, *Camera Lucida: Reflections on Photography*, p. 81.
53. Connor, *The Book of Skin*, p. 59.
54. Edelstein, 'Limp trysts', p. 58.
55. Barker, *The Tactile Eye: Touch and the Cinematic Experience*, p. 12.
56. Connor, *The Book of Skin*, p. 275.
57. Marks, *The Skin of the Film: Intercultural Cinema, Embodiment, and the Senses*, p. 169.
58. Barker, *The Tactile Eye*, p. 31.
59. Barthes, *Camera Lucida*, pp. 26–7.
60. Connor, *The Book of Skin*, p. 26.
61. Ibid. p. 28.
62. Serres, *Les cinq sens*, p. 97.
63. Connor, *The Book of Skin*, p. 38.
64. Barker, *The Tactile Eye*, p. 31.
65. Connor, *The Book of Skin*, p. 65.
66. Ibid. p. 155.
67. Beugnet, *Cinema and Sensation: French Film and the Art of Transgression*, p. 140.
68. Connor, *The Book of Skin*, p. 155.
69. Silver and Ursini, *The Vampire Film*, p. 135.
70. As Nina Auerbach observes, in *Near Dark* 'the primary sensory experience is neither biting nor bloodsucking, but the sun's rending of tender vampire flesh'. Auerbach, *Our Vampires, Ourselves*, p. 122.

CHAPTER 2

Zombie Media:
Transmission, Reproduction, Disintegration

The modern zombie is a media zombie. Beginning with George Romero's 1968 classic *Night of the Living Dead*, zombie films have drawn attention with insistent frequency to the role of recording and broadcast media.[1] Most conspicuously, they have focused on the inability of news media to communicate the nature, scale and imminence of the zombie threat. In *Night of the Living Dead*, radio and television reports funnel out-of-date information to the embattled survivors, leading them into fatal misjudgements. In Romero's sequel *Dawn of the Dead* (1978) television again represents organised society's failure to come to terms with the unfolding disaster. The film opens with chaotic scenes at a network news studio, where the staff is in open revolt, apparently having lost faith in the authorities' ability to make sense of the crisis. To some extent, though, ordinary citizens in these films are also apparently to blame for their over-dependence on media. The protagonist of the comedy-horror *Shaun of the Dead* (Edgar Wright, 2004) lazily channel-surfs through an assortment of television shows, accidentally stitching together random yet coherent phrases describing the unfolding disaster, while remaining oblivious to their import. In *Dawn of the Dead*, one character's compulsion to leave the television set on, even though broadcasts have long since stopped, prompts another to ask in desperation, 'what have we done to ourselves?' With even nastier satirical intent, the British miniseries *Dead Set* (E4, 2008) establishes the set of the reality TV show *Big Brother* as the ultimate refuge from a zombie outbreak, allowing for amusing parallels to be drawn between the screaming, celebrity-fixated fans of the show and the manic, flesh-eating ghouls they so quickly become.

Yet the zombie film's engagement with media extends well beyond these obvious examples of social critique and the associated notion that media are capable of 'zombifying' their audiences. This engagement, I argue, extends to the very materiality of recording and broadcast media. It is concerned with grain and pixelation, with static and speed, with the transmission and reproduction of signals. It demonstrates an ongoing fascination with vision and the body, and the way that technology often underpins the relationship between them. Underlying the most sophisticated examples of the zombie subgenre is a highly developed media ontology, in which the zombie body and the 'body' of the medium are metaphorically connected in a reversible relationship. Alongside this ontological thread runs an associated media phenomenology, in which pleasures and fears associated with the breakdown of media are channelled through the spectacle of the disintegrating zombie body.

In foregrounding the body's ontological and phenomenological connections with media, the zombie film overlaps with its generic neighbours, in particular the vampire. However, in contrast to the zombie, the vampire's tendency to oscillate between absence and presence marks a connection, however equivocal, to Gothic conceptions of disembodiment. Such conceptions are evident in a thread of ontological uncertainty that runs from nineteenth-century spirit photography to cinema to digital media. As Tom Gunning outlines, this thread is typified by ghostly mediated visions of the past, which commonly present the viewer with 'a phantasmatic body', an absent presence that undermines the reliability of the senses.[2] Similarly, Jeffrey Sconce notes that electrical and electronic communications technologies have often been linked, in public discourse and popular narrative media, with spectacular and spectral disembodiment.[3] This Gothic-derived tradition of haunted media, in which a particular medium (such as a cursed videotape or movie theatre) is invested with negative forces, is not the dominant template for the zombie film. Indeed, zombie media present a particular configuration of the monster and the medium that is *not* premised upon such notions of disembodiment or haunting. Placed alongside the examples discussed by Gunning and Sconce, zombie films seem instead to insist upon a radically *embodied* ontological vision. In the contemporary zombie film, the spirit rarely, if ever, leaves the body, and the monstrous affliction does not, generally speaking, occasion the unearthing of Gothic secrets.[4]

Moreover, despite its firm basis within the horror genre, zombie cinema is aligned with science fiction in its tendency to frame media, and the failure of media, in social terms. Comparing *Night of the Living Dead*'s representation of the media with that of mainstream science fiction films, Vivian Sobchack notes that radio and TV in Romero's film 'are seen as negatively, even fatally, influential'.[5] Furthermore, zombie films parallel science fiction's concern with imaging technologies and the body, particularly in contexts of surveillance and mass communication. As Garrett Stewart argues, 'science fiction cinema . . . has always taken media as its subject', while 'the human body has typically served as placeholder for [the] science of imaging'.[6] Yet whereas science fiction cinema is generally concerned with showcasing cutting edge or speculative technologies, zombie films are focused instead on present-day media forms and channels. Furthermore, although science fiction films single out electronic media as providing the greatest threat to bodily integrity (as opposed to the apparent 'normality' of the photographic),[7] I would argue that zombie films place *all* media under suspicion. In other words, any form of audio-visual mediation may be associated with the zombie film's representations of physical, social and hermeneutical disorder. As some of my later examples will illustrate, this sense of disorder extends across text-based media as well, from erasable whiteboards to reprogrammable digital signs. The moving image, however, is central to zombie cinema's exploration of mediation.

The Media Zombie

The weaving together of media and bodily metaphors is most evident in those zombie films influenced by the works of George Romero. It becomes clear particularly at moments where the boundaries between the human and the zombie are challenged: where human characters lose the facility for verbal and gestural communication, or zombies flicker with the remnants of human understanding. In Romero's own *Day of the Dead* (1985), it is the figure of the captive zombie Bub that encapsulates the idea of the 'media zombie'. Bub is the subject of experiments by Dr Logan, who is attempting to 'cure' the zombie affliction through a type of reprogramming. Dr Logan provides Bub with various everyday items – a razor, a book, a telephone, a tape recorder – and encourages him to interact with them. Although unable to completely overcome his hunger for flesh, Bub flicks curiously through the pages of the book, holds the telephone receiver to his ear and listens appreciatively to a musical recording on the tape recorder. Significantly, Bub is being reformed through media experiences. The room where he is confined, which features a large glass window on one side and a microphone suspended from the ceiling, resembles nothing so much as a recording studio. In this space, Bub is submitted to a process of re-registration. Eventually, he is able to organise his chaotic body into meaningful communication: he 'salutes' the hostile military captain Rhodes, mumbles a few words, and eventually uses the gun to shoot Rhodes. Dr Logan's success is in revealing Bub's vestigial memory (the traces of his past life that have not been erased) and in rewriting his consciousness with new behavioural norms and expectations. Here, the

Figure 2.1 Media play a crucial role in Bub's 'reprogramming' in *Day of the Dead* (George Romero, 1985).

zombie is not only remade through media, but also functions itself like a type of medium.

Romero's *Diary of the Dead* (2007) displays an even more emphatic parallel between zombies and media. The story is told from the perspective of a group of film students, who happen to be shooting a horror film when the outbreak occurs. Going on the road, the students use their video cameras to record the horrors and upload the footage to their MySpace accounts. This endeavour effectively becomes part of a global project to document the events as they unfold. Importantly, the students' project is one of both reproduction (recording the events for posterity) and transmission (quickly disseminating audiovisual materials to an international viewership). The rapidity with which this information is shared, along with its ready reproducibility, parallels closely the properties of the zombie virus itself. At the same time, the film foregrounds the role of bodies and media as vehicles for meaning, and the potential for that meaning to become lost or corrupted.

In one particularly revealing sequence, the students encounter an old man who stumbles out from behind a barn, making unintelligible noises. Assuming him to be one of the zombies, they prepare to fire, but something stops them. It turns out that their new acquaintance is an Amish man named Samuel, and their introduction to him immediately invokes problems of mediation. First of all, he is unable to speak. He does, however, have a small chalkboard with which he communicates. In the first instance, the chalkboard is used to confirm that he is Amish and deaf-mute. Before long, Samuel scrawls the word 'hurry' on the chalk-board. The students are baffled at first, but Samuel points behind them and a reverse shot reveals a horde of shambling zombies. Here, communication is displaced from the body (Samuel lacks hearing and speech) before being suddenly returned to it, in the form of physical gesture. In this way, the body's role as a medium of communication is foregrounded. Despite initial appearances, Samuel is not like the zombies, and it is his capacity for communication that marks him apart, alongside his use of communication technologies (his chalkboard constitutes an analogue of sorts to the cameras and websites of the film students). The zombies, by contrast, communicate nothing other than their own empty and mean-ingless desire—they are, in effect, blank media. Steven Shaviro makes a similar observation when he states that the zombies in Romero's original trilogy 'could almost be said to be quintessential media images, since they are vacuous, mimetic replications of the human beings they once were'.[8]

The 2004 remake of *Dawn of the Dead* (Zack Snyder), maligned in some quarters for failing to take up the satirical slant of George Romero's 1978 original, inventively extends the notion of the media zombie. In one memorable scene, a group of survivors atop a besieged shopping mall use whiteboards to communicate with a solitary survivor named Andy who is stranded in an adjacent building. A favourite game involves members of the shopping mall group writing the name of a celebrity on a whiteboard before holding it aloft for Andy to read. Andy must then pick out the zombie that resembles said celebrity (examples include Burt Reynolds, Jay Leno and Rosie O'Donnell) and dispatch it with a rifle shot to the head. The game thus depends upon a particular configuration of identity and non-identity, sense and non-sense. The unfortunate zombies are selected as targets based upon their resemblance to media images, but they now exist in a milieu where social signification has become redundant. This is, indeed, the subgenre's enduring joke: the particular features and behav-ioural quirks of individual zombies merely serve to highlight the fact that they are now indistinguishable from the mass. Like a buzzing frame filled with television static, they constitute a field of non-identity, pure teeming media. Meanwhile, the survivors use the whiteboards to play a game of signification that is both literally and figuratively over the zombies' heads.

When Andy is eventually claimed by the zombie virus, signification again comes into play. The survivors wait for his next message as he scrawls frantically on the whiteboard. When he raises it above his head, however, they see that it is completely smeared with blood. This gesture effectively presents non-signification as signification. It is either Andy's final signifying act as a human (warning the others of his impending

Figure 2.2 The blood–smeared whiteboard signals Andy's zombification in
Dawn of the Dead (Zack Snyder, 2004).

transformation), or the first random act of a being that has moved beyond
language. In any case, Andy's whiteboard both frames and provides an
index for the breakdown of sense, and it highlights zombification's intimate connection with media. The media zombie and zombie media thus
act as reversible metaphors.

Although these reversible metaphors are generally based upon visual
aspects of media, this is not exclusively the case. In the Canadian film
Pontypool (Bruce McDonald, 2008), a radio announcer and his co-workers
become aware of a zombie outbreak in their town via radio transmissions and phone calls from those experiencing them first-hand. The initial
symptoms of zombification involve the breakdown of language, with
victims beginning to repeat words or phrases. Although the spread of
the virus does not depend upon media, the connection is implied by the
almost total confinement of the diegesis to the radio station itself, so that
the consequences of the outbreak are communicated, for the most part,
via audio transmissions. The film's submerged media metaphor is further
foregrounded by the description of one victim as 'a crude radio signal',
suggesting that an ontological equivalence between bodies and media has
somehow been uncovered by the collapse of signification. Similarly, in
the final scene of *Dawn of the Dead* (2004), which consists of a zombie
attack recorded on a camcorder, the sound of zombies (guttural grunts
and snarls) is blended almost seamlessly with the sound of media failure
(blips, glitches, static and buzzing noises). The disintegration of language
and sense that accompanies the zombies' arrival is thus associated with the
disintegration of media.

In highlighting the question of mediation in this way, the zombie film
carves out a unique generic space. It is distinct from Gothic horror (with

its special relationship to the past) and from science fiction (with its special relationship to the future). Media are, in the case of the former, the potential vehicle for Gothic curses and, in the case of the latter, 'posthuman' ontological crises. Unlike both of these genres, however, zombie cinema is focused on the present and does not express an anxiety about mediation *per se*. Rather, it seems to hint at mediation's power to reveal the materiality and potential meaninglessness of bodies.

Speed, Stillness and the Body

Given the subgenre's insistence on mediation and bodily materiality, it seems appropriate that many zombie films highlight the visibility of their material form. This extends from the rough and grainy high-contrast 35 mm of *Night of the Living Dead* (1968)[9] to the pixelated digital video of Danny Boyle's quasi-zombie film *28 Days Later* (2002), as well as the digital 'documentary' footage of *Diary of the Dead* and the Spanish viral outbreak films *REC* and *REC 2* (Jaume Balagueró and Paco Plaza, 2007 and 2009).[10] In many cases, the materiality of media is foregrounded at the moment of lethal attack. For example, the 1971 film *Tombs of the Blind Dead* (Amando de Ossorio) applies slow motion effects to its imagery of horse-riding skeletal knights, while *28 Days Later* and *28 Weeks Later* (Juan Carlos Fresnadillo, 2007) both make use of fast shutter speeds to add velocity and violence to the attacks of the infected.

The importance of speed in zombie cinema has been emphatically underlined by fan debates. In particular, both the UK television series *Dead Set* and Zack Snyder's *Dawn of the Dead* remake were criticised for featuring fast zombies.[11] In a diegetic universe where the distinction between the quick and the dead is often blurred, some fans appeared to feel nonetheless that the dead should not be quick. Twenty-first-century zombie films have thus been attacked for failing to reproduce the correct technical standards regarding zombie behaviour. In extreme cases, these debates begin to resemble a gathering of Society of Motion Picture and Television Engineers (SMPTE) technicians. The body is figured as a medium, to which norms of playback and resolution apply. Indeed, it might be suggested that the emergence of the high-speed zombie introduces a digital aesthetic to zombie media. If Romero's shambling figures replicate the slow and steady unspooling of low-resolution analogue media, then the contemporary zombie reflects digital media's capacity for speed and random access. Tanya Krzywinska makes a related point about fast zombies in contemporary films (*28 Days Later* and *Dawn of the Dead*) and video games (*Doom3* and *Painkiller*), suggesting that advances in graphics and animation explain the change: 'If Romero's shuffling flesh-eating zombies are second generation to the worker-zombies of 1930s horror (as illustrated by the passive worker-zombies of *White Zombie*), then these are third-generation zombies, born of the digital era'.[12] Meanwhile, the zombie comedy *Shaun of the Dead* underlines the analogue connotations of slow zombies by having its protagonists hurl vinyl LPs at them (the challenge is then to decide which albums are sufficiently dispensable to qualify as weapons).

Indeed, despite the existence of fleet-footed forerunners in *Nightmare City* (Umberto Lenzi, 1980) and *The Return of the Living Dead* (Dan O'Bannon, 1985), it is only since the onset of the digital era that fast zombies have become commonplace. Yet as I will go on to argue, the zombie film does not generally propose a strong or consistent ontological distinction between analogue and digital media. Rather, the emergence of these 'third generation zombies' may simply reveal the subgenre's continued engagement with media materiality. Before turning fully to the question of digital media, however, I will first reflect upon the way that zombie cinema intersects with what leading theorists of film and photography have proposed as the privileged relationship between death and the mediated image.

Laura Mulvey[13] and Garrett Stewart[14] have both highlighted the ways in which cinema has tended to conceal its technical basis in still imagery and, by extension, its link to photography's relationship to death, outlined most notably by Roland Barthes[15] and Andre Bazin.[16] Mulvey and Stewart are therefore both interested in films that take up still photography as a narrative subject, while Mulvey dwells at length on the way that domestic video equipment (the VCR, the DVD player, and the remote control) has placed the power of stillness in the hands of viewers. For Mulvey, electronic and digital technologies allow viewers unprecedented access to the 'hidden stillness of the film frame'. Although the electronic freeze-frame is not literally still, it nonetheless 'restores to the moving image the heavy presence of passing time and of the mortality that Bazin and Barthes associate with the still photograph'.[17] This, in turn, serves to highlight the way that cinema combines 'two human fascinations: one with the boundary between life and death and the other with the mechanical animation of the inanimate, particularly the human, figure'.[18] In *Between Film and Screen*, Stewart focusses specifically on cinema's relationship to photography, again with a strong emphasis on death: 'Photography is death in replica; cinema a dying away in progress, hence death in serial abeyance . . . The isolated photo or photogram is the still work of death; cinema is death always still at work'.[19] With its focus on media technologies and with the zombie as a literal figure of death, the zombie film offers a useful representational frame within which to consider such ideas.

Do zombie films articulate a media ontology consistent with Stewart and Mulvey's emphasis on death and stillness? *Dead and Buried* (Gary Sherman, 1981) appears to affirm this perspective, proffering a particularly literal analogy between zombies and analogue media. In this film, unfortunate visitors to a small American town find themselves surrounded by a posse of locals who take flash photographs of their victims before attacking them violently. These victims are then subjected to the attentions of the local mortician, who removes their hearts and, with a vaguely outlined combination of science and black magic, contrives to reanimate them. One of the film's most memorable sequences shows the mortician breaking down and reconstructing the face of a young woman. The woman's face is framed by the metallic surface of the mortuary table, and her transformation is depicted in medium close-up via a series of lap dissolves. In this way, the process is designed to evoke the development of a still photograph. Facial reconstruction and still image reproduction are joined together via the cinematic device of the dissolve. The unfortunate young woman's transformation is at once cinematic, photographic, surgical and alchemical.

In the film's final scene, the town sheriff (the film's protagonist) confronts the mortician in his reanimation chamber, where the walls teem with multiple projected film clips revealing the truth of the town's gradual collective mortification (it transpires that the sheriff and his wife are among the victims, too). The capture and projection of these images thus mirrors the fate of the townsfolk, in particular their passage through stillness and back into movement. Departing from the dominant zombie mythos of Romero's films (in which the zombies are flesh-eating, mindless ghouls), *Dead and Buried* posits cinema as the conjunction of science and black magic, where the deadly stillness of the photographic unites with the ghostly quasi-presence of the moving image. It therefore presents a media configuration that is strikingly consonant with Garrett Stewart's account. As if to underline Stewart's argument, the film begins and ends with still images: the first a photograph of the town, and the last a freeze-frame on the sheriff as he looks at his fingers, realising that he is now reliant on the mortician's technical interventions to keep them from decaying.

Dead and Buried thus articulates a media ontology that is specifically grounded in cinema and photography. The media zombie is, here, a celluloid zombie. Moreover, its ontological properties hinge upon the relationship between cinematic and still images. For Garrett Stewart, cinema and photography evoke death in distinct but related ways. 'What is dead about a corpse', he writes, 'is not only its stasis but the sense of subtracted life it conveys, the sense of what has been evacuated from behind its eyes. Moving pictures no less than static ones are a visible function of nonpresence, a trace of the passed away'.[20] Thus, both media are marked by death as absence, but photography has a stronger attachment to the 'cadaverous' in the sense that it offers us the stilled bodies of its subjects. Cinema, meanwhile, tends to the 'ghostly' in its ephemerality, characterised by 'death's perpetual encroachment'.[21] *Dead and Buried* references both of these media, and both of these senses of death, shifting between the 'encorpsed' death of the still image (the bodies in the mortuary) and the ephemeral death of the cinematic image (with the chilling realisation that both the undead hero and his wife have been suspended in the spectral projection of a marriage).

Dead and Buried, however, is not a typical example of the contemporary zombie film. In contrast with the works of George Romero, electronic and broadcast media are de-emphasised, and the small coastal town depicted in the film seems cut off from the wider mediascape. Furthermore, while the dominant trend in zombie cinema is for the outbreak to spread virally from city to city, in *Dead and Buried* the affliction is a secret that belongs to the townsfolk and is spread as a result of their conscious efforts. As such, the film provides an illuminating counterexample, highlighting by contrast the subgenre's customary approach to the questions of transmission and reproduction. In the dominant, Romero-influenced strand of zombie cinema, zombieism is transmitted virally and reproduces itself as a limited repertoire of blank, dehumanised behaviours. At the same time, this phenomenon is paralleled by the reproduction and transmission of zombie-inflicted chaos, public panic and disinformation via recording and broadcast media. The associated ontology is quite distinct from Stewart's pairing of the encorpsed and the ephemeral. Rather, the most prominent zombie films insist upon the embodiment of the cadaverous in the moving image itself, while doing away with the sense of absence and pastness that lends such a ghostly quality to the films Stewart discusses. In zombie and viral outbreak films, moving images present the threat, not of absence, but rather of pure *presence*.

Night of the Living Dead, for example, renders its constantly advancing zombies in rough 35 mm, implicitly aligning celluloid grain with the pressing proximity of the undead. In the concluding scene of *Diary of the Dead*, this sense of presence is conveyed through the use of video surveillance. Locked in a 'panic room' walled with monitors, the last of the surviving characters look on as external security cameras relay images of zombies encircling the house where they are hiding. The survivors thus find themselves trapped by the convergence of zombies and mediation, as the array of video screens produces an effect of overwhelming closeness, underlining the imminence of the zombie threat. In a number of films, this sense of presence is supplied by embedded sequences of live or pre-recorded media images. In the scene that opens *28 Days Later*, a chimpanzee sits shackled to monitoring equipment before a bank of screens displaying violent news footage. This cruel media-based experiment is soon revealed to be the cause of the devastating 'rage' virus that will shortly be transmitted to humankind. Although the footage is apparently pre-recorded, the juxtaposition of screens playing different clips simultaneously, combined with the choppy and chaotic nature of the footage, evokes an overwhelming sense of liveness and material presence. Indeed, the emphatic materiality of media is associated with the bodily effects of the virus itself, as the jerky, disjunctive news footage mirrors the chaotic, violent movements of these mediatised chimpanzees and their subsequent human victims. The affective charge of the images thus lies not in spectral distance but in visceral proximity.

Zack Snyder's *Dawn of the Dead* (2004) further develops this perspective on zombie media. Here, the deathly connotations of media are based not in photographic stillness (as in *Dead and Buried*) but in a type of absolute, undifferentiated movement. This sense of movement as a static flux is applicable both to the chaotic movements of the zombies themselves and to the disordered images which appear within the film at key moments. At these moments of flux, what emerges is the zero degree of the moving image, comparable with the visual noise of static: total difference as no difference at all. In this regard, the film's opening credits are exemplary. As a Johnny Cash song plays in ironic counterpoint, we see a plethora of images showing the consequences of the zombie outbreak. These include frantic news reports and interviews with confused government officials, along with footage of riots, looting, violence and general devastation. Most of the footage is marked by scan lines, as if filmed directly from a television monitor, and it incorporates a host of analogue and digital flaws and artifacts, including static, pixelation, colour desaturation and fluctuations in brightness. The effect is enhanced by the insertion of single-frame shots taken through broken glass. The sequence culminates with stuttering images of a zombie face looming in the frame.

This opening sequence, then, aims at an account of the zombie apocalypse as an outbreak of mediation itself. As opposed to the revived stillness of *Dead and Buried*'s photographic/cinematic analogy, *Dawn of the Dead* offers the random grain and digital breakup of media images. Although stillness is certainly a feature of these images (the broken stills of the zombie face are a case in point), the relationship between movement and stillness is different. Rather than the haunted 'absence' of Stewart's moving images, we are confronted with the visceral presence of images without memory. The 'cadaverous' mortality of the still photograph infects these moving images, but it infects them as a form of chaotic movement. This example may remind us that death itself is never, in a literal sense, still, but marked instead by the busy movements of decomposition. In this case, zombie media embody the liveliness of death, in the form of a cadaverousness that is visceral and very much present.

While Stewart's account of movement and stillness is grounded in the relationship between photography and celluloid film, it is productive to push it into electronic and digital media. Here, the image itself is constituted in a host of different ways, from video fields that 'write' themselves across the screen to digital compression, which uses complex calculations to predict the content of subsequent frames. Such imaging technologies, I would argue, do not negate the dialectic between stillness and movement, but they introduce new layers of *technical* movement into the image. Zombie media, by positing an analogy between the materiality of the image and the materiality of the body, suggest that the conceptual pairing of death and stillness is not sufficient to explain their characteristic effects. Nor is the absence/presence dialectic sufficient to account for the role of death in zombie cinema. As Steven Shaviro argues, 'The image cannot be opposed to the body, as representation is opposed to its unattainable referent. For a fugitive, supplemental materiality haunts the (allegedly) idealising processes of mechanical reproduction'.[22] It is materiality and movement, I suggest, that 'haunt' zombie media, rather than the absence and stillness described by Stewart and Mulvey.

The Phenomenology of Zombie Vision

The zombie film's engagement with media produces an ontological alignment of the technological and the physical. Yet by exploring the bodily manifestations of media, it also reflects upon the relationship between mediated images and embodied viewers. In particular, it suggests the potential for such relationships to be overtaken by the collapse of signification. Through its dual focus on mediated embodiment and embodied mediation, the zombie film brings its distinctive ontology into contact with a corresponding phenomenology.

For Vivian Sobchack, film itself has a body, constituted by the entire technological apparatus of camera, screen, projector, and so forth. This apparatus forms a 'ground' for the film's 'perceptive and expressive activity'.[23] In Sobchack's phenomenologically-based account, to watch a film is to look both at and through it via an intersubjective process: the film is both an 'object' and a 'subject' of vision. Cinema thus encapsulates the 'address of the eye' in two senses. It constitutes a form of address, an intersubjective communication that calls upon spectatorial vision. At the same time, it situates that vision within the body, at a specific address. 'Thus, *address*, as noun and verb, both denotes a location where one resides and the activity of transcending the body's location, originating from it to exceed beyond it as a projection bent on spanning the worldly space between one body-subject and another'.[24]

Sobchack's account is extremely suggestive in the context of this discussion because it proposes a two-way relationship between embodiment and media. Her emphasis on the bodily address of cinema and the liveliness of intersubjective experience provides an antidote of sorts to Garrett Stewart's overemphasis on stillness and pastness. Most importantly, it is also consonant with the zombie film's insistence upon the intimate connections among the bodies of characters and viewers, the 'body' of the film itself, and the physical locus of vision. Zombie films are often concerned very literally with the address of the eye, in both senses. Eyes are in jeopardy in a number of these films; a threat to the characters' eyes is invariably addressed toward spectators' vision as well. Perhaps most famous is the scene in Lucio Fulci's *Zombi 2* (1979) in which a zombie pulls a woman's face close to a large splinter, which is shown penetrating her eyeball in close-up. Other notable examples include eyeballs being skewered with a hypodermic needle in *Dead and Buried*, violently enucleated in *Nightmare City*, and burned out with quicklime and eaten by tarantulas in *The Beyond* (Lucio Fulci, 1981). In the crudest sense, viewers of these films are confronted with the bodily location of vision.

However, while Sobchack insists upon the 'intentionality' of cinematic vision, zombie films often work to show vision separated from intentionality. For Sobchack, 'perception is a living and *organising organisation* of the world, a *textualising* of the sensing body in its contact with a sensible world. Thus, perception is always already the *expression* of intentionality in the world and, as such, always already a judgment, an interpretation . . .'.[25] The identification of a frame, the separation of figure and ground – these things mark an intentional relationship with the visual world. Zombie films partially undermine this relationship by putting forward, at key moments, a zombie vision devoid of sense and intentionality. At the end of *REC*, for example, the protagonist (a news reporter) is dragged out of frame by an unseen representative of the infected as the camera, *sans* operator, continues to record whatever lies in front of it. In *Dead Set*, the

unmanned cameras of the reality TV series *Big Brother* relay images of
zombification to an audience that is itself already zombified. *Dawn of the
Dead* (2004) concludes with amateur video footage shot by the remaining survivors, documenting their encounter with an unexpected horde
of zombies. The abandoned camera bears witness to their final moments
as the frame fills with undead attackers. In *28 Weeks Later*, a character
stumbles in the dark before one of the 'infected', wielding her own rifle,
bludgeons her to death. The killing is depicted through the rifle's green-
tinted infrared sight as it rises and falls violently. Disturbingly, the address
of the eye here passes through a disembodied visual technology, wielded
by the attacker but in no way connected to anything resembling an intentional consciousness. Similarly, surveillance footage presages the escape
of the infected chimpanzee at the start of *28 Days Later* and frames the
bleak, claustrophobic conclusion of *Diary of the Dead*. In these films, the
automated vision of security cameras looks blankly towards the eclipse of
human consciousness.

Zombie cinema thus raises the question of phenomenological experience via a distinctive configuration of mediated vision and bodily experience. Its intensive focus on disorder and meaninglessness produces a *de
facto* theorisation of spectatorship, in which the notion of intersubjectivity
collapses into a vision of media as chaotic and disarticulated from human
subjectivity. For Vivian Sobchack, 'sense' denotes both the means by
which we experience stimuli and the order associated with meaning; these
two things are intimately connected. Zombie cinema, by contrast, repeatedly returns to the moments when these two types of sense pull apart,
foregrounding the breakdown of meaning and intentionality. In its most
extreme moments of violent excess, zombie cinema confronts us with
sensory experiences that make no sense, with matter that doesn't matter.

This collapse of sense and intentionality has a transmedia dimension.
In his brilliant analysis of Romero's trilogy, Steven Shaviro makes the case
that 'perception itself becomes infected, and is transformed into a kind
of magical, contagious contact'.[26] This infection, I would argue, is also
transmissible across media formats. In the hypermediated credit sequence
of *Dawn of the Dead* (2004), for example, analogue and digital media in
various states of disintegration are juxtaposed almost at random. This
transmedia infection lies beyond intentionality because it is beyond communication: it is *communicable* but it does not *communicate* (indeed, this
paradox underpins the fact that the zombies act *en masse* but generally
speaking fail to constitute a society).[27] Intention is also sidelined because
it depends upon temporal relations involving pastness and futurity. As
Shaviro puts it, the fragmentation and blending of the zombies' bodies

with those of their victims 'causes the living time of memory and anticipation to converge with the zombie time of empty motion'.[28] The temporality of the zombie is thus the temporality of the (mediated) present.

Contingent Threats, Contingent Pleasures

Zombie and viral outbreak films present a scenario in which a contagious menace threatens to overtake the human body and to remake it as
mere media, erasing sense and intentionality. Under these conditions, the
zombified body becomes subject to a sudden evacuation of meaning that
is both comparable and coextensive with the mediated image's capacity
for embodying non-sense. By comparison with neighbouring subgenres,
zombie cinema therefore places a particularly marked emphasis on chance
and the contingent. Unlike such classic movie monsters as the vampire
and the werewolf, the zombie lacks a truly intentional relationship with its
victims. Confrontations with zombies are generally speaking shaped and
propelled not by fate or planning but by chance or bad luck. Furthermore,
the zombie is not an individual threat to the same degree as other monsters
(taken alone, it is often dispatched relatively easily). Rather, by virtue of its
viral provenance and its generic behaviours, the zombie is always already
a multitude. In this context, the iconic image of the zombie attack is the
undifferentiated mass of undead faces or hands, filling the frame with
random movement and foreclosing three-dimensional space. These recurring images in zombie cinema, I will argue, denote moments of contingent
threat.

In the previous chapter, I discussed the vampire's relationship to the
contingent, in which optics gives way to haptics, focus gives way to diffusion, and the geometry of the gaze is overtaken by epidermal contact.
The vampire, I argued, is involved in a relay between vision and touch,
meaning and nonmeaning. The zombie's particular brand of the contingent is more immediate and visceral, involving the violent disorganisation
of bodies, media and meaning. This more concrete, intensive mode of
contingency can be understood in relation to Mary Ann Doane's theorisation of the concept. According to Doane, contingency is inherent in
film and video technologies, which allow the irruption of chance and the
ephemeral within the frame. Doane describes the modern era's domestication of time through social and technological means, and cinema's dual
role in relation to this domestication. On the one hand, cinema provided a
standardised temporal record at 24 frames per second. On the other hand,
it recorded unplanned or random movements within its visual field, providing an opening for chance and contingency.[29] Doane goes on to suggest

that electronic and digital media are also vehicles for contingency, despite the different technologies of registration.[30] Zombie films, I argue, gesture towards contingency in terms of the undirected and multitudinous nature of the zombie threat, but also through the practical immediacy of their recording formats (both analogue and digital), which are ideally equipped to register the chaos and randomness of the outbreaks. By emphasising format, either narratively (the characters are filming the events) or materially (the resolution or speed of the format is foregrounded), these films remind us not only of the temporalities of narrative or reception, but also of the temporality of physical registration – the time at which actors, props and locations were placed before the lens. To be aware of the time of registration in this way is to be conscious of the contingent, of the way that chance inflects every aspect of the image.

Crucially, the raw and pervasive contingency of zombie cinema offers an alternative way of understanding the relationships among death, movement and signification. While Garrett Stewart's analysis suggests that the deathliness of cinematic images is located in their underlying stillness, zombie cinema, as I have already argued, also presents death as a type of movement. Although it might be objected that zombies are not 'dead' at all but 'undead', this argument would overlook the way that zombies (and the infected hordes in 'viral outbreak' films) function as stand-ins for mortality itself. From this perspective, 'undeath' is not the negation of death but its hypertrophic fulfilment. In zombie cinema, this movement towards and through death is often mirrored by a movement away from sense and order, as both bodies and images lose their ability to communicate. Contingency is integral to this crisis of signification. For Mary Ann Doane, contingency is connected with death insofar as both 'are often situated as that which is unassimilable to meaning'.[31] This hidden connection is amplified in the zombie film, which stages the contingent threat as a type of contagious death that heralds the collapse of signification. The arbitrariness of the deadly zombie attacks is thus paralleled by their meaninglessness. Zombie cinema's media ontology and phenomenology are both inflected by this logic of contingency and non-sense. The zombie's disordered physical form and the breakdown of the visual field are, ultimately, quintessential embodiments of the contingent. Whereas the vampire's relationship to contingency is typically communicated by optical diffusion, zombie contingency entails the wholesale disintegration of the media-body.

Moreover, the concept of contingency may take us to the very heart of the pleasures offered by zombie cinema. In other words, the fear and fascination provoked by the figure of the zombie are channelled through a type of second order cinephilia that is focused on the instability and contingency of cinematic images. In his philosophical exploration of the horror genre, Noël Carroll dwells at length on the way that the emotions of disgust and fascination are connected to the figure of the monster. Drawing upon the work of Mary Douglas, he suggests that monsters in horror fiction gain their particular force from their impurity, and the way that they traverse different 'schemes of cultural categorisation'.[32] Indeed, in their equivocations between the terms living and dead or human and nonhuman, monsters represent 'categorical violations'.[33] Carroll admits that his 'theory of art-horror' is essentially 'entity-based', depending on the figure of the monster as a conduit for the strong feelings of repulsion and attraction experienced by consumers of the genre.[34] While in agreement with Carroll's articulation of the ambivalent pleasures offered by horror, I want to suggest that his entity-based account of this ambivalence can be productively extended into a media-based account. In this account, the aesthetic 'ugliness' of degraded media images is at once also a source of attraction and pleasure. The zombie's categorical uncertainty (at once dead and alive, human and nonhuman, whole and fragmentary) is paralleled by the categorical uncertainty of zombie cinema's moving images, which equivocate between the flat immediacy of documentary reportage and the layered hypermediacy of multiple recording and transmission formats. From the grainy stills that conclude *Night of the Living Dead* to the low-resolution video of *28 Days Later* and shaky Handycam of *Diary of the Dead* and *REC*, zombie films foreground both the utilitarian plainness and the material sensuality of degraded media.

Zombie Formats: Between Digital and Analogue

Zombie cinema's ontological alignment of bodies and media invites reflection not only on questions of death, stillness, and cinematic movement, but also on the status of embodiment in the context of digital media. I have already suggested that it may be possible to see contemporary 'fast zombies' as loosely connected to the speed and random access of digital media, but that this connection does not, in itself, draw a definitive ontological line between analogue and digital zombies. Some contemporary films and television shows, however, associate zombies not with digital media but with the material traces of analogue media. Frank Darabont, for example, creator of television series *The Walking Dead* (AMC, 2010–), is at pains to emphasise the show's 'analogue feel', both in terms of zombies ('We're not doing CGI monsters') and media (the show was shot on 16 mm film, producing 'that analogue bit of grain in the image').[35] Despite this, digital effects are not absent altogether. Talking about the first zombie encountered by the show's protagonist, Darabont says: 'We use traditional make-up effects, combined with some digital visual trickery, to make the creature you're seeing far more horrible than it would otherwise be'.[36] The 'feel' of the show may be analogue, but it also bears the visible imprint of digital postproduction. This is evident during a number of the zombie attacks, but also at other key moments, such as the iconic shot of Sheriff Rick Grimes riding on horseback along a deserted Atlanta freeway, which makes heavy use of digital compositing.

Robert Rodriguez's film *Planet Terror* (2007) is even more overt in exploring the connections between zombies and analogue media. It deploys an aesthetic of analogue visual degradation, attaching it very directly to a heightened type of 'zombie cinephilia'. Initially released as part of a double feature alongside Quentin Tarantino's *Death Proof* under the umbrella title *Grindhouse*, this film chronicles a zombie outbreak that takes place in a small Texas town in the course of a single night. Harking back to the look and feel of 1970s and 1980s exploitation cinema, these films foreground the paraphernalia of cinematic experience, from the lurid titles to the fake trailers for other films, and the vintage title cards announcing 'prevues of upcoming attractions'. The film's story is a deliberately flimsy construction, built around a toxic chemical leak from a military base and including a host of exaggerated types. The main character, Cherry Darling, is a go-go dancer who loses her leg to a zombie attack and has it replaced first with a table leg and ultimately (and spectacularly) with a fully functioning submachine gun. Indeed, bodies in general are vulnerable to amputation, mutilation, and decomposition in *Planet Terror*. One character's testicles are cut off, and another's hands are immobilised by a paralyzing injection, while a police deputy (played by George Romero's special effects wizard Tom Savini) has two fingers severed by a zombie bite. Quentin Tarantino appears as a military officer intent on rape who loses an eyeball to Cherry's splintered table-leg prosthesis (in a direct reference to Fulci's *Zombi 2*) and his penis, in one memorably disgusting moment, to the flesh-melting effects of the toxic gas.

It is the body of the film itself, however, that displays the greatest evidence of decay and corruption. Scratches and marks, flares and discolouration, bad splices and bubbling celluloid: *Planet Terror* constantly foregrounds the materiality of traditional cinema *as* cinema and connects it with the deterioration of zombie flesh. It even features a 'missing reel', highlighting both the unfolding temporality of cinemagoing and the notion of the film itself as another amputee. The intensity of these 'contingent' effects is most notable at moments of heightened drama and spectacle. The missing reel is in fact preceded by a sex scene in which the erotic imagery appears responsible for jamming the 'projector': the film flares, jitters and bubbles before a final frame is caught in the gate and burnt through. Similarly, the scene where military leader Lt Muldoon's body is bloated and blistered beyond all recognition (after he deliberately breathes in the toxic gas) is accompanied by colour shifts and an analogous warping effect on the 'print', as if the filmstrip has been subjected to high temperatures. The film's nostalgic evocation of grindhouse cinemagoing is grounded in its mimicry of the contingent flaws and artifacts of analogue media. The foregrounding of celluloid materiality thus underlines the explicitly cinephilic project of *Planet Terror* (and the *Grindhouse* 'double-bill').

Tellingly, however, the film's production of cinematic contingency is almost entirely artificial, and its technical underpinnings overwhelmingly digital. *Planet Terror* was in fact shot on a Panavision Genesis digital video camera. The 'damage', explains the director Robert Rodriguez, 'is really just a series of layers, of real film print damage, artifacts, dust passes, scratches, and using different brightness levels and other just trickery to keep it looking random'.[37] Thus, the combination of digital plug-ins and effects with 'real' film deterioration creates an effect that appears almost, but not quite, as an example of analogue contingency. What is important here is the preservation of a sense of the 'randomness' of these effects, even though they are deliberately crafted. With this in mind, Rodriguez asked different effects teams to work separately on the film and refrain from sharing resources, in order to combine a number of

Figure 2.3 Digital and analogue techniques were combined to add scratches and other 'damage' to this shot from *Planet Terror* (Robert Rodriguez, 2007).

distinct and varied ageing effects. Contingency was also mimicked via software. Comments visual effects (VFX) artist Rod Brunet, 'we found it looked much more realistic by using a host of compositing techniques. We wrote noise expressions to alter individual colour channels randomly over time as one example'.[38] Thus, the flesh of the film is marked by a complex layering of digital and analogue processes. *Planet Terror* provides an exemplary instance of zombie cinephilia that is marked by the intimate contact between media formats. It invites a knowing audience to partake in a direct engagement with the physical materiality of media and their basis in contingency (even if it is an *ersatz* contingency).[39]

The 'analogue dead' of *The Walking Dead* and *Planet Terror* are therefore substantially digital, even as both texts appear to suggest that zombie bodies are best rendered via the visual and tactile materiality of analogue media. This apparent insistence on analogue embodiment indirectly recalls, in turn, arguments within film and media theory associating digital media with dematerialisation. Vivian Sobchack, drawing together electronic and digital media and opposing them to cinema, argues that, 'unlike cinematic representation, electronic representation by its very structure phenomenologically diffuses the fleshly presence of the human body and the dimensions of that body's material world'.[40] Similarly, much subsequent writing on electronic media tends to treat digital media separately from analogue electronic media, while reflecting the same essential opposition between embodied (traditional) and abstracted (new) media formats. Ewan Kirkland, for example, writing about the deployment of 'analogue' media effects in horror video games including the *Resident Evil* (Capcom, 1996–) and *Silent Hill* (Konami, 1999–2014) franchises, suggests that such effects produce the effect of an encounter with some external, material reality: 'emulating the dirty, scratchy, or corroded audiovisual effects associated with analogue media communicates a sense of something malevolent and corrupting contaminating the clean digital world'.[41]

Yet in spite of ongoing arguments suggesting that electronic or digital media have augured a decisive shift in the mediation of the human body,[42] many zombie films do not uphold this dichotomy between embodiment and abstraction. While *Planet Terror* makes use of digital media in order to reproduce the material traces of analogue technology, the 'digital dead' in such films as *Dawn of the Dead* (2004), *Diary of the Dead*, *REC* and *28 Days Later* are generally represented, much like their analogue counterparts, in terms of contingent materiality. Furthermore, although analogue media, with their visual and tactile presence, may seem to be the natural home of the contingent, it is easy to overlook the fact that digital media also depend upon material constraints in terms of hardware and software and are thus vulnerable to glitches and flaws (for an illustration of this, think of the way that the images of interlocutors on video calls can break apart in the face of restricted bandwidth). Accordingly, in many zombie films, digital media provide the occasion not for abstraction or disembodiment but for enhanced representations of visceral and visual disintegration. Both *Dawn of the Dead* (2004) and *Diary of the Dead* feature montage sequences that underline this point by blending analogue and digital media sources, so that analogue static mixes freely with digital pixelation.

Moreover, the retrospective association of analogue media with zombi-fication in *Planet Terror* and *The Walking Dead* is complicated by the fact that the 'evidence' of analogue materiality in such texts is increas-ingly generated via digital technologies of representation. Similarly, in the comedy horror *Dead Snow* (Tommy Wirkola, 2009), digital compositing is combined with practical effects in order to show a squadron of Nazi zombies emerging from the icy Norwegian landscape. Regarded col-lectively, zombie films thus confound any comprehensive attempts to generalise about the shift from an analogue to a digital ontology or phenomenology. Furthermore, as I hope to have demonstrated by now, zombie cinema's spectacular incarnations of the analogue and digital dead are strikingly consonant in terms of their emphasis on contingency and material embodiment.

Although I argue here that contingency is a persistent thematic, stylistic and narrative trope in many zombie films, this is not to suggest that they can be read uniformly as subversive texts (either politically or aestheti-cally). Significantly, Mary Ann Doane opposes contingency to cinematic spectacle, which 'functions to localise desire, fantasy, and longing in a timeless time, outside contingency'.[43] For Doane, spectacle is inherently conservative because it neutralises time. However, in zombie films gen-erally (and *Planet Terror* in particular), we are witness to contingency *itself* as a form of spectacle. Here, the image is infiltrated by zombie time and turned inside out, so that spectacle threatens to overwhelm itself. Certainly, it is possible to see zombie cinema as a ground for subversive ideas (as Steven Shaviro's analysis of Romero's trilogy indicates), but my purpose is not to suggest that zombie films are inherently progressive. Instead, I argue that contingency offers a recurrent locus of pleasure and anxiety in zombie films, a zone of unstable vision where mediaphobia and mediaphilia appear as two sides of the same coin.

The protean nature of zombie media allows this affective structure to extend well beyond film and television. Indeed, the sense of contingent materiality that grounds zombie mediaphilia/mediaphobia is refracted and magnified by the movement of zombie films into new digital formats.

One can understand the workings of this process by considering the online circulation of an extract from Lucio Fulci's 1979 'masterpiece' *Zombi 2* (aka *Zombie Flesh Eaters* or *Zombie*), namely the notorious 'zombie vs shark' scene. This scene consists of a brief and unexplained subaquatic confrontation between a zombie and a shark that interrupts the main storyline without having any real bearing on subsequent events. Contingency saturates this scene at multiple levels, from the arbitrariness of the narrative to the material traces of the film's production process (highlighted by the sharp contrast between the actor's thickly applied zombie make-up and his evident, and very human, wariness of the shark). Like many other examples of B-movie excess, the 'zombie vs shark' scene has been uploaded to YouTube. One version of the clip appears to have been produced by pointing a video camera at a TV monitor. It includes two layers of letterboxing: one horizontal set produced through letterboxing on a 4:3 screen; the second vertical set through YouTube's recent adoption of the 16:9 aspect ratio as a default. The image thus bears the evidence of multiple contingent layers of mediation, both analogue and digital. The lost resolution and dropped frames in this clip draw attention to the material limitations of its various layered formats, contributing to the image of a shared media sickness affecting both old and new media. Here, the figure of the zombie is diminished, viewed through layers of mediation and information loss, even as this degradation itself serves as a metaphorical embodiment of the zombie threat. Like many of the films discussed above, this clip provides access to a type of zombie mediaphilia that thrives upon contingent materiality. Here, the disintegration of meaning, the image, and the human body incarnates both the horror and the joyous possibilities of the contingent.

Zombitextuality

Ultimately, contingency inflects not only the zombie's audiovisual manifestation but also its narrative forms. At this level, the zombie's tendency towards entropic disorder can be mirrored or, as in some recent examples I will discuss below, managed and mitigated. In Romero's original trilogy and its most direct descendants, a sense of contingent, unfolding time is communicated via the flatness of the narrative. The stories tend to be linear and flatly paced, lack flashbacks, and are often restricted to a limited period, as if the events were recorded in real time. The titles are indicative: alongside Romero's *Night*, *Dawn* and *Day of the Dead* sit *28 Days Later* and *28 Weeks Later*, *REC* and *Diary of the Dead*. The chronicle format of these films indicates an orientation towards what literary critic Frank

Kermode identifies as *chronos* (passing time), as opposed to *kairos* (time structured according to some ultimate meaning).[44] While *kairos* derives its resonance, according to Kermode, from the Biblical orientation towards the Apocalypse as the final revelation of meaning, *chronos* unfolds sequentially and is not shaped prospectively or retrospectively by the imposition of signification. Unlike conventional Gothic narratives, with their characteristic mysteries, rituals and backstories, these zombie films are not strongly anchored around retrospective revelations or anticipatory prophesies. With their contingent, unfolding chrono-logic and their orientation towards 'passing time', these films therefore embrace *chronos* rather than *kairos*. Conversely, their scenes of social breakdown and hellish brutality evoke nothing less than the Apocalypse itself. As David Pagano points out, Romero's zombie films effectively bring forward the Apocalypse into the present moment, unleashing the End of Days among the everyday. Romero's most subversive ploy, according to Pagano, is to allow this apocalyptic narrative to play out as *chronos*, thereby depriving it of its transcendent significance.[45] By virtue of its narrative articulation (which tends towards the chronicle format and emphasises chance events), as well as its visual aesthetic (which gravitates towards disorder), 'post-Romero' zombie cinema is thus a cinema of the contingent.[46]

However, beyond the core group of post-Romero films, there is considerable variation in the narrational and generic framing of the contingent. At one end of the scale are the films of Lucio Fulci: as illustrated by *Zombi 2*, Fulci specialises in arbitrary outbreaks of violence and surreal imagery. In this and other films, including *City of the Living Dead* (1980) and *The House by the Cemetery* (1981), Fulci presents contradictory explanations for the zombies' emergence, while flaunting breaches in narrative logic. In the inconsistency of his plots, themes and characters, argue Steven Zani and Kevin Meaux, Fulci is the quintessential zombie director: 'his films are themselves the breakdown of order and understanding, repeating in their form (or rather, in their breakdown of form) the same thing that they represent in their content'.[47] Here, the zombie functions 'as a tool for subverting narrative itself, along with our presumptions about what narrative is, and the sense of order and meaning inherent within the narrative framework'.[48] Similarly, at the end of *The Beyond* (1981), where the final survivors of a zombie onslaught find themselves stranded in a vast wasteland with no apparent hope of escape, Roger Luckhurst comments that Fulci presents 'not just social apocalypse but the very end of meaning itself'.[49] Here, the bodily dissolution of the zombie finds full narrative expression in a metatextual disordering that I will refer to as 'zombitextuality'.

At the other end of the scale are those films that attempt to manage and mitigate zombitextuality, primarily through the recombination of generic categories, which, as scholars including Ian Olney and Sherryl Vint have noted, has been a notable feature of zombie cinema since the early 2000s.[50] Hybrid forms have included zombie melodrama (*Maggie* [Henry Hobson, 2013]), zombie romance (*Warm Bodies* [Jonathan Levine, 2013]), zombie comedy (*Zombieland* and *Zombieland: Double Tap* [Ruben Fleischer, 2009/2019]), zombie Christmas coming-of-age musical (*Anna and the Apocalypse* [John McPhail, 2017]), zombie literary adaptation (*Pride and Prejudice and Zombies* [Burr Steers, 2016]), zombie anime (*Seoul Station* [Yeon Sang-ho, 2016]) and zombie action film (*World War Z* [Marc Forster, 2013]). Within this group of films, zombitextuality comes into contact with other generic structures, in ways that can sometimes involve the partial containment or neutralisation of contingency. One way in which this occurs is via character development. 'Since about 2010,' Luckhurst argues, 'some zombies have also been acquiring a flickering of consciousness, intelligence, halting speech and conflicted emotional lives, soliloquising and even falling in love'.[51] In films like *Warm Bodies* and *The Girl with All the Gifts* (Colm McCarthy, 2016), the emergence of undead protagonists guides the zombie along a more ordered path. In the former film, the zombie's romantic desire causes his heart to start beating again (in this case, the specific trigger is a vinyl record, which he treasures because it sounds 'more alive' than digital media). In the latter, a young girl who is the offspring of an 'infected' mother survives a postapocalyptic confrontation between mistrustful soldiers and feral 'hungries', and ends up, in the film's final scene, sitting together for a school lesson together with other hybrid children (as the teacher is safely ensconced behind glass). The narrative dynamics, in each case, thus ameliorate the more disruptive aspects of zombitextuality, its tendency towards disorder and nonmeaning.

In a more general sense, the zombie's cultural ubiquity has also served to diminish its contingent threat. Roger Luckhurst questions whether our immersion in the 'zombie apocalypse', in everything from video games to zombie walks, has caused a cultural domestication of the zombie.[52] Nonetheless, the zombie itself still appears as an identifiable agent of contingency, which can be introduced to a vast range of narrative contexts, often for comedic effect. The additive logic of this zombitextual approach is encapsulated in the title of *Pride and Prejudice and Zombies*, itself an adaptation of Seth Grahame-Smith's 2009 novel, in which Jane Austen's original work is 'infected' by an outbreak of narrational and textual disorder.[53] Both Austen's novel and its depicted world of nineteenth-century manners and social propriety are menaced by the abject presence of the zombies. This threat, however, is managed via the maintenance of the core romantic plot, combined with the operation of action and comedy tropes. Not only are Elizabeth and Darcy successfully united at the end; they are also, it transpires, expert zombie slayers. Nonetheless, in a flourish of zombitextuality, the closing credit sequence is interrupted briefly by a shot of Darcy's romantic rival Wickham leading a zombie horde on horseback: a final gesture towards the contingent, additive logic expressed in the title's 'and zombies'.

Perhaps the most extreme example of zombitextuality's neutralisation is provided by the blockbuster *World War Z*. Departing from the chronicle format of Max Brooks's original novel, and centring its story on a single heroic protagonist, the film sets out to contain zombies in multiple ways: narratively, spatially and ontologically. Sought out by the military, Gerry Lane is tasked with assisting in efforts to locate a vaccine for the zombie virus that has overtaken the planet. Although the story unfolds as a chain of episodes strung out across international locations, the action–suspense narrative takes precedence. Confidently traversing various sites of conflict, Gerry successfully isolates a vaccine, seeing off the entropic threat of the zombie before rejoining his family. Meanwhile, the key military command centre is located on an aircraft carrier, and thus insulated from the zombie threat, and it is here that Gerry's wife and children are housed in exchange for his involvement. Spatial containment thus preserves the military and the family, two social institutions which are regularly presented in other zombie films as rotting from within. Even consumer culture, the satirical target of countless zombie films from *Dawn of the Dead* to *The Dead Don't Die* (Jim Jarmusch, 2019), is left intact, as the freshly inoculated Gerry pauses for a can of Pepsi before strolling past the zombies unmolested. Ultimately, the neutralisation of zombitextuality is mirrored in the film's depiction of media and communication technologies, which ultimately work as a means of combatting the outbreak, from the massive data screens at the command centre, to Gerry's Iridium satellite phone, to the surveillance system at the Welsh research facility that allows the scientists to monitor the zombies' behaviour. The effectiveness of mediated communication against the zombies is underlined in the film's final montage when Gerry has been reunited with his family in Nova Scotia. Here, a mediatised sonic weave of radio messages and public information broadcasts is combined with the qualified optimism of Gerry's voiceover and with visual footage of mass exterminations and military strikes. Rather than unleashing the threat of disorder and nonmeaning, this sequence suggests instead a militarised cleansing operation, in which the lines separating

zombies from humans and zombitextuality from signification are reinforced rather than challenged.

Nonetheless, zombitextuality has continued to flourish in other texts
and contexts, even as the zombie film has undergone transformations and
recombinations. *Train to Busan* (Yeon Sang-ho, 2016) incorporates elements of family melodrama; its protagonist, Seok-woo, is a self-absorbed
fund manager who must accompany his daughter on a train trip to visit
his estranged wife. When zombies overrun the train, it becomes clear that
cooperation is the only way to fend off the zombies, so Seok-woo must
unlearn his selfish ways in order to protect his daughter. Although the film
is tightly plotted and eventually produces a moment of character redemp-
tion for Seok-woo (after we discover that his company was somehow
responsible for the outbreak), other aspects of the film, including the
real-time narrative, the linear progression of the train and the ambivalent, half-resolved ending, suggest *chronos* rather than *kairos*. Contingency
is multiplied via other means too, including communication channels.
The civil defence report broadcast via the train's onboard screens is not
only glitchy but clearly misleading, as is the official advice that leads the
characters to disembark at Daejeon, where the protective military force
turn out to have already been zombified. Cell phones are also a central
element, linked both to the careless individualism of Seok-woo and the
other characters (which allows the zombies to multiply) and also to the
viral spread of panic and misinformation (illustrated at one point by a
close-up of cascading text messages, apparently in contravention of an
official announcement discouraging the spread of rumours). Unlike *World
War Z*, *Train to Busan* embraces contingency as fundamental to its rendering of characters, concepts, technologies and stories.

Zombitextuality has even been employed in the absence of zombies.
In *One Cut of the Dead* (Shin'ichirô Ueda, 2017), a group of filmmakers
making a low-budget zombie film are apparently attacked by real zombies
and end up capturing the events in a single take on handheld video.
However, this formula, familiar from *Diary of the Dead*, undergoes a
further metatextual twist when it is revealed that the whole zombie attack
and real-time recording of it were in fact staged by the diegetic filmmakers.
The remaining two-thirds of the film details the process of planning and
executing this single-take exercise, which is broadcast live on television.
In the final section, we are given a 'behind-the-scenes' perspective on the
zombie film, replete with missed cues, feats of resourcefulness and just-in-
time arrivals. From this angle, contingency takes centre stage, in the form
of unexpected events and encounters. One of the performers has shown
up drunk, another is diverted by an upset stomach, and two others are

prevented from attending by a car accident *en route* to the location. The film constantly threatens to fall apart: from the dummy's head that falls off at the wrong moment, to the on-the-fly script revisions that are devised and communicated from the control centre. Although *One Cut of the Dead* is a zombie film without zombies, it is nonetheless pervaded by zombitextuality, from its countless brushes with contingency to its multimedia patchwork structure.

Zombitextuality thus posits the zombie as an agent of disorder and contingency. Lurking behind this textual disorder, as I have argued, is the figure of the 'media zombie' and the associated notion of 'zombie media'. Through this figuration, media are overlaid with bodily metaphors, and are seen as vulnerable, like human bodies, to ageing, disease and dismemberment. In zombie films, bodies are menaced not only by contingent encounters with the undead but also by the contingent signs of mediation, including film grain, colour shifts, distortion, dropped frames, and digital artefacts. Media's capacity for capturing, transmitting and reproducing contingency is connected with a loss of meaning and order which also plays out across human bodies. This bodily orientation towards the contingent may serve to explain in part the appeal of the zombie film, which hinges, as per Carroll's argument, on the zombie's equivocation between ontological categories, but also on the medium's equivocation among speeds, resolutions, and formats. Traversing digital and analogue media, the films discussed here explore the shared media sickness that connects the glitches and information loss of the digital with the traces of analogue decay. Zombie media are thus central to the subgenre's fascination with the breakdown of bodies and meaning.

The intertwining of contingent reality and media materiality extends beyond the cinematic examples I have discussed here. Public zombie parades, for example, performed in countless cities around the world, and replayed in countless amateur videos on YouTube, offer a humorous gloss on contingency. Bringing together large numbers of strangers, many of them sporting gory makeup and dishevelled clothes, these parades establish urban spaces as potential venues for random zombie encounters. As clips of these events disperse across the web, they produce other contingent encounters among viewers, participants and media. The image of a viral outbreak, sustained by chance encounters, is entirely appropriate to this fan activity and its online consumption. Similarly, in 2009, a group of Texan pranksters captured the ubiquity and contingent materiality of zombie media by reprogramming digital road signs to warn against zombie attacks.[54] Wittingly or unwittingly, these hackers provided recognition of the modern zombie's intimate connection with media technology and its material limitations. Ultimately, these digitally constituted warnings signal that technology has already failed as a defence against the contingent, because contingency always already infects our technologies, making all media zombie media.

Notes

1. Zombie cinema has an extensive history preceding Romero's watershed film. Roger Luckhurst points out the zombie's origins in the transatlantic slave trade, with its imposition of forced labour, dehumanisation and colonial violence, and argues that contemporary readings should acknowledge this history. Nonetheless, my focus here is on developments in the imagination of the zombie that are tied more narrowly to the development of postwar media culture. See Luckhurst, *Zombies: A Cultural History*. Other comprehensive accounts can be found in Dendle, *The Zombie Movie Encyclopedia*; McIntosh, 'The evolution of the zombie: the monster that keeps coming back', pp. 1–17; and Russell, *Book of the Dead: The Complete History of Zombie Cinema*.
2. Gunning, 'To scan a ghost: the ontology of mediated vision', p. 100.
3. Sconce, *Haunted Media: Electronic Presence from Telegraphy to Television*, pp. 8–9.
4. There are exceptions to this general rule. Lucio Fulci's zombie films, for example, are based upon the return of forces from the past. In Fulci's *Zombi 2* (1979) a curse causes the dead, including a band of long-dead Spanish conquistadors, to rise from beneath the ground, while evil acts in *City of the Living Dead* (1980) and *The Beyond* (1981) open the gates of Hell, unleashing hordes of undead attackers. More recently, *Rec 2* (Jaume Balagueró and Paco Plaza, 2009) uses demonic possession to explain a viral outbreak that turns ordinary citizens into zombie-like creatures.
5. Sobchack, *Screening Space: The American Science Fiction Film*, p. 190.
6. Stewart, 'Body snatching: science fiction's photographic trace', p. 226.
7. Ibid. p. 247.
8. Shaviro, *The Cinematic Body*, p. 85.
9. Recent film and digital releases have somewhat de-emphasised the 'roughness' of *Night of the Living Dead*, although Ben Hervey argues that this was part of the film's aesthetic from the start. See Hervey, *Night of the Living Dead*. Hervey notes that Romero 'deliberately chose unsuitable, over-grainy stock for some scenes' (p. 26), and that the film's concluding still images, showing the dead bodies of the main characters being carried out on meat-hooks and thrown on to a bonfire, were printed through cheesecloth 'to make them coarse and grainy, like newsprint' (p. 113).
10. Although some of these examples are not strictly speaking zombie films, they are virtually identical in terms of their narrative set-up (a viral outbreak turns humans into mindless, flesh-eating monsters), their bleak, apocalyptic tone,

and their fascination with the visceral materiality of bodies and the techno-logical materiality of media.

11. Simon Pegg, *Shaun of the Dead*'s co-writer and lead actor, launched a modest but serious polemic against fast zombies in a newspaper opinion piece. See Pegg, 'The dead and the quick'. Many fans posting to online forums were less circumspect.

12. Krzywinska, 'Zombies in gamespace: form, content, and meaning in zombie-based video games', p. 159.

13. Mulvey, *Death 24x a Second: Stillness and the Moving Image*.

14. Stewart, *Between Film and Screen: Modernism's Photo Synthesis*.

15. Barthes, *Camera Lucida*.

16. Bazin, *What Is Cinema?*. For Bazin, 'photography does not create eternity, as art does, it embalms time, rescuing it simply from its proper corruption' (p. 14).

17. Mulvey, *Death 24x a Second*, p. 66.

18. Ibid. p. 11.

19. Stewart, *Between Film and Screen*, p. xi.

20. Ibid. p. 37.

21. Ibid. p. 37.

22. Shaviro, *The Cinematic Body*, p. 256.

23. Sobchack, *The Address of the Eye: A Phenomenology of Film Experience*, p. 171.

24. Ibid. p. 25.

25. Ibid. p. 69–70.

26. Shaviro, *The Cinematic Body*, p. 96.

27. Romero's *Land of the Dead* (2005) is one substantial exception. It features a group of zombies who collectively teach themselves how to swim, thus making possible an assault on a besieged group of the living.

28. Shaviro, *The Cinematic Body*, p. 77.

29. Doane, *The Emergence of Cinematic Time: Modernity, Contingency, the Archive*, p. 32.

30. Ibid. p. 29.

31. Ibid. p. 145.

32. Carroll, *The Philosophy of Horror; or, Paradoxes of the Heart*, p. 31.

33. Ibid. p. 191.

34. Ibid. p. 41.

35. Quoted in Karlin, 'How *The Walking Dead* Brings New Life to Zombies—Without CGI'.

36. Ibid.

37. *Planet Terror* DVD commentary track.

38. Quoted in Bielik, '*Grindhouse*: Pistol-Packing VFX'.

39. Ersatz contingency is also a feature of contemporary video games. See, for example, game designer Mike Booth's retrospective reflection on the popular zombie game *Left 4 Dead* (Valve, 2008), which incorporates a sophisticated 'AI director' that changes the pace and difficulty of play in response to player

inputs in order to maximise engagement, fear and surprise. See Freeman-Mills, 'Mike Booth, the architect of *Left 4 Dead*'s AI director, explains why it's so bloody good'.

40. Sobchack, *Carnal Thoughts: Embodiment and Moving Image Culture*, p. 161.

41. Kirkland, '*Resident Evil*'s typewriter: survival horror and its remediations', p. 124.

42. See also Rodowick, *The Virtual Life of Film* and Stewart, *Framed Time: Toward a Postfilmic Cinema*; both writers propose that digital media have a fundamentally different relationship to temporality than their analogue counterparts.

43. Doane, *The Emergence of Cinematic Time*, p. 170.

44. Kermode, *The Sense of an Ending*, p. 47.

45. Pagano, 'The space of apocalypse in zombie cinema', p. 72.

46. Max Brooks's popular novel *World War Z* also uses a chronicle format to narrate the arrival and aftermath of a zombie apocalypse. The book takes the form of a series of reports and interviews with witnesses from various countries.

47. Zani and Meaux, 'Lucio Fulci and the decaying definition of zombie narratives', p. 110.

48. Ibid. p. 99.

49. Luckhurst, *Zombies*, p. 166.

50. Olney, *Zombie Cinema*, pp. 1-2; Vint, 'Abject posthumanism: neoliberalism, biopolitics, and zombies', p. 173.

51. Luckhurst, *Zombies*, p. 14.

52. Ibid. p. 167–9.

53. Grahame-Smith and Austen, *Pride and Prejudice and Zombies*.

54. See 'Zombies! Run! (TxDOT is not amused)'.

CHAPTER 3

Corporeal Frames: Found-Footage Horror and the Dislocated Image

Despite their deliberately unrefined aesthetic means, found-footage horror films like *Paranormal Activity* (Oren Peli, 2007), *Cloverfield* (Matt Reeves, 2008), *Unfriended* (Leo Gabriadze, 2014) and *Host* (Rob Savage, 2020) offer an intensive formal reflection on the frame's capacity to capture and articulate bodily relations. Here, the visual perspective is provided by video cameras within the narrative itself, whether wielded by the characters themselves or installed as instruments of surveillance. These cameras become our interface to the diegetic world, revealing evidence of a poltergeist, capturing the damage wrought by a rampaging monster, or relaying the 'live' content of video chat sessions. The video frame, as epistemological and phenomenological boundary, takes on heightened significance, outlining various kinds of 'image-bodies', including those captured onscreen but also those that hover out of frame, including camera operators, and, looking further afield, even spectators. A subgenre founded on an overt invocation of the raw and the real, found-footage horror nonetheless presents the body itself as a textual effect, generated at the boundary between film discourse and the material world.

My use of the term 'frame' here is primarily visual-spatial, but it will also include the technical (the framing role of different media formats) and the temporal (the sequential arrangement of film or video frames). In each case, the relationship between whole and part, between totality and fragment, is central to the film's aesthetic and narrational logic. Although found-footage horror tends to invoke a total 'world' that is unfolding in real time, it also presents us with a deliberately partial, limited view of that world, shaped by borders and limits. These are tales told via media remnants and narrative scraps. Moreover, such films often work to produce what I refer to as a 'media differential', evident in various spatiotemporal misalignments between recording and viewing, digital and analogue media, and human and technological vision. Rather than establishing some core ontological *difference* between these various elements, however, the media *differential* invokes an inaugural split underlying mediation, sensation and sense-making. Mediation, from this perspective, is not an external threat that menaces human characters from outside. Rather, the camera is always already present and mediation always already implicit.

Cameras, Bodies, Frames

The foregrounding of mediation in found-footage horror is ambiguous: on the one hand, it seems to vouch for an underlying temporal continuity, captured by the camera as observer; on the other, it highlights various kinds of discontinuity, embedded in the movement between formats, frames and contexts. In *The Blair Witch Project* (Daniel Myrick and Eduardo Sanchez, 1999), the film generally credited with kick-starting the millennial found-footage cycle, a trio of student filmmakers becomes lost in the woods while investigating the eponymous witch. Using a 16 mm camera (with black-and-white film stock) alongside a Hi8 video camera, they document their own conflict, disorientation and terror as they encounter strange noises, disturbing artifacts and impenetrable darkness. Footage from these two cameras has, according to the opening title cards, been retrieved after the filmmakers' disappearance, hence the designation of this film and others like it as found-footage films. The partial, unstable view afforded by each camera, combined with recurring periods of darkness, hints at an amorphous threat that seems always to lie just beyond the boundaries of the frame. Ultimately, the witch's existence is never definitively confirmed, and the agent of the filmmakers' apparent demise remains out of view. The stability and orientation of the visual field is thus an ongoing dramatic problem. As night presses in, the filmmakers' frantic handheld camerawork fails again and again to capture the source of the strange noises emanating from the woods. Huddled in her tent, one of the characters resorts to delivering a frightened monologue direct to camera, her face looming awkwardly at the bottom of the image as if to illustrate the frame's inability to contain or manage the threat pressing in from outside.

In such scenes, the relationship between the body and the camera (both as a material presence and a framing device) is central. As Barry Keith Grant points out, the foregrounding of the 'camera as apparatus' marks a crucial departure from the camera's 'invisible or effaced presence' in classic narrative cinema.[1] Using the audiovisual language of amateur video to deliver cinematic narrative, *The Blair Witch Project* makes its audience aware of the camera's limited capacity for representing the world, as well as its material vulnerability. Caetlin Benson-Allott observes that found-footage films menace viewers by aligning them not only with the camera-wielding protagonists but also the camera itself: as it 'gets shaken, dropped, beaten, and otherwise abused over the course of the movie, the spectator experiences its trauma as a personal assault'.[2] This account assigns a kind of bodily presence to the camera, whether it is carried by characters within the diegesis or stationed, as in *Paranormal Activity*, as a surveillance device. Indeed, *The Blair Witch Project* helps to establish the victimised camera as a signature trope of the subgenre: after the characters have been fatally dispatched, the fallen device lies on the ground, documenting the film's empty final moments.

The presence of the camera as a virtual 'body' within the diegesis both simplifies and complicates its relationship with the visual frame. According to Edward Branigan, the concept 'camera' reaches beyond the technical or material or even visual dimension, encompassing 'the schematic and abstract wherein lies language and the language of film'.[3] The operations of film language, he suggests, can require the spectator to engage in 'imagining a camera'.[4] By contrast, in *The Blair Witch Project* this aspect of film language is short-circuited, since the imagined camera is granted a literal presence within the diegesis. In a radical streamlining of film form, the visual frame is aligned with a material camera, producing an overt 'reality effect'. Conversely, the resulting departures from classical cinematic language also produce a commensurate foregrounding of the film's material and rhetorical structure. As Steven Shaviro argues regarding found-footage horror's use of both handheld and surveillance imagery, '[n]either sort of camera gives us the raw material needed for the conventional continuity style'.[5] Instead of the orchestrated back-and-forth of the shot-reverse shot and the effacement of spatiotemporal disjunctures, found-footage films offer extremes of fragmentation on the one hand and protracted duration on the other. In this context, the visual frame is no longer a 'natural' effect of film grammar but becomes a central discursive concern. Here, the camera's supplementary 'body' needs to be accounted for within the viewer's apprehension of the narrative.

Despite this overt departure from classical conventions, however, some scholars have associated the found-footage film's camera-centred aesthetic with a heightened sense of continuity. Barry Keith Grant, for example, argues that such films are Bazinian in their commitment to the idea of a world beyond the frame.[6] Similarly, Cecilia Sayad claims that in placing the camera inside the world of the story, the found-footage horror 'merges the film and the extra filmic'.[7] While suture theory 'presupposes the perception of the film image as a cut-out from a unified whole', for Sayad these films suggest an extended model of space, which is not controlled, delimited and defined by the frame.[8] This view aligns with film theorist Dudley Andrew's rejection of the flat, abstracted 2D frame of classical film theory,[9] and his corresponding embrace of the screen as a 'threshold', which 'adds a third dimension to the frame, taken either as depth or as time'.[10] Found-footage horror would seem to provide a concrete affirmation of this perspective: *The Blair Witch Project*'s unpredictable camerawork, for example, emphasises unfettered spatial exploration over abstract order. Expanding on her argument, Sayad argues that the extension of the frame in found-footage horror is contextual as well as visual. It is evident not only in the films' exploration of physical space, but also in the apparent blurring of boundaries between fiction and documentary, and in the use of online content (such as websites and social media profiles) to suggest an expansive diegetic universe.[11]

The problem with such continuity-based readings, however, is that they overlook the deliberate dislocations of found-footage horror, from the juxtaposition of formats to the incomplete alignment between human and camera vision. The frame may be shifting and subject to dizzying movements, but this does not entail its wholesale dissolution. Indeed, it is the very mobility of the image across media that makes the frame an important concept in relation to these films. As Edward Branigan points out, there are many different kinds of 'frame' used to refer to film, from the physical to the conceptual, and these are overlapping rather than neatly aligned.[12] In understanding the found-footage film's articulation of frames, one could draw on a number of Branigan's proposed definitions, from 'the *real edge* of an image on the screen' and 'the *view* that is given on a fictive action', to the '*narration* or discourse' that produces the story and 'the relevant subset of our world knowledge' that bears upon its reception.[13] Accordingly, the spectator's reading of the frame *as* a frame in found-footage horror is qualified by their awareness of the camera as a diegetic element, a narrative gimmick and a mediating device. In *The Blair Witch Project*, the visual-spatial framing of the image needs to be read in relation to the various technical frames surrounding its capture and display. These are not reducible to a single screen or interface; rather, the image's movement across different types of screen (both diegetic and extra-diegetic) is what defines it.

Like other found-footage horror films, *The Blair Witch Project* generates what might be termed a *dramatic irony of the frame*, which derives from a deliberate misalignment between the ostensible production and exhibition contexts. An intertitle at the beginning of the film informs us that the footage was discovered after the disappearance of the three filmmakers. What we are watching is an edited assembly of this raw footage, interleaving the material from both cameras and thus producing a final version which has not been anticipated by the diegetic 'filmmakers' (who are, we must assume, now dead). Our interpretation of the material depends on our understanding that it is not being screened in its intended context. The foregrounding of medium specificity (stipulating cameras, stocks and so forth) draws attention to the movement of the framed image across screens and systems, and thus, paradoxically, to its loss of material identity. The framed image we are watching never seems to 'know' its ultimate context.

By contrast, Dudley Andrew's Bazinian account of cinematic depth depends heavily on an architectural reading, which incorporates not only the screen itself but also the theatre lobby, the curtains, the opening credits and other related thresholds.[14] For this reason, he sets the 'expanded three-dimensional frame of cinema' apart from the 'TV monitor, which works by a succession of instant recognitions put together in montage'.[15] This rigid medial demarcation, however, is of little use in the context of found-footage cinema, which works by blending *different* types of screen, from the projection screen to the video monitor to the digital interface. Human bodies have different implied relationships to each of these screens: regulated distance in a cinema, proximity in relationship to television, intimacy with a laptop or mobile. The frame is carried across each of these screens, often existing in ironic relation to them. This is not the deterministic frame of suture theory; rather, it is a frame that moves across formats and contexts, revealing spatial and temporal disjunctures in the process.

Composite Mediality

The frame as delimiting visual form, then, is not the only signifying boundary in these films. In a broad sense, found-footage horror oversees a multiplication of technical frames, as the infrastructure of mediation provides an array of inputs, outputs and formats, each of which inscribe their own material limits. In this section, I will explore found-footage horror's composite form in more detail, before considering how its varied technical frames might align, or fail to align, with the diegetic characters' bodily experiences. In *The Blair Witch Project*, the alternation between film and video renders the film a media patchwork: the two cameras provide views of the same fundamental 'reality', even as they foreground the partial and contrasting nature of the two perspectives. In the opening scenes, a mutual interrogation of formats takes place, as the filmmakers grapple with their camera and sound equipment, trying to learn the settings. The alternations between film and video suggest a fragmented portrait of reality, and also amplify the conflicts that erupt among the characters. However, there is no decisive ontological differentiation between these different formats. Instead, *The Blair Witch Project* concentrates on their mutual inability to capture the events unfolding in front of them. Indeed, as David Banash notes, the film shows a general breakdown afflicting all technological affordances, with cameras, maps and compasses all failing to help orient the characters.[16] In this way, the juxtaposition of different technologies serves to highlight their mutual failings.

Moreover, media in the found-footage film are riven with internal differences. These differences have to do with the movement between first-person and third-person perspectives, with the migration of images across different screens and formats, and with the relay between 'real' and 'delayed' time in recording and reviewing the footage. This complex structure of thresholds and boundaries naturally intersects with theoretical questions of intermediality and intramediality. For Irina O. Rajewsky, intermediality 'designates those configurations which have to do with a crossing of borders between media, and which thereby can be differentiated from *intra*medial phenomena as well as from *trans*medial phenomena (i.e. the appearance of a certain motif, aesthetic, or discourse across a variety of different media)'.[17] In this instance, however, the borders are unclear. Is the primary encounter between technical formats (16 mm film and digital video, for example), or between cinematic and videographic conventions (feature film narrative and home movie)? Which boundaries are significant?

Found-footage horror, I argue, displays what Ágnes Pethő refers to a 'structural' mode of intermediality, which 'makes the media components of cinema visible, and exposes the layers of multimediality that constitute the "fabric" of the cinematic medium, revealing at the same time the mesh of their complex interactions'.[18] Indeed, the most prominent differences here are internal, involving the patchwork of media inputs that constitute not only cinematic narratives, but also home movies and evidentiary videos. This particular kind of intermediality is thus also a kind of *intramediality*, since it focuses on differences that are internal to moving image media. Rather than one medium interrogating another discrete medium, we are presented with a wholesale interpenetration of media. The found-footage film produces encounters between video and cinema, digital and analogue, and production and reception, multiplying both overlaps and divisions. This dynamic accords with Jihoon Kim's assessment of contemporary encounters between film, video and digital media as grounded in a 'dialectic of medium specificity and hybridity'.[19] It is not that medium specificity itself is denied, but that distinct media formats are reconfigured into new hybrid forms, producing an array of comminglings and dislocations.

It is therefore important not to reduce the found-footage film to a manifestation of 'digital horror', even though most of its recent exemplars have been created with digital cameras and postproduction equipment. For one, there are notable pre-digital examples of the form. Most famously, *Cannibal Holocaust* (Ruggero Deodato, 1980) contains segments of 16 mm footage ostensibly shot by a documentary crew in the lead-up to their grisly deaths at the hands of Amazonian cannibals. Similarly, *Man Bites Dog* (Rémy Belvaux, André Bonzel and Benoît Poelvoorde, 1992) consists of 'real' 16 mm footage shot by a film crew chronicling the daily life of a serial killer. Similarly, although the creators of *The Blair Witch Project* made innovative use of a website to disseminate and promote the film's documentary 'evidence', the film itself is composed of analogue film and video footage.

Moreover, some contemporary examples deliberately blur the ontological distinctions between digital and analogue media. In the process, they present the film itself as a kind of composite 'media-body', an assemblage of inputs and formats. *V/H/S/2* (2013) is one such film. It operates according to a logic of multiplication and seriality, focusing attention on the ironic relation between frame and screen.[20] This work is not only a sequel to the original *V/H/S/* but also, like its earlier counterpart, an anthology, in which four found-footage artefacts are all discovered at one location. In the frame tale, a private investigator and his sidekick, searching for a missing boy named Kyle, infiltrate his house and find a collection of VHS tapes, a bank of monitors screening video static, and a laptop containing video clips of Kyle himself. These digital clips begin with Kyle's exhortation to watch the VHS tapes, and culminate with his apparent attempted suicide. At the end of the film, however, Kyle emerges from the shadows to attack the investigators. The film's media-intensive setup thus involves a structure of nested frames: the digital recordings provide an initial frame for the VHS recordings, which in turn serve as frames for the various narrative episodes. Meanwhile, the technological array of screens, files and tapes provides a frame for Kyle's narrative. In a further instance of dramatic irony, it transpires that Kyle has escaped all media frames, and instead waits literally behind the investigators' backs.

Interleaved with this clumsy narrative, the VHS tapes themselves reveal yet another layer of irony: all of the recordings consist of digitally-shot footage. Despite the title's overt reference to analogue media, *V/H/S/2* is saturated with the digital, both in the format of the recordings and the central role played by the laptop computer as media machine. Highlighting the materiality of media, the film simultaneously blurs the boundaries separating analogue and digital formats. It begins by presenting media as

Figure 3.1 An array of media screens greets the investigators in *V/H/S/2/* (Simon Barrett et al, 2013).

threatening, via the eerie tableau of static-filled monitors, stacked videotapes and laptop computer, but this threat is assigned neither to old nor to new media exclusively. Rather, it is mediation itself that menaces the characters, via a recursive relay between different screens, formats and archives, including analogue tapes alongside digital files. Furthermore, much as the unearthed video footage in *The Blair Witch Project* serves as a material stand-in for the bodies of the missing filmmakers, the tableau of media technologies discovered by the investigators provides a material analogue for the absent body of Kyle. This threatening media assemblage anticipates, and provides a spatial mirror for, Kyle's physical emergence from the background at the end of the film.

The ironic relationship between cameras, frames and bodies is carried over into each of *V/H/S/2*'s embedded narratives. In the first of these, the main character is furnished with an optical implant, which soon begins to glitch, revealing fleeting images of demonic figures. The film's visual perspective is identical to that of the implant, producing a thorough alignment of physical and mechanical vision. The positioning of the implant in the subject's orbital cavity leads, conversely, to an experience of dislocated vision, since the otherworldly images it produces fail to match up with other aspects of his bodily experience. As if to underline this point, the film has the protagonist meet another character with a cochlear implant, who can hear but not see the same ghosts that plague his visual field. Here, the investigation of technologized experience leads to a teasing apart of sound and image. The image is grounded in the physical frame of the subject's body, yet also menaces the body with sensory contradictions.

The other episodes, similarly, play with the misalignment of cameras and bodies. In the second film, a mountain biker's helmet-mounted GoPro documents his encounter with roving zombies as well as his own subsequent zombification. The elevated camera thus presents a kind of zombie vision, which never quite matches the character's optical perspective. This effect becomes apparent following his transformation, when he begins to vomit blood. As his hands and his effluvium enter the frame, both are clearly misaligned with what we 'know' about the spatial organisation of the human body: this is the camera's view and not the protagonist's. Contact with other characters, particularly when he bites them, further illustrates this misalignment. The third and most complex instalment in *V/H/S/2* shows a camera crew recording the activities of a religious cult, using conventional documentary cameras, hidden shirt-button cameras and the cult's own surveillance system. The bloody massacre that culminates this instalment presents numerous opportunities for dislocated perspectives, showing what happens when the human actors lose control of technologized vision. In the final tape, a group of children take turns filming as they perform pranks on each other. The camera thus becomes an instrument of shaming and retaliation that is exchanged between the characters. Ultimately, the device in question is attached to a dog, which is then, in a ludicrous twist, abducted by aliens. The visual alignment of the camera thus shifts across human, canine and extra-terrestrial perspectives.

At the end of every one of *V/H/S/2*'s portmanteau episodes, a camera that has been attached to the body is detached and ends up recording a key character's mortal moment. In the first instalment, the optical implant is cut out by the victim himself, after which the camera is picked up by one of the demons and thrust down his throat. The zombie from the second instalment shoots himself in the head, thus blasting off the helmet so that the GoPro captures his bloodied, inhuman face. At the end of the final instalment, the aliens drop the dog back to earth, at which point the detached camera documents the sad spectacle of the canine corpse. In sum, *V/H/S/2* represents a kind of a baroque turn in the found-footage genre, which involves cameras moving dynamically between alignment and misalignment with human perception. The various reversals and dislocations of perspective demonstrate the central role played by the ironic frame and suggest a kind of ontological mutability. Just as the stack of videotapes embodies a kind of confusion of analogue and digital technologies, *V/H/S/2*'s various narratives play upon the confusion between mediated and 'native' perception, as cameras and eyelines fall in and out of alignment.

Dislocated Bodies

The sensory dislocations of found-footage horror might suggest a negation of the human body as a conceptual and experiential frame. Accordingly, Shane Denson has argued that in our contemporary 'digital and more broadly post-cinematic media environment, moving images have undergone [. . . a . . .] "discorrelation" from human embodied subjectivities and (phenomenological, narrative, and visual) perspectives'.[21] For Denson, 'post-cinematic cameras' (which include both real and virtual cameras and screens) 'deviate from the perceptual norms established by human embodiment'.[22] The post-cinematic camera 'has shed the perceptually commensurate "body" that ensured cinematic communication' under the phenomenological model proposed by Vivian Sobchack.[23] These cameras show us things that we can't see, they occupy positions we cannot reach and they manifestly fail to perform the function of conventional point-of-view shots. However, although dislocated perspectives are certainly part of the found-footage horror's stylistic inventory, Denson underemphasises the extent to which these films maintain reference to the body as a perceptual frame. Indeed, one of the central affective strategies of such films is to *reincorporate* the uncanniness of the technical image, rendering it physical. The alien phenomenology of the camera and screen is folded into experiences and representations that are emphatically body-centred.

For example, in *Paranormal Activity 4* (Ariel Schulman and Henry Joost, 2012), the relation of body to frame is a central structuring dynamic. This film (which Denson himself draws upon in support of his argument) features a similar scenario to earlier instalments in the franchise: some sort of ghostly presence appears to have infiltrated a suburban family home, and the occupants make use of video recording technology to capture it. This technology includes a handheld digital camcorder as well as cameras on laptop computers, which provide simple video recordings and also relay live chat sessions between the main character, Alex, and her boyfriend, Ben. These laptops are sometimes stationary and sometimes carried around by characters. They also take on the function of screening devices, as the characters review previously shot footage. Moreover, the film makes innovative use of an X-Box Kinect, as I will discuss below. While Denson sees in *Paranormal Activity 4*'s use of new technologies 'the discorrelation of computational from human perception',[24] I argue that he underemphasises the close engagement between human bodies, cameras and computers in this film.

In *Paranormal Activity 4*, the body is a problem in relation to the frame: it is often conspicuously absent or excessively present. There are numerous examples of awkward framing, in which legs or faces appear at the periphery of the image. These uses of the frame invoke the epistemological questions that increasingly bedevil the characters: what else is present beyond the frame; what can or cannot be seen? They also heighten our awareness of the various cameras and screens that both occupy and articulate the characters' spatial environments. At one point, Ben, with whom Alex is trying to converse via video chat, is obscured by interference, until, to Alex's surprise, he appears abruptly in her room and seizes her from behind. This scene refers to the epistemological problem of Alex's immediate spatial environment, but also to the ontological problem of her media environment, in which Ben's distant, mediated body is transformed suddenly into a fleshly presence at the frame's periphery. By alternating between different cameras and recording scenarios, the film suggests an array of roles for the offscreen body, from distant spectator to hands-on operator. In one scene the video–chat perspective on Alex is coloured by Ben's verbal request for a peek at her breast, making us aware of his bodily (desiring) presence outside the frame. In another scene the camera shifts around as Alex's younger brother Wyatt insists on moving the laptop (and thus the laptop's onboard camera) closer to the bath, before Alex moves it away again. We are thus made conscious of the material presence of the recording technology, but also the vital bodily presence of its users.

Since Ben, in an attempt to capture visual evidence of the ghost, has set up the laptops to record video automatically, users often interact with their computers while unaware that they are also functioning as cameras. We witness Wyatt watching cartoons, and Alex's mother Holly looking up recipes online, each one of them unwittingly facing the laptop's reversed surveillant gaze. These cameras and screens are thus intimate. They can be cradled, reversed, handled, placed, exchanged. They look both ways. They are both seeing and seen. Even when they are just sitting in place, we are aware of the human actions that have determined their location. At the same time, these moments make us aware of our own spectatorial 'presence', placing us, via the literalism of the found-footage conceit, both 'inside' the screen at the moment of recording and, as witnesses after the fact, in our own lived location, where we are to imagine ourselves as first viewers of a documentary artefact. The *mise-en-abîme* of this camera-screen sets off a chain of bodily enquiries: not just 'where is the object of the gaze now?' (are they still alive or have they been dispatched by the demon?) but also 'where is its subject?' (watching alongside us, or already eliminated?) and also 'where am I to *imagine* my viewing body?' (at the filming location, hidden inside the apparatus of recording, projected into some diegetic space where I am watching the tapes or, indeed, right here, at my literal location?). The film further encourages such questions by showing the characters reviewing their own footage on laptop computers.

Paranormal Activity 4 thus replays a process of looking-at-looking, turning both cameras and inquisitive eyes back on themselves recursively. The body, as both optical and haptic presence, is folded into these multi-modal encounters: not just looking upon the mediated gaze, but holding it and physically directing it; not just in front of the camera but also behind and alongside it. Rather than viewing the film as overturning Sobchack's model of film-body relationality, as Denson suggests, we should regard it as intensifying and complicating it. In Sobchack's model, film itself has a body, consisting of the accumulation of technical affordances that enables film's registration of the visible world. Like the human viewing subject, and yet distinct from it, Sobchack argues that the film possesses a 'percep-tive and expressive *intention*' which is grounded in the 'material *instrumen-tality*' of cinematic technology.[25] Film's technical body thus parallels the viewer's physiological body, as each provides the ground for shared per-ceptual/expressive acts. In found-footage horror, however, this relation is further literalised and concretised, as the human body and cinematic body enter into direct tactile encounters. Sobchack uses the term 'address of the eye' to invoke both the 'locatedness' of vision in a bodily 'address' and the communicative act that connects cinematic and human vision.[26] Here, the address of the eye is reflexively complicated in both senses: these films place in question the location of the viewing body (of characters and spectators alike) in relation to the camera/screen, and transform the expressivity of cinematic vision by submitting it to the tactile interven-tions of diegetic characters. The corporeal 'frame' of embodied vision is thus rendered concrete and literal.

In *Paranormal Activity 4*, the frame-body relation is further complicated through the use of the Microsoft Kinect gaming console, as the characters exploit its infrared motion detection technology to reveal the presence of a ghost. Ben points out that when viewed through an infrared camera, the Kinect's light-point sensory system (which enables the machine to detect and respond to human movement) becomes visible. Through this technical trick, the room becomes filled with little green dots. Eventually, the little ghost, a small boy named Toby, manifests as a disturbance in these virtual pixels. These luminous dots are measures of spatial depth but also, in this form, produce a flattening of the space and an abstraction

Figure 3.2 The X-Box Kinect stipples the characters with infrared light in
Paranormal Activity 4 (Ariel Schulman and Henry Joost, 2012).

of its contents: in a sense, they turn space itself into media. Here, within
the stippled field of the frame, there are two optical systems at work: the
Kinect's projection of light, and the infrared camera's reception of that
light. In this zone, supplementary bodies are produced. It is here that
we see the only visual manifestation of Toby's physical form. This is also
where Katie, a key character from the earlier films who has been pos-
sessed by a demon, first materialises. Although Denson is right to point
out that this camera technology does not correspond, in a literal sense, to
an equivalent human sensory input, it nonetheless produces an engagement with space that is grounded in bodily experience, evoking ephemeral
apprehensions that trace the line between the visible and the invisible,
the seen and the felt. This scene reminds us of the Kinect game system's detection of players' physical movements and the translation of such
movements into virtual electronic 'bodies'. At the same time, through the
intervention of the infrared camera, we see the projection of such bodies
into physical space. This process is reminiscent of Sobchack's description
of the viewer's engagement with the film image: in watching cinema, she
proposes, 'we see seeing writing itself'.[27] In *Paranormal Activity 4*, the
pixelated field with its phantom bodes appears as a form of digital 'writing'
that speaks to our own embodied vision. Bodies are written into the frame,
both as arrangements of pixels, and as a form of agentic presence (whether
of operators or viewers) that hovers just out of view.

However, Denson's discussion of digital imaging technologies raises a related issue: although the 'discorrelated' images of found-footage horror are folded into corporeal frames of human action and perception, they do not leave undisturbed the question of signification. Like the dead surveillance monitors and discarded cameras of zombie cinema, audiovisual technologies in found-footage horror films evoke a gaze that lacks both meaning and intentionality. In this way, they contrast with Sobchack's phenomenological account, which 'demands that we consider the embodied and 'enworlded' subject as always already immersed in meaning, both supported and constrained by the inherited "fortune" of language'.[28] This sense of meaning, insists Sobchack, spans both human and technological actors: '[t]he film's body, like our own, is a *subjective object*. It is an intentional instrument able to perceive and express perception, to have sense and make sense'.[29] However, the distributed and fragmentary audiovisual assemblages of found-footage cinema suggest something other than an intentional subject. Rather, in these films both human and technological bodies are susceptible to disorder and non-sense. Thus, on one hand, the frame-bodies of *Paranormal Activity 4* reject a sharp division between human and digital audiovision (Denson); on the other, they fail to resolve into an integrated sensorial experience (Sobchack). In this context, internal divisions and sensory disarticulations are central to *both* technological mediation *and* human experience.

Indexical Frames

The internal divisions shaping phenomenal experience and audiovisual mediation in found-footage horror accord with Jean-Luc Nancy's post-phenomenological theorisation of the body. For Nancy, the body is produced via a process of 'exscription', which places the body outside, but at the margin of, discourse: it is 'placed *outside the text* as the most *proper* movement of its text; the text *itself* being abandoned, left at its limit'.[30] Here, I argue that the 'corporeal frames' of found-footage horror serve as a literalisation of Nancy's argument, providing an encounter between material forms and discursive (cinematic) figures that persistently 'write' the body at the margins of the image. At the same time, found-footage horror aligns with Nancy's use of a second metaphor that is based not in writing but in images. According to this metaphor, the body is 'the *coming to presence*, like an image coming on a movie or a TV *screen – coming from* nowhere behind the screen, *being* the spacing of this screen, existing as its extension'.[31] Accordingly, the body-as-image is not simply a discrete form, a figure that discloses itself to us in its entirety. Rather, it also invokes the action of our own eyes and body, 'themselves coming into this coming, spaced, spacing, themselves a screen – less "vision" than *video*'.[32] This process of bodily apprehension thus involves both a projection of space and an unfolding of time. At the curious intersection of Nancy's textual and visual metaphors, the body can be understood as combining material, phenomenal, textual and technical aspects.

Found-footage horror works to produce a similar textual-technical formation of the body, in particular through an intensive focus on the signifying function of the index. The index, per C. S. Peirce's influential account, is a sign that is materially connected to its referent, with examples including footprints, sundials, weathervanes and photographs. Media theorists have taken intense interest in the idea that images supply an indexical 'trace' of the visible world. Offering a particularly vivid manifestation of found-footage horror's indexical orientation, the found-footage film *Cloverfield* stages a documentary-style depiction of a monster attack on New York City, captured in 'real time' on a digital video camera. Including *Cloverfield* in his account of 'the verité horror and sf film', Barry Keith Grant argues that such works express 'a postmodern anxiety about the indexical truthfulness of the image that has been exacerbated by the ubiquity of digital technology'.[33] Indeed, the questioning of digital imagery's indexicality has been a theme in contemporary film theory, with writers such as D. N. Rodowick[34] and Mary Ann Doane[35] arguing that digital media interrupt the direct analogical connection between media and their referents.

Cloverfield foregrounds the 'problem' of the digital index. First of all, it invokes indexicality by overtly referencing well-known documentary footage, in particular imagery of the 9/11 attacks on New York City, including the collapsing buildings, the billowing dust and the use of the subway as a source of refuge. The 'reality effect' here is enhanced by digital video's connotations of immediacy. However, this invocation of the index is underwritten by postproduction trickery, as the film relies on CGI to create virtual 'indexical' traces of the monster and the damage it inflicts on New York City. In one scene, the Statue of Liberty's head is hurled into a Manhattan street. Here, digital effects work is used to make this event appear as an artefact of documentary realism. The statue's head is gashed in a number of places, apparently providing material evidence of the monster's swiping claws. The film thus produces a simulacrum of the indexical trace, even as its viewers are presumably quite aware of the artifice involved in producing it.

Yet *Cloverfield* is engaged with the index in another way that speaks more directly to the frame and its relationship to the body. C.S. Peirce's definition of the index, notes Tom Gunning, is not confined to the index understood as 'trace' but also incorporates the notion of 'deixis', which refers to anything that points or indicates.[36] In *Cloverfield*, the entire aesthetic suggests a deictic mode of representation, in which zooms, camera moves and character reactions point to events and objects both on and off-screen. From this perspective, *Cloverfield* can be viewed not only or primarily as about the truth-value of images, but also as engaged with the indexical articulation of various bodies, both human and monstrous, both via the trace and deixis. The monster's destructive force is conveyed via fleeting and partial views. Daniel North comments that 'news footage seen through a shop window provides the first clear sight of the creature's body' – as a result, the picture of the monster is kept 'maddeningly incomplete'.[37] The film's monster never fully reveals itself, so for the bulk of the film we encounter it indexically, through its effects, including the hordes of rats that flee the monster and the CGI parasites that accompany it. Contributing to the film's 'aesthetic of glimpses', flash-frames from classic monster films are woven into the texture of the film, impossible to see clearly without a remote control: *King Kong, The Beast from 20,000 Fathoms, Them*.[38] These flash-frames point beyond the text towards a broader field of cinematic monstrosity.

In *Cloverfield*, the human body is also represented indexically, producing parallels with the monster. In one particularly fraught scene, a young woman who has been bitten by a parasite is whisked behind a fabric barrier by military personnel. Seconds later, a shot is heard and there is a splatter of blood visible through the sheet. This bodily trace is thus *also* a deictic gesture that points beyond the field of immediate visibility. Moreover, like other found-footage films, *Cloverfield* gestures deictically towards the presence of the camera operator, a vital presence who is nonetheless invisible throughout most of the film's running time. The presence of bodies (whether human or monstrous) beyond the boundaries of the frame is crucial to the film's game with visibility and invisibility. This deictic gesturing beyond the frame aligns with Nancy's theorisation of the body as a particular kind of screen-image, a *'coming to presence'* which manifests as a kind of spatial projection but also implicates the projective, screen-like aspect of vision itself.[39] *Cloverfield*'s indexical bodies, whether indicated by a blood-spattered sheet or a clumsy movement of the camera, literalise Nancy's mediatised conception of embodiment, presenting bodily manifestations as an *effect* produced by screens and frames. At the same time, they involve exscription, a *writing* of the body along the boundary between materiality and the discursive operations of film grammar.

This literalisation of 'coming-to-presence' and bodily exscription is enacted not just spatially but also temporally. Writing about *Paranormal*

Activity, Cecilia Sayad notes that the digital time codes visible on the recordings capture the duration of the recorded image but also make evident 'the artificial manipulation of time, as their numbers reveal the seconds, minutes, and hours that are skipped both at each cut and at each artificial speeding of the image'.[40] This form of numerical inscription thus underwrites bodily exscription, pointing towards the characters' material presence in the missing interstitial frames. Meanwhile, *Cloverfield* uses a different kind of temporal gap to write bodies in and out of existence. One of the film's most distinctive narrative gimmicks involves the appearance of previously recorded footage during breaks in the camera's recording of the present-day events. Anchored temporally by the time-code recorded on the footage, these unerased fragments of the characters' past moments serve both as 'real time' raw footage and as memorial artefact, offering *de facto* flashbacks to happier times. The imaged bodies appear as a fleeting 'coming-to-presence', written in and out of being at the boundary between real time and archive. These characters are already missing bodies, unaware of their circumscribed fate, suspended between past and present.

Moreover, befitting its provenance, the film itself appears as a temporally suspended narrative fragment, lacking a proper exposition and denouement. We never learn the ultimate fate of the monster or the city, although we can infer that the main characters have all perished. On this level, the film itself serves as an index, gesturing towards a partially obscured storyworld with its array of missing bodies. Meanwhile, mysterious online extensions of *Cloverfield*'s narrative, from abandoned social media accounts to fake news videos and corporate websites, have served a similar function, pointing towards narrative questions that are never fully resolved. *Cloverfield*'s indexical production of bodies thus parallels Nancy's notion of exscription by writing the body outside of various frames: visual, spatiotemporal, technical and narrational.

Creep (Patrick Brice, 2014) extends this indexical model by introducing another bodily presence that hovers just out of frame: the editor. Initially, however, the focus is on the camera operator. In this case, that is Aaron, a budding filmmaker who has answered an advertisement seeking a videographer. His client is Josef, who lives alone in a secluded, forested area and is, by turns, exceedingly friendly and menacing. Josef claims to be terminally ill and asks Aaron to record a video of him that will serve as an extended message to Josef's young son when he is old enough to view it. Josef's ongoing chatter is directed not only at the future attention of this alleged son, but more emphatically, directly and presently, at Aaron behind the camera. The camera's framing is determined not only by Aaron's choices as operator, but also by Josef's overt and insistent interventions.

Control over the film thus oscillates between the videographer and his subject. Attempting to leave after Josef's bizarre and threatening behaviour escalates, Aaron finds himself in a scuffle that ends with the camera glitching and blacking out. After this point, the struggle between the two men takes on additional temporal complexity, as the film deliberately blurs the distinction between real-time and archival footage.

Creep then proceeds via a series of reversals, in which the production and reception contexts are revealed to be different than initially presented. For example, a sequence captured with a fixed camera in which Josef prepares to bury the contents of two large black plastic bags would appear to provide evidence that Josef has murdered Aaron. However, the screen image is suddenly paused and, following an abrupt pan, we are face to face with Aaron, who is watching the footage on a DVD sent to him by Josef. The footage we were viewing is thus literally and figuratively reframed. Aaron's body, which we were invited to assume was in the bags, is in fact very much alive and present. Josef's deliberately-staged scene of posthumous horror turns out to be a performance of future-oriented menace. After further ironic frame-reversals, including a scene in which Josef films Aaron in his sleep, Aaron receives a final DVD from Josef, which is captured by Aaron's camera so that we are presented with a frame within a frame. In full confessional mode, Josef proclaims his need to present 'the truth of me', while the nested frames of the camera/screen indicate both spatial and temporal dislocations. Josef is here and not-here, now and not-now.

Eventually, Josef convinces the thoroughly alienated Aaron to meet with him again, at which point the grounding of the film's plot in postproduction becomes fully apparent. Aaron captures the lakeside meeting from a camera in his own vehicle. After a long wait, Josef appears behind Aaron and deals a fatal blow to his head with an axe. As he is halfway through a second swing of the axe, the image pauses abruptly, and the camera pans away from the stilled frame to Josef, who is watching this footage in his postproduction suite. This freshly ironised frame thus demonstrates a hidden temporal split, presenting the footage as suspended between real-time recording and posthumous playback. In the frozen image, Aaron is both under attack and already dispatched. *Creep*'s faux-factual images thus partake simultaneously of the contemporaneous and the retrospective, the present and the absent, the living and the dead. Meanwhile, the camera movement that wrenches us away from this paused image links two temporally distinct manifestations of Josef: one (stilled) in which he acts as an onscreen performer and director, and another (moving) in which he watches and reacts to the recording, exerting a retroactive influence as the film's editor.

The dramatic irony of the frame in *Creep* thus hinges on the relationship between production and postproduction. The film has reminded us throughout of the physical presence of the camera operator: invisible and yet indexically present in the movements of the frame. Ultimately, it insists on the physical presence and authorial role of the editor. Josef's control over the film, and Aaron's bodily fate, is underlined by the concluding point-of-view (POV) shot, which appears to show Josef adding Aaron's DVD to his collection of tapes and discs. This array of media artefacts reveals that Josef's murderous scheme has been executed many times before, spanning the waxing and waning of different video formats. The DVD acts as a posthumous stand-in for Aaron, with the filing away of the disc serving as a kind of de facto burial. It also indicates the pre-planned nature of his fate. Regarding Aaron's function within the film as both 'real time' witness and posthumous subject, one might suggest that the worst has not yet happened, will definitely happen, and has already happened. This ironic temporal overlay is produced by the film's construction around an array of indexical frame-bodies. These include Aaron as videographer, as living and posthumous subject, and as dead media; ultimately, however, they are determined by the film's ostensible subject, Josef, who hovers at the edge of frame as director and editor. To borrow Nancy's term, *Creep* thus offers a dual *exscription* of the body, which involves the 'writing' of posthumous presence into the video image but also the acknowledgement of offscreen bodies as determining agents.

Writing the Frame

The intersection of visual and textual expressions of embodiment is nowhere more evident than in *Unfriended* (Leo Gabriadze, 2014). This is not, strictly speaking, a found-footage film, since it presents the viewer with a real-time interaction that runs for the duration of the film itself. While *Cloverfield* and *Creep* depend on a structure of temporal delay and revision, *Unfriended* is defined by linear temporality and the coexistence of multiple spatialised media frames. An online interaction among a group of high school friends goes badly awry when their various communication interfaces (including Skype, Facebook and email) are hijacked by an unidentified presence. This presence is eventually revealed as the spirit of Laura Barns, a fellow student who committed suicide after being bullied. Laura is able to control the behaviour of digital applications and interfaces, but also the characters' fates in the material world. As each of the friends is violently dispatched, their complicity in Laura's bullying is made clear. These narrative revelations are delivered exclusively via the multi-windowed environment of a single Macintosh laptop, belonging to Blaire, one of the students. Yet despite its structural differences from found-footage films, *Unfriended* depends on a similar interplay between the conventions of cinema and domestic media. Just as *The Blair Witch Project* combines the signifiers of amateur video with the articulation of a cinematic story, this film works both as a carefully crafted narrative and as a simulation of everyday human–computer interaction.

Unfriended, like the other films I have been discussing, also sets up an ambiguous relation between the body and the frame. The characters are almost exclusively viewed through the Skype video interface, privileging the face and presenting it through windows of various sizes (including thumbnails).[41] The rest of the body, which remains largely out of frame, is invoked frequently, particularly when Laura begins to exact vengeance. As characters attempt to exit the interaction, they involuntarily perform actions of self-directed violence, which occur mostly off-frame and are glimpsed only momentarily via the Skype window. Here, the facially-oriented frame of the interface is placed in tension with the bodily action that it fails to capture. One scene, in particular, expands the bodily parameters of the video chat frame, but only to insist more emphatically on violent consequences. As Ken, the group's resident tech guru, plans his departure, Laura's Skype window begins to show an alternative camera angle from within his own room, which presents an oblique view of his entire body seated in front of the computer. Immediately before his death, Ken goes searching for this unexplained hidden camera. However, the uncovering of this supplementary 'bodily' frame presages his death, which, like the others, occurs largely beyond the margins of the image.

The film is thus similar to *Host* (Rob Savage, 2020), in which a group of friends conduct a live séance via Zoom, with deadly consequences unfolding across the video chat platform's windowed interface. In that film, the recurrent toggling between Zoom's single 'speaker view' and panelled 'gallery view' contributes to the sense that the characters have lost control of their respective frames, as demonic forces hover at the boundaries of visible space. *Unfriended*, however, is distinguished by its embrace of multifarious digital 'frames', incorporating not only video chat but also text-based applications. This approach creates a more marked departure from cinematic conventions regarding space and perspective, underlining the film's abstract treatment of point of view. This is particularly evident in the implied body–screen relationship between the protagonist, Blaire, and her MacBook. Ostensibly, the camera's perspective on the windowed interface corresponds to her own, embodied perspective. Yet given the fixity of the framed image and the fact that the camera never directly takes in anything of Blaire's immediate environment, it does not seem accurate to refer to this as a conventional POV shot. What is reproduced is the content of the screen, with its nested array of interfacial frames, but not the situation of that screen in a three-dimensional, material space.

The effect is to render Blaire's body both as a concrete off-screen presence (responsible for the activity taking place on the computer) and as an abstraction (notionally present but lacking immediate spatial or sensorial grounding). Thus, the 'dramatic irony' of the media frame, as in *Creep*, involves a virtual splitting of the body. However, whereas the split in *Creep* was between the (contemporaneous) videographer and the (retroactive) editor, here it is between two kinds of onlooker: *Unfriended* projects both a cinematic spectator and a digital user into the same space, but without uniting them through the mechanism of the POV shot. The ambiguous status of the screen space is only truly resolved at the end of the film when Blaire is finally attacked (and presumably killed). At this point, the laptop abruptly closes as the mysterious threat lunges at her. With the disappearance of the computer screen and the materialisation of a previously excluded three-dimensional reality, the image finally, at the last possible moment, takes on the qualities of a POV shot. Blaire's body is thus granted an existence in a coherent physical space only at the moment of death.

Elsewhere in the film, bodies also signal their presence via textual traces, as the characters type messages to each other using Facebook Messenger, Apple Messages and Gmail. Dramatic suspense is heightened by the animated dots that signal another character composing a message, as well as by the pauses between messages. Meanwhile, Blaire's own composition, deletion and revision of messages is fully visible onscreen, and reveals a great deal about what she is thinking and what she would prefer to conceal from the other characters. At these moments, the 'real-time' production of typed text points indexically beyond the windowed frame of the interface, suggesting the outline of an embodied figure beyond the screen. A kind of bodily exscription thus takes place, as the discursive-material interactions of the chat interface write the body outside the image. This process is rendered particularly fraught by the film's ghost narrative, since Laura Barns appears almost entirely as a haunting of the interface. Hers is a supplementary body that hovers out of sight and yet is written into existence via its textual effects.

Ultimately, Laura's absent body is returned to retrospective visibility, in a way that highlights the significance of frames (visual, textual and discursive). Towards the end of the film, Blaire's computer is overtaken by a YouTube video revealing the events preceding Laura's suicide: in a drunken state, Laura had soiled herself, and Blaire, visibly laughing, was party to her collective shaming. Given the film's reliance on the tight, facially-oriented frame of the Skype interface, the full depiction of Laura's prostrate figure in YouTube's 16:9 aspect ratio appears particularly shocking. The multiplication of this clip across an array of pop-up browser windows further underlines the role of the media frame in facilitating Laura's public humiliation. Furthermore, the video has been given the title 'Leaky Laura', thus layering a textual frame over a visual one. The 'meaning' of the video is further circumscribed by a great deal of prior discussion (both verbal and typed) among the members of the group.

Unfriended thus explores the intersections between visual, textual and social frames, connecting them all to an abject mode of embodiment. The abject, in Julia Kristeva's terms, refers to that which 'disturbs identity, system, order. What does not respect borders, positions, rules. The in-between, the ambiguous, the composite'.[42] In cultural terms, the abject is associated with notions of impurity, filth and disorder, and is defined as 'other' to the subject. Despite this rejection, however, the abject is never fully excluded. Indeed, the subject is defined by its attempts to cast aside the abject. In *Unfriended*, the footage of Laura's soiled body presents an image of abjection *par excellence*. It not only documents physical abjection (in the form of uncontained waste), but also indexes Laura's social abjection (she is other than the group but resists ejection) and metaphysical abjection (she is a dead presence that haunts the world of the living). Moreover, Laura represents a kind of interfacial abjection, serving as an in-between, supplementary body that emerges at the margins of digital applications and windows. The abject failure to respect 'borders' here manifests itself via the literal borders of the computer's windowed interface. Laura's presence is thus not merely off-frame but also *via* the frame and *as* a frame.

This abject presence manifests itself within an array of malfunctioning digital interfaces, both textual and audiovisual. Upon requesting the archiving of Laura's Facebook page, Blaire is confronted by text boxes filled with perplexing repetition: 'I GOT HER I GOT HER I GOT HER'. Elsewhere in the film, textual fields and other aspects of the interface fail to behave in a logical or usable way, producing a kind of abject textuality. Such moments illustrate the threat to signification and subjective coherence posed by the abject: in Kristeva's words, it 'draws me toward the place where meaning collapses'.[43] Video interfaces are no less susceptible to this breakdown of coherence. Particularly as characters become distressed or threatened, their faces become marred by random glitches, rendering them as horrific and distorted forms. These glitches also suggest a fluid relationship between digital images and text: here we see the images

Figure 3.3 Blaire's face is broken up by digital glitches in *Unfriended* (Leo Gabriadze, 2014).

themselves being written into being, as they reveal their basis in code and their vulnerability to error. *Unfriended*'s distinctive brand of interfacial horror thus presents nested frames of abjection, from these glitching images and text to the cascade of multiplying browser windows that fill Blaire's screen as she tries to close the incriminating YouTube clip.

The body is implicated in all of these abject frames, which partake both of image and of text, of Jean-Luc Nancy's formulations of the visual 'coming-to-presence' and the textual 'writing outside'. In a passage that recalls Kristeva's framing of the abject as something that is cast out, Nancy suggests that the body itself is constantly engaged in a type of expulsion via becoming, an 'absolute rejection of the self that *is* the world of bodies'.[44] This is a spatiotemporal process: '[a] body expels itself: as corpus, as spasmic space, distended, subject-reject, *"im-mundus"*'.[45] In *Unfriended,* this process of expulsion is conveyed by the various glitches and ruptures that deframe and disfigure the characters. Similarly, in other found-footage horrors, the kinetic movements of the handheld camera generate an image of space itself as saturated with bodily presence. The frame and the body thus collaborate in the expulsive production of space.

For Nancy, the radical conclusion of this theoretical trajectory is that 'places are dead bodies'. The coming-to-presence of the body is a temporal process that produces spatial indexical effects: traces and indications of bodily involvement. In *The Blair Witch Project, Cloverfield* and *Creep,* the dramatic irony of the frame, with its split between formats, contexts and temporal modes, is central to this process. Their various recording devices document a real-time emergence that is also a retrospective petrification: these living bodies, and by extension the spaces they both frame and inhabit, are already dead. This mortal fate, moreover, is written into the metaphorical 'bodies' of the discarded cameras, tapes and digital files that frame each of these narratives. Interfacial horrors like *Unfriended*, despite operating in a different temporal mode, also entail a virtual deadening of space. Here, the DCT blocks of digital compression overflow the characters' glitched faces, generating tiny, fleeting frames that produce further boundaries within the image itself. These blocky forms serve as abject projections of bodily matter, inscribing space itself with necrotic extrusions. Both bodies and places are thus subjected to a fatal reckoning that is expressed as a particular kind of frame effect.

If, in Jean-Luc Nancy's terms, the body is produced at the seam joining materiality to discourse, then found-footage horror films literalise and spatialise this relationship. These films reflect on the multiplication of frames produced both through recording and exhibition, from the camera's viewfinder, to the video monitor, to the windowed interfaces of digital media. In this context, the spatial presence of the body is written into being through disjunctures, absences and oscillations. There is a relay between frames and bodies, bodies-as-frames and frames-as-bodies. Written 'outside', *exscribed* along the boundary between discourse and matter, the body is never fully contained within the frame of a unified subjectivity. It is thus presented, in Nancy's words, as 'infinitely other'.[46] Found-footage horror, with its array of mobile and mutable frames (visual, technical, discursive and narrational), provides a metaphorical realisation of this otherness, a reflexive foregrounding of the body's fraught, borderline existence.

Notes

1. Grant, 'Digital anxiety and the new verité horror and SF film', p. 154.
2. Benson-Allott, *Killer Tapes and Shattered Screens: Video Spectatorship from VHS to File Sharing*, p. 191.
3. Branigan, *Projecting a Camera: Language Games in Film Theory*, p. 149.
4. Ibid. p. 149.
5. Shaviro, 'The glitch dimension: *Paranormal Activity* and the technologies of vision', p. 321.
6. Grant, 'Digital anxiety and the new verité horror and SF film', p. 165.
7. Sayad, 'Found-footage horror and the frame's undoing', p. 58.

8. Ibid. p. 56.
9. Andrew, *What Cinema Is!: Bazin's Quest and Its Charge*, p. 82.
10. Ibid. p. 84.
11. Sayad, 'Found-footage horror and the frame's undoing', p. 66.
12. Branigan, *Projecting a Camera*, p. 145.
13. Ibid. p. 103–13.
14. Andrew, *What Cinema Is!*, p. 85.
15. Ibid. p. 85.
16. Banash, '*The Blair Witch Project*: technology, repression, and the evisceration of mimesis'.
17. Rajewsky, 'Intermediality, intertextuality, and remediation: a literary perspective on intermediality', p. 46.
18. Pethő, *Cinema and Intermediality: The Passion for the In-Between*, p. 99.
19. Kim, *Between Film, Video, and the Digital: Hybrid Moving Images in the Post-Media Age*, p. 7.
20. The film featured a roster of different directors: Adam Wingard, Simon Barrett, Gareth Evans, Jason Eisener, Eduardo Sánchez, Timo Tjahjanto and Gregg Hale.
21. Denson, 'Crazy cameras, discorrelated images, and the post-perceptual mediation of post-cinematic affect', p. 193.
22. Ibid. p. 196.
23. Ibid. p. 202.
24. Ibid. p. 202.
25. Sobchack, *The Address of the Eye: A Phenomenology of Film Experience*, p. 171.
26. Ibid. p. 24.
27. Ibid. p. 217.
28. Ibid. p. 44.
29. Ibid. p. 247–8.
30. Nancy, *Corpus*, p. 11.
31. Ibid. p. 63.
32. Ibid. p. 65.
33. Grant, 'Digital anxiety and the new verité horror and SF film', p. 154.
34. Rodowick, *The Virtual Life of Film*.
35. Doane, 'The indexical and the concept of medium specificity', p. 142.
36. Gunning, 'Moving away from the index: cinema and the impression of reality', p. 30.
37. North, 'Evidence of things not quite seen: *Cloverfield*'s obstructed spectacle', p. 84.
38. Ibid. p. 85.
39. Nancy, *Corpus*, p. 65.
40. Sayad, 'Found-footage horror and the frame's undoing', p. 62.
41. For a more detailed discussion of faciality in this film, specifically in relation to the digital glitch, see Cameron, 'Facing the glitch; abstraction, abjection and the digital image', pp. 345–8.

42. Kristeva, *Powers of Horror: An Essay on Abjection*, p. 4.
43. Ibid. p. 2.
44. Nancy, *Corpus*, p. 107.
45. Ibid. p. 107.
46. Ibid. p. 13.

CHAPTER 4

Aesthetic Incisions:
Giallo Cinema and the Matter of the Cut

A doorknob turning. A black gloved hand. A gleaming razor, held to catch the light. A scream, a raised arm. A splash of blood. The vicious narrative economy of the Italian *giallo* film is instantly recognisable in its iconic murder sequences. This cycle of films borrows its name and its basic plot conventions from crime and mystery fiction novels of the mid-twentieth century, which were published in Italy with yellow (that is, 'giallo') covers. The films are often highly stylised, with common features including convoluted mystery plots, shadowy killers, pop-Freudian flashbacks, lurid sex scenes and spectacular deaths.[1] The start of the cycle is usually thought to be marked by Mario Bava's *The Girl Who Knew Too Much* (1963) or *Blood and Black Lace* (1964), although the conventions are arguably refined and consolidated in Dario Argento's influential 1970 film *The Bird with the Crystal Plumage*. Following a rapid flourishing, the *giallo* had largely petered out by the mid-1970s, although there are notable later examples, including Argento's *Tenebrae* (1982), as well as more recent revisionist *gialli* such as Helène Cattet and Bruno Forzani's films *Amer* (2009) and *The Strange Colour of Your Body's Tears* (2012), and Yann Gonzalez's *Knife+Heart* (2018).

In the previous chapter I considered how found-footage films present a composite image-body, in which various frames (visual and technical) work as hinges or as lines of articulation, both dislocating and connecting aspects of spatial experience. Here, I proceed along a related but quite different seam, looking at films in which the frame serves not as a spatial-experiential hinge but rather as a sharply definitive edge. Here, the metaphorical image-body is constituted not by an opening into space, but by an operation of flattening and cutting out. In this sense, the process of producing and consuming images is itself conceived as a kind of mediatised violence. In key examples of the *giallo*, questions of mediation are focused on the boundaries of the body and of the image, as the integrity of both is periodically threatened by spatio-temporal operations of cutting.

This cutting or separation takes several forms: it is the explicitly violent cutting of the killer, but also the cutting of the film's editor, as well as the evaluative cutting of aesthetic judgement which separates the art object from the flux of the everyday. Thus, processes of delineation and separation are applied both to bodies and to images, slicing across the corporeal and the representational. Image production and aesthetic consideration alike are implicated in acts of violence. What is emphasised here is not the composite bodily articulation of found-footage horror, but a severing, a cutting out, a rendering of the body as a discrete image-object. Therefore, such films also linger on the relationship between figure and ground, on the way that bodies can be pared away from or pressed into their surroundings. These are films, ultimately, about edgework, about the spatial cut-out and the temporal ellipsis.

This chapter will therefore concentrate on the boundaries of bodies, images and aesthetic spaces, and the way that *gialli* enact the fragmentation of *matter*, understood both as materiality and as meaning. I will discuss a number of the most significant *gialli*, showing how they not only frame the body as an aesthetic image-object but also present aesthetics as fundamentally violent and shocking. I will then explore how such films depict both bodies and images as discrete, bounded shapes, and the way this is reflected in the thematic recurrence of still photography as well as the structuring of stories around seriality and subtraction (via the narrative mechanism of the 'body count'). Finally, I consider the fraught relationship between matter and meaning, concluding with an analysis of the 'neo-*giallo*' film *Amer* and its kaleidoscopic multiplication of impressions and events. Although the *giallo* forms a diverse generic grouping, I argue that these films can be connected via their insistence on the violent power of aesthetic edges to cut around and across the mediatised 'image-body'.

Cutting Up the Screen

Although the array of violent acts in *giallo* films ranges from suffocations to drownings, burnings and beatings, the blade serves as the subgenre's most iconic mortal instrument. In key examples, this emphasis on cutting extends to the very fabric of the narrative, where the work of the editor takes on a violent, assaultive cast. *The Bird with the Crystal Plumage*'s stylised, elliptical murder sequences direct the killer's slashing razor towards the camera and, hence, the viewer. In *giallo* films more generally, murder scenes are often constructed as a succession of discrete close-ups featuring body parts and murder weapons in stark, stylised configurations. Narrative ellipsis (motivated by the need to conceal the killer's identity) is translated into a more fundamental type of spatiotemporal fragmentation. The dynamic, dislocated feel of these cinematic deaths bears a close relation to the shower scene in Alfred Hitchcock's *Psycho* (1960), in which a staccato series of shots, some of them featuring very little physical movement, generates a violent effect through sheer disjuncture. Hitchcock famously wrote in the margins of *Psycho*'s shooting script that he wanted 'an impression of a knife slashing, as if tearing at the very screen, ripping the film'. An assault on a character thus becomes an assault on the spectator, mediated by the screen itself. Moreover, foreshadowed by Norman Bates's tearing aside of the shower curtain in *Psycho*, a concern with screens and surfaces flourishes in *giallo*. Windows in particular offer scant protection, as illustrated by the deadly defenestrations that punctuate several of Argento's films.[2] The 'cut', whether depicted within the frame (as a swinging blade or pane of shattering glass), or, by virtue of editing, embodied in the transition between shots, is thus a key motif of the *giallo*.

Dario Argento's *Deep Red* (1975) provides a particularly strong concentration of these various aspects, with each of its spectacular murder scenes subjecting space, time and narrative to violent fragmentation. In the film's first fully-rendered slaying, a psychic named Helga finds her own premonitions of a killer on the loose proven correct when she is attacked in her apartment by a figure in a dark coat wielding a meat cleaver. The murderer's imminent arrival is first heralded by off-kilter framing and editing. This includes an awkward profile shot placing Helga's forehead and anxiously darting eye in the bottom corner of the frame, and a jump cut shifting a large scallop-shaped artwork abruptly from frame left to frame right. The attack itself is conveyed in a rapid series of tightly framed shots, as the swinging open of the door gives way to the downward trajectory of the cleaver and the infliction of bloody wounds across Helga's body. Save for close-ups of shoes and gloved hands, the killer remains largely out of frame. These disorienting perspectives on objects and details, combined with 'empty' frames devoid of human characters, enact a cutting up of space that both prefigures and accompanies the cutting up of the body.[3]

Although Helga's murder appears to have concluded by this point, the following scene extends it into a further narrative performance, witnessed initially by the main character Marcus, who is standing in the public square outside. A rapid shot-reverse shot sequence, in which the framing alternates awkwardly between tighter and wider views, shows Marcus looking up at Helga's apartment as she is struck from behind with the cleaver, sending her head smashing through a window. An extreme close-up from inside the apartment presents a profile view of Helga's neck as it is forced, fatally, onto the jagged glass, a movement that is repeated in two almost identical but slightly mismatched shots. The (dis)articulation of the cut is theorised within the film itself, as a fundamental disruption that unites the work of the killer with the work of the editor. Film grammar itself thus functions as a kind of violence: via the logic of the cut, the killer's victims give up their bodies as material to be acted upon – as media, in other words.

Deep Red produces a fragmentation of space and time, in which each spectacular death is punctuated by moments of artificial stillness, as if to reveal the hidden stasis that haunts both bodies and cinema. For example, Mikel Koven observes that the 'rhythm and flow' of Helga's murder scene is broken up by 'inert' close-ups on mutilated body parts: the editing thus alternates 'between the fluid movement (of the actor) and the non-movement (of the special effect)'.[4] This stillness is further underlined by the presence of stilled objects and figures in adjacent scenes, from the scallop-shaped sculpture to the dummy-like bar patrons overlooking Marcus as he loiters in the square below Helga's apartment. Although *Deep Red* presents a particularly pronounced example of this aesthetic, the representation of violence as a sequence of abstracted close-ups is found in many other examples. As in *Psycho*'s famous shower scene, acts of violence in *giallo* are commonly presented via sharply delineated, static, almost de-animated moments. Cinema, from this perspective, is a mechanism that harbours the ability to halt time: it both stills and kills. The editor's cut thus takes on a supplementary re-animating role, chaining together the succession of disjointed moments and subjecting these inert bodies to an aggressive form of abstract movement.

Deep Red's disjunctive aesthetic is crystallised even further by the extension of the logic of the cut into the *mise-en-scène*, as visual dislocation and separation serve to turn elements of the image into discrete components. Helga's murder is preceded by an unexplained and decontextualised tracking shot exploring a number of items displayed against a black background: a yarn doll impaled with needles, a child's drawing of a violent stabbing, a devil figurine, marbles and knives. This interpolated sequence both interrupts the flow of the narrative and prepares the ground for the following scene's overt violence. The black surface beneath the objects renders them distinct and disconnected. Their layout, including the distance between them, is motivated neither by narrative nor spatial necessity. It is, rather, a form of disarticulated spatial montage. Mikel Koven sees this sequence as 'set entirely within the killer's mind' since it involves 'abstract images from the killer's childhood',[5] but even in retrospect these objects hardly serve to advance our understanding of the central mystery,

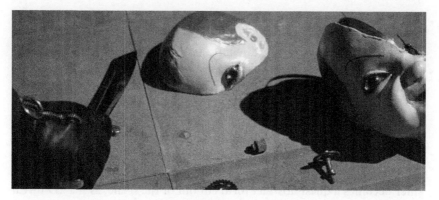

Figure 4.1 The anonymous killer seizes a weapon from the floor in *Deep Red* (Dario Argento, 1975).

and the weaving of the camera is never decisively anchored in any character's perspective. Rather, this shot seems to convey a sense of disarticulation, suggesting via extreme close-up a magnified, non-anthropocentric view of the world. This view finds ultimate expression in the array of inert objects and dispassionate perspectives that mediate Helga's subsequent death. Anticipated by dolls and knives but undertaken by cleaver and windowpane, this murder is depicted through a series of disjunctures which break up the scene across perspectives and locations. *Deep Red* displays an excess of dislocation, as the editing and *mise-en-scène* carve up space in anticipation of the more visceral cuts of the murderer.

Films like Argento's can be regarded not simply as representations of murder conveyed via thematically appropriate cutting but also as a kind of aesthetic reflection. The *giallo*, by virtue of its singling out of aesthetic objects and its graphic and thematic deployment of the cut, drags the invisible work of the editor into the visible spaces of the diegesis. As Karla Oeler writes,

> Montage famously serves as a vehicle for conveying violence (e.g. the shower sequence in *Psycho*). What often escapes consideration, however, is that the reverse is also true: deadly violence, throughout the history of film-theoretical writing, has . . . often served as a metaphor *for* montage.[6]

This is the case not only for film theorists but also for filmmakers. That is, in certain *giallo* films, murder is presented as a way to think about the aesthetic implications of the cut. Viewed in this way, Helga's murder provides the ground for an intensive exploration of representational violence that not only mirrors but also exceeds the violent acts of the killer.

Accordingly, the killer in *giallo* can serve not only as a character in the narrative but also as a proxy for film grammar. By virtue of the need to conceal their identity, they present a fragmented form both temporally and spatially. The dark figure manifests a kind of *coupure*, a cut-out, a shadowy absence within the shot, represented by discrete elements that function largely as signifiers of negation, such as the gloved hands, the mask and the dark hat. It is as if there is nobody (no *body*) there. In this respect, these films recall the appearance of Norman Bates in *Psycho*'s shower scene: Norman is depicted in silhouette while Marion is fully lit; he is a flattened abstracted form, while her vulnerability is expressed via her occupation of three-dimensional space. Similarly, in the *giallo* the killer becomes a quasi-abstract form cut out of the scene, as if a 2D threat has intruded into a 3D world. The killer, indeed, seems like a formal arte-fact of the film itself – a force that emerges from within film form and its structure of ellipses.[7] As a counterpart to the *cutting up* of the victim, then, there is the *cutting out* of the killer. The material presence of the killer is communicated, to a large extent, via the objects with which they interact: typewriter, photograph, doorhandle, knife, wire. Each of these objects takes on a discrete identity and even a sense of agency, singled out by the camera (whether as a murder weapon or a token of psychological crisis) but also given rhetorical prominence via the mechanism of the cut. In the absence of the killer's complete physical form, the editing articulates a treacherous *mise-en-scène* populated by quasi-autonomous objects.[8]

In the examples I have discussed here, cinematic 'suture' is pushed to breaking point. The term 'suture', as proposed by psychoanalytic theo-rists, denotes the ways in which film overcomes narrational and ideological discontinuity by 'stitching' the spectator into a field of spatial relations through its system of framing and cutting.[9] According to Stephen Heath, suture produces perspectival images that 'bind the spectator in place' and prompt her/him to fill in the gaps.[10] Significantly, it is disjuncture and negation that allow this sense of wholeness and narrative unity to flourish: 'the fiction film disrespects space in order to construct a unity that will bind spectator and film in its fiction'.[11] From a Lacanian perspective, the missing visual field serves as a kind of 'wound' which is stitched together through narrative signification. As Kaja Silverman puts it, 'it is only by inflicting the wound to begin with that the viewing subject can be made to want the restorative of meaning and narrative'.[12] How, though, does suture function in the face of the *giallo*'s disjunctive excesses?

In *Deep Red*, the 'multiple cuts and negations'[13] that Silverman posits as the basis for cinematic meaning are not always organised into patterns of spatiotemporal or narrative unity. The ambiguous presence/non-presence of the killer might thus be linked with the 'absent one' in suture theory –

the figure of the other that haunts the cinematic system of signification. But rather than working to fix the gap threatened by this absence, the *giallo* instead turns it into a figure of disarticulation. In its disjunctive movements from one scene and one perspective to another, *Deep Red* appears to unstitch suture, refusing to close the wounds that are opened up by its acts of bodily and textual violence. The disorienting movement between perspectives, the foregrounding of nonhuman objects and the privileging of empty space suggest a fundamental disarticulation, a wounding that cannot be stitched back together.

Moreover, the disjunctive aesthetic moments that punctuate certain *gialli* suggest a decentring of the human form that pushes past suture theory's anthropocentric orientation. As Karla Oeler argues, the montage aesthetic is not easily compatible with Christian Metz's theory of identification, founded on the metaphor of the mirror, where the spectator encounters 'his ego ideal, his better coordinated and more powerful self'.[14] Breaking up the body into parts inhibits both secondary identification (in which we identify with characters on screen) and primary identification (in which we identify with the camera itself as presenting a coherent view of the action).[15] Similarly, Ian Olney argues that *gialli* often feature a multiplication of visual perspectives that are not aligned with a particular character, thus working against conventional suture and decentring human subjectivity.[16] Olney cites a scene from Mario Bava's *Blood and Black Lace,* in which a young woman is stalked by the killer inside an antique shop. He remarks on the disorienting cuts between different perspectival views: some anchored in the character's point-of-view, others omniscient and others ambiguous.[17] The human figures are thus placed on the same ontological plane as the antique shop's panoply of dead artefacts. Editing is central to this emphasis on the world of things: in films like *Blood and Black Lace* and *Deep Red*, the sudden cutaway to inert objects or empty spaces serves to undermine human agency and subjectivity.

Shock, Modernity, Aesthetics

Deep Red and other *gialli* make frequent use of the 'shock cut', a device that Scott Diffrient defines by its 'predilection for violent imagery' and its production of 'violent rupture in the diegesis'.[18] Diffrient links the shock cut with the modern experience of 'shock itself' as theorised by Walter Benjamin and others.[19] Shock is associated with new modes of transport and communication that appeared at the beginning of the twentieth century, with transforming social roles, with art movements like Cubism and Dada, and with cinema itself. Although often connected with 'death

and the dangerous undertow of the supernatural',[20] shock also expresses
'both the vitality and triviality of modern life',[21] providing 'a revitalising
jolt that galvanises the senses'.[22] In a passage that captures the affective
charge of both montage and modernity, Diffrient compares the shock cut
to breaking glass, and comments on how 'the sharp, glassy quality of the
device is literalised in numerous films'.[23] Here, he cites the moment in
Argento's (non-*giallo*) film *Inferno* where a woman's guillotining by glass
is followed by a shot of beef being minced.[24] Diffrient's description reflects
a dominant aesthetic tendency within the *giallo*, and in Argento's films in
particular, according to which windows, screens and other surfaces are
susceptible to sudden fragmentation.

This framing of *giallo*'s aesthetics as 'modern' accords with Mikel
Koven's argument that the subgenre's overarching theme is 'a marked
ambivalence toward modernity'.[25] Koven notes that the early 1970s 'was a
period of marked change within Italian culture and society', and brought
to the surface 'issues pertaining to identity, sexuality, increasing levels
of violence, women's control over their own lives and bodies, history,
the state'.[26] Accordingly, *giallo*'s fascination with the accoutrements of
modernity – fashion, industrial design, cars, cameras and telephones –
supplies the objective correlative for this ambivalence. These elements not
only embody the erotic appeal of the modern but also provide the backdrop
to acts of abject cruelty and violence. The *giallo*'s disjunctive editing, in
particular its foregrounding of material objects, contributes to this sense of
novelty and shock. Indeed, Koven himself points out the disruptive nature
of *giallo* aesthetics, comparing the subgenre's use of excessive style to
interrupt cinematic narrative continuity with the self-reflexive gestures of
modernism.[27] In particular, he notes the preponderance of point-of-view
shots in the *giallo*, claiming that this 'highly artificial device . . . ruptures
the classical text, and calls attention to its own constructedness'.[28]

This link between modernity and shock can be further elaborated by
considering the *giallo*'s overt concentration on aesthetics. Steven Schneider
argues that contemporary horror cinema grants a special place to the aesthetic, which is attended by notions of modern art as shocking and disruptive. Whereas earlier horror narratives present the monstrous as a failed
aesthetic project (in the mode of *Frankenstein*), the contemporary horror
often presents horrific deeds and scenes as aesthetic articulations: 'what
used to be the monster as corrupt or degraded work of art has become
[. . .] the monster as corrupt or degraded artist'.[29] Schneider links this tendency to changing perspectives on art heralded by the modern era.[30] The
'rise and popularisation of modern and avant-garde artistic practice', he
suggests, has linked art with 'notions of "shock," transgression, and offen-

siveness', as opposed to 'traditional notions of aesthetic technique, form, and beauty'.[31] Similarly, Karla Oeler argues that the 'under-theorised self-referential tendency' of the horror genre[32] has its parallel in the aesthetic theories of writers like Viktor Shklovsky and Sergei Eisenstein, which often 'invoke examples involving shock and horror' in illustrating the radical potential of art or cinema.[33] With its aesthetics of shock and rupture, and its intense focus on aesthetic display, *giallo* cinema is a particularly marked example of this second-order reflexivity. Moreover, Schneider finds evidence of an aesthetic sensibility in the characters of Mark in *Peeping Tom*[34] and Norman in *Psycho*,[35] both of whom can be seen as forerunners of the *giallo*'s secretive assailants. The *giallo*, with its focus on fashion and modernity, and its depiction of violence through formal excess, communicates the shock of aesthetics.

In *giallo* films the spatiotemporal disorder associated with montage's violent interventions is thus counterbalanced by an emphasis on aesthetic unity, emblematised by the killer's diabolical creativity and the staging of murders against the backdrop of art exhibits, galleries, fashion shows, and theatrical performances. Meanwhile, the intervening cut (of the editor as well as the killer) renders these non-cinematic spaces of exhibition properly cinematic, producing a prismatic refraction of these different aesthetic spheres. Argento's *The Bird with the Crystal Plumage* provides a fine example in its most famous scene, in which Sam, the main character, witnesses an attempted murder inside an art gallery. Walking along the street at night, Sam is attracted to the well-lit gallery's large plate glass window. As he looks in, he sees a violent confrontation between a man and a woman, resulting in an apparent stabbing. Before he can react, however, a large glass partition closes behind him, trapping him. Here, the murder itself takes on the quality of an aesthetic performance, while Sam, forced to occupy a space in front of the gallery window, becomes like an immobilised cinema spectator. As L. Andrew Cooper puts it, 'since he cannot enter the scene he is witnessing, he becomes, like the moviegoing audience, a passive voyeur'.[36] However, Argento also cuts into the space of the gallery, offering us high-angle and reverse shots of the scene which prompt us to consider the injured woman and the artworks as equivalent. By the end of the film, one of the art works in the gallery, a large spiky slab, is itself transformed into a murder weapon and turned against Sam. Thus, the body, the art object and the weapon are all placed in the same ontological frame. Via the aesthetic incisions of the killer and the editor, human subjects are rendered mute or inert, while material objects take on their own expressive agency.

Bava's *Blood and Black Lace* provides an earlier template for the linking

Figure 4.2 Sam witnesses an attempted murder at the art gallery in
The Bird with the Crystal Plumage (Dario Argento, 1970).

of murder with contexts of aesthetic display. It takes place inside a fashion
house, with the runway models falling victim to the actions of a serial
murderer. While the victims are presented as visible, appealing bodies,
the killer remains concealed, with a dark coat and hat, along with a layer
of fabric covering the face. Once again, the masking of the killer not
only serves to conceal their identity and gender but also frames them, as
Leon Hunt puts it, 'as a function within the text'.[37] The primary visual
focus, then, is on the bodies of the victims as glamorous objects. Indeed,
the treatment of the body as aesthetic object is announced by the film's
famous opening sequence, in which shots of the performers are intercut
with mannequins. Alexia Kannas comments that the static poses of the
film's characters in this sequence replicate the flatness of the playing cards
in *Cluedo*.[38] This aspect of the film mirrors the *giallo*'s frequent focus on
objectified figures and figurines, including dolls in *Deep Red, The Red
Queen Kills Seven Times* (Emilio Miraglia, 1972*), Don't Torture a Duckling*
(Lucio Fulci, 1972), *Torso* (Sergio Martine, 1973) and *The Perfume of
the Lady in Black* (Francesco Barilli, 1974), and mannequins in *Spasmo*
(Umberto Lenzi, 1974). These figures often concentrate narrative concerns with childhood trauma and the uncanny, but also serve as harbingers
of the *giallo*'s treatment of mortal bodies as aesthetic objects. Meanwhile,
the association between fashion and murder is replicated in subsequent
gialli, including *Strip Nude for Your Killer* (Andrea Bianchi, 1975) and
the neo-*giallo The Neon Demon* (Nicolas Winding Refn, 2016), which
makes use of angular forms and bright colours in its depiction of amoral-
ity and murder in the modelling industry. The latter film's luminous,

kaleidoscopic aesthetic can be traced back in turn to *Blood and Black Lace*, which Kannas describes as 'perpetually threatening to explode in jewel-toned patterns'.[39] Bava's use of exaggerated red, green and purple lighting combines with high-fashion outfits to enhance the perverse appeal of the models' murders, evoking a lethal orchestration of line and colour.

This focus on aesthetics is also associated with *giallo*'s peculiarly dis-located handling of narrative and optical point of view. Joel Black sug-gests that the aestheticisation of murder often goes hand-in-hand with the positioning of spectators or readers as witnesses, an idea that he finds articulated in Thomas De Quincey's famous 1827 essay, 'On Murder Considered as One of the Fine Arts'. Black locates variations on this central idea across a range of contemporary aesthetic disciplines, including cinema.[40] He argues that the experience of violence as aesthetic is particu-larly foregrounded in works where the reader/viewer identifies neither with the murderer nor the victim, nor the detective investigating with the case, and occupies instead the role of witness.[41] As an example, Black cites a scene from Brian De Palma's *giallo*-influenced *Dressed to Kill* (1980). In this scene, Kate, the protagonist of the first part of the film, is murdered in an elevator by a mysterious black-clad figure. Rather than showing the events from Kate's perspective, or indeed from that of the killer, the cam-erawork is oriented around the point-of-view of Liz, a younger woman who will soon take over as the main protagonist. As she is about to assist Kate, Liz spies the reflection of the attacker in the elevator's curved glass mirror, and thus manages to avoid his lethal razorblade altogether, even as she sees Kate fall prey to it. Liz, then, is 'less a victim than a witness'.[42] The witness, in this narrative form, 'is at once vulnerable and immune to the murderer whose devastation he or she witnesses'.[43] For Black, '[t]he device of having the reader-viewer identify with the witness (in a murder story) or with the voyeur (in an erotic narrative) serves to thematise the reader-viewer's own experience *as* observer'.[44] This detached perspective provides a frame in which viewers might take pleasure in the aesthetic spectacle of the murder itself.

Another illustration of this dynamic is offered by Luciano Ercoli's *Death Walks on High Heels* (1971), which destabilises narrative point-of-view but also thematises it through an overt concentration on optics and aesthetics. The main character, a burlesque performer named Nicole, is threatened by a knife-wielding balaclava-clad man with piercing blue eyes, who demands to know the location of the jewels that were stolen from her father on the occasion of his murder. The anonymous attacker may be Nicole's boyfriend Michel, in whose bathroom cabinet she finds some blue contact lenses, or her new lover Robert, a British eye surgeon and erstwhile fan of her show. The film is thus aligned with the *giallo*'s frequent return to optical concerns, which is evident, as Gary Needham points out, in titles featuring the word 'eyes', in violence inflicted on the eyes, and in failures of vision and visual witnessing.[45] In *Death Walks on High Heels,* this optical theme parallels the film's positioning of the viewer as witness. At key points we are placed at an optical distance from Nicole, as when we watch her inside her apartment through the striking curved form of the leadlight window as her attacker closes in, and when a crucial interaction with Robert's wife Vanessa is depicted via the telescope of a voyeur across the street.

The narrative, broken up by flashbacks that are anchored in different characters' perspectives, produces a commensurate distancing effect. Ultimately, after both Nicole and Vanessa (whom she strongly resembles) turn up dead, the mystery continues to unfold, but without being strongly grounded in the subjective perspective of Michel, Robert or the police. The prolongation of the narrative mystery is achieved by keeping all possible suspects at a distance, while the resulting sense of perspectival fragmentation is counterbalanced by a strong aesthetic vision that ties together bodies, garments and architectural spaces. As per Black's argument, the lack of a clearly anchored narrative perspective in *Death Walks on High Heels* enhances the focus on décor, design and the artful demise. Thus, although unity often fails to eventuate on the *giallo* film's narrational or signifying plane, it appears instead on the aesthetic plane.

Violent Frames

Although the *giallo* is diverse, I have argued that a number of recurrent features are discernible: visual and perspectival fragmentation, a concern with modernity and aesthetics, and a general sense of aesthetics as violent. The dominant style and thematic tendency of the *giallo* is thus characterised by a focus on edges and divisions. This can be linked not only to modernity but also to a more general second-order reflexivity encompassing art, the image and the body. Indeed, the *giallo* bonds together the body and the image, rendering the body as a violently stilled or abstracted representation. This framing of the image-body's violent provenance can be related to what Jean-Luc Nancy refers to as 'the distinct': a definitive boundary that is formed in the creation of any image. For Nancy, the image is distinct in two ways: 'it must be detached, placed outside and before one's eyes', and 'it must be different from the thing' it represents.[46] At the same time, the image involves a kind of cutting or separation: 'It is detached from a ground [*fond*] and it is cut out within a ground. It is pulled away and clipped or cut out'.[47] In other words, the image frame severs that which is selected for view from that which is not; and it also presents a disruption of the backdrop against which it is displayed. The image, pulled away and brought forward, becomes 'a separate frontal surface'.[48] Thus, 'the ground disappears' and 'passes entirely into the image'.[49]

In the production of images, then, there is an inherent violence that has two key dimensions: the object represented is displaced by its representation, and the ground of the image is cut away both from its field of reference and its field of display. Punning on the French word 'monstrer' (to show), Nancy argues that there is 'a monstrosity of the image' involving 'unity and force'.[50] The violence and 'excessive power' of an image, exerted via its functions of selecting and showing, produces a 'unity of force that the thing merely at hand does not represent'.[51] The act of framing, he argues, produces a kind of contraction, in which 'the image never stops tightening and condensing into itself'.[52] Cinematic *gialli*, I argue, play upon this 'tightening and condensing' of the image and direct it against the human body. The fatal stilling of the victim, the concentration on aesthetic presentation and the striking juxtaposition of visual perspectives combine to suggest a notion of the body itself as an image.

Although Nancy's argument is addressed primarily towards still images, he is at pains to suggest a broader application spanning both cinema and the performing arts. There is thus an immobility of the image, even in the context of music, dance, cinema or kinetics: 'it is the distension of a present of intensity, in which succession is also a simultaneity'.[53] Indeed, the *giallo*'s general interest in scenes of artistic performance and display (incorporating artforms like opera, music, painting and dance), involves a particularly intense fascination with various kinds of aesthetic frame. In other words, it is not just that these films feature performances of the aesthetic; they are also strongly arranged around particular kinds of spaces, which are demarcated and sharply cut off from the mundane: the stage, the gallery, the painter's canvas. The thematic of the frame links all of these various art forms in particular to the still image as a kind of aesthetic master metaphor. From the art gallery in *Bird with the Crystal Plumage* to the opera house in *Opera* (Dario Argento, 1987), demarcated spaces of aesthetic display crystallise into images of violence.

In Argento's *Four Flies on Grey Velvet* (1971), the violent frame is expressed via a bizarre plot twist, in a relay between moving and still images. Following a murder, police investigators remove the victim's eye and scan it with a special beam. Based on the ludicrous premise that the retina retains its final view for several hours after death, they extract the image of four flies arranged in a line. This mysterious image provides the evidentiary trace of a pendant worn by the killer, which has a fly encased at its centre. The form of this trace is explained by an audacious cinematic metaphor: the victim's eye has 'recorded' four 'frames' of the necklace swinging from left to right. The killer's act of violence is thus paralleled by the metaphorical violence of this spatiotemporal frame, which fragments vision and wrenches it away from the other senses (in this case, literally, by enucleating the victim's eyeball). Here, the violence of this quasi-cinematic frame recalls Pascal Bonitzer's idea of the 'deframed' image. As Edward Branigan puts it, '[i]n a deframed image, something human has been lost or drained away, cruelly disfigured, but the spectator has arrived too late to witness how the frame/frame lines were broken and used "as a cutting edge"'.[54] This 'sadism' produces a mysterious wounding that is neither revealed nor mended by subsequent shots: 'The 'wound' to the film, as it were, will not be fully exposed or sutured, even temporarily'.[55]

However, it is not just cinematic frames that turn violent. At the conclusion of *Deep Red*, Marcus revisits the apartment where Helga was killed, lingering in front of an array of paintings depicting grotesque faces. It is here that Marcus realises he has already seen the killer. Among the paintings is a mirror, which Marcus had previously taken to be another painting. He now realises that the face in that frame was not a painted one; rather, it was the face of the killer. At this moment, the killer appears once again in the same frame, revealing herself to be the mother of Marcus's friend Carlo, and attacks Marcus. She comes to a nasty end, however, when her necklace becomes entangled in the door of an elevator. The definitive cut of the mirror's frame is gruesomely replicated in a much more material, visceral form, as the murderer is decapitated by her own necklace. This conceptual alignment of the image-boundary and the fatal necklace literalises Nancy's theorisation of the frame's 'tightening and condensing'. The physical frame, which marks the elevation of the artwork from the mundane and into the space of aesthetics, is depicted by association as violent.

The violent condensation of the image in *giallo* spans both painterly and photographic contexts. In *The House with Laughing Windows* (Pupi Avati, 1976), a painting of the death of St Sebastian serves a prominent role within the film's plot, which links art and the Catholic Church with murder. *Torso* (Sergio Martino, 1973), which features an art historian as its elusive killer, aligns both painting and photography with its framing of aestheticised death. In *Torso*'s lurid opening scene, we hear the art historian delivering a lecture on a Perugino painting (again, St Sebastian is the subject), while we witness a *ménage à trois* taking place. Here, the painterly discourse on the soundtrack is deliberately linked with the photographic. The erotic spectacle is depicted via a series of oblique and soft-focus shots which hint at the action without disclosing the identities of all the participants. One, it will be revealed, is the art historian himself, while the two women present are his future victims. Eventually, a photographic viewfinder and lens enter into view, providing glimpses of a reflexive 'camera eye' on the proceedings and injecting photographic stillness into the *mise-en-scène*. Later, it is revealed that the resulting still photographs were used to blackmail the killer, thus providing him with a partial motivation for his subsequent crimes. The sexual vitality of this scene is haunted by the stilled bodies of painting (St Sebastian) and photography (the two victims-to-be). Later in the film, the still image's link to mortality and aesthetics is again underlined when the police use a slide projector to display crucial evidence for the students. Here, the police chief feels compelled to note that the projected slide is not, as it might appear, an example of expressionist art but rather represents a scrap of cloth retrieved from beneath a murder victim's fingernails. The framed and projected photographic image, presented in the dedicated setting of the lecture hall, represents the violent extraction of aesthetic content from the ground of the everyday.

The notion of photographs (and photographic frames) as inherently violent is also suggested by the photographic mediation of fashion in a number of *gialli*. Prominent examples include *The Case of the Bloody Iris* (Giuliano Carnimeo, 1972), *The Red Queen Kills Seven Times* (Emilio Miraglia, 1972) and *Strip Nude for Your Killer* (Andrea Bianchi, 1975). In the first of these three, which revolves around the murders of several young women, a model named Jennifer is troubled by memories of her abusive ex-husband Adam. Two scenes early in the film imply a connection between photography and violence. Firstly, during an erotically charged photo-shoot, Jennifer becomes disoriented and seems to imagine that Adam is watching her. Here, Jennifer experiences the photographer's use of camera and lights as an assault that renders her dazed and immobile, as if she herself is turning into a stilled image, becoming photographic. Secondly, when Jennifer encounters Adam on her way home, she experiences a flashback depicting their sexually coercive relationship. In this flashback, multiple exposures are used to create a kaleidoscopic effect, as Adam tosses bunches of flowers onto Jennifer's naked recumbent body. Both the shot and reverse shot of this action are broken up into a revolving array of overlapping frames. Although this dizzying effect is a brief moment in the sequence, it suggests a certain reflexivity regarding the filmic-photographic image, a multiplication of optical frames that is

associated with psychological disorder but also the flattening and subjuga-
tion of the body. A very similar visual effect is applied in *The Red Queen
Kills Seven Times*, as a montage sequence shows the protagonist Kitty
photographing a fashion model. Here, the film cuts between close-ups
of the still camera's shutter opening and closing with multiple rotating
vignettes of the model's likeness being captured. These examples of com-
pound imagery further highlight *giallo* cinema's affinity for visual edges,
along with their threatening connotations. Such sequences provide a
direct manifestation of what Alexia Kannas has identified as *giallo*'s kaleidoscopic aspect,[56] but also, in pulling the external frame into visibility,
underline Nancy's emphasis on the image's *distinctness* and its associated
representational violence. Here, in moments of extreme aesthetic condensation, the cutting edge of the frame is multiplied within the image itself.

Subtractive Seriality

The *giallo*'s concern with visual edges, discrete forms and fragmentation is replicated at the narrative level, via an emphasis on repetition and
segmentation. In particular, the arrangement of the plot around a series
of spectacular deaths (a structure common both to many *giallo* films and
to the American 'slashers' they influenced) produces a logic of subtractive
seriality. Elsewhere, Adam Lowenstein has used the term 'subtractive
spectatorship' to describe how *giallo* and slasher films express 'a desire to
subtract or erase human beings from the landscape, to leave it empty'.[57]
Concentrating on Mario Bava's *A Bay of Blood* (which, with its high body-
count and inventive murders, is a clear precursor to the *Friday the 13th*
franchise), Lowenstein argues that the subtractive mode does not elide the
film's special effects and spectacular deaths, but instead works 'in tandem'
with them.[58] According to Lowenstein, Bava's 'gory spectacles are both
sensationally present and artificially absent: they are images to feel in the
flesh as well as compositions to contemplate in the abstract'.[59] One can see
this abstraction reproduced at the narrational level in a form of editorial
seriality, which involves a successive cutting away of victims and narrative
possibilities. These serial formations suggest a kind of violence inherent
to aesthetic patterning. Here, the spatiotemporal 'cutting edge' of *giallo*
aesthetics manifests itself within the structure of the story itself, providing
a threat to order, continuity and meaning.

Subtractive seriality is exemplified by the lurid 1975 thriller *Strip Nude
for Your Killer*. The film's chain of murder scenes frames the victims'
bodies as disposable objects of consumption, rendering them as inert
matter but also, by excising each character sequentially, suggesting that

they are *of no matter*. Beginning with a botched abortion that leaves the patient dead, the film depicts a series of killings that claims the abortionist as its first victim, followed by several personnel from a modelling agency. This performance of subtractive seriality is linked to the *giallo*'s thematic imbrication of photography, aesthetics and death: having acquired a photographic print showing the agency's staff gathered together, the killer works through this array of still figures, rendering each one literally inert, one after another. As in other *gialli*, this subtractive work is aided by the killer's dark attire: here, a black motorcycle helmet and leathers facilitates the silhouetted absence more commonly afforded by hats and long coats. Meanwhile, a photographer's assistant named Magda helps her lensman boyfriend Carlo try to solve the case. The killer is ultimately unmasked as Patrizia, a model whose sister Evelyn was the victim of the mishandled abortion. Patrizia blames Carlo for his role in covering up the death, and although Carlo tells Magda that he does not know who got Evelyn pregnant, his leering and boorish behaviour throughout the film suggests the possibility that it was him.

The two key thematic threads in the film are to do with abortion and photography. Indeed, the film immediately connects the two by casting the abortion scene in a monochrome blue that parallels the red glow of the agency's darkroom. Moreover, Carlo and the doctor dispose of Evelyn's body by placing it in her bathtub to simulate drowning, an action that resembles the submerging of prints in a photographic 'bath'. Here, the abortion and the developing process both serve as a kind of uncanny gestation, resulting not in life but in the stilling of bodies. Accordingly, the agency's darkroom not only serves as a central location for the film's lurid plot, but also furthers the film's thematic engagement with death. When Magda strips off her clothes in the darkroom to demonstrate her suitability for a modelling career, Carlo replies dismissively that 'fashion models are finished in a couple of years'. In Carlo's terms, the longevity of Magda's career (and, by implication, her life) is linked with the decision to stay on the 'right' side of the camera. Later in the film, when Carlo thinks he has snapped a fleeting picture of the murderer, he has Magda rush to the lab to develop it. Violently interrupting this process, the murderer takes the trouble to burn the negatives. Manifesting exclusively as a visual negation, a black cut-out or void, the killer is evidently all too aware of the fatal consequences of appearing as a recognisable image.

Meanwhile, the use of the abortion scene as a frame for the narrative produces further thematic resonances, not only foreshadowing the deaths to come but also suggesting a desire for elimination that recalls Lowenstein's notion of 'subtractive spectatorship'. Towards the middle of the film, one death in particular illustrates this idea. Maurizio, the obese husband of the agency's owner Gisella, has attempted unsuccessfully to seduce one of the models. Unable to perform sexually, he wanders around his house in his underpants, weeping pitifully for his 'mama'. Retrieving a blow-up doll in anticipation of some compensatory pleasures, he becomes increasingly unnerved by the sound of running water, a sonic detail which has served as a harbinger of previous killings. After several minutes of this grotesque spectacle, the killer brings Maurizio's life to its sad conclusion. In the context of a film and genre predicated on the thrills of the aesthetic death, Maurizio's prolonged torment is resolutely anti-aesthetic. In this context, particularly given his infantile mannerisms and language, we are invited to see him as worthy of excision, or in the film's brutal terms, as an unwanted foetus.

The end of the film once again ties together the themes of abortion and photography. Having unmasked the killer and survived their ordeal, Carlo and Magda relax at home, going over the details of the story and enjoying a growing state of mutual arousal. Despite Magda making clear that she is taking contraceptive pills, Carlo's final suggestion is that they have anal sex in order to avoid any risk of pregnancy. His subsequent claim that he is 'only joking' does little to counter Magda's shocked protestations, particularly in the context of his rough and boorish behaviour earlier in the film. At this precise moment, the final freeze-frame of the two together returns fatal stillness to the image, while linking it to the negation of reproductive processes. Despite surviving the killer's onslaught, it seems that Carlo and Magda have fallen prey to the serial return of the motionless image. The expression of aesthetic qualities and enjoyment of sexual pleasure seem in this film to require a cancellation of life, as articulated via the paired metaphors of abortion and photography.

Death and significance are thus prised apart, as the film's series of aesthetically motivated fatalities fails to build towards a meaningful resolution. The unveiling of Patrizia as the killer is abrupt and cursory, and the revelation of her motivation (as Evelyn's sister) is delivered via an offhand chunk of dialogue as Carlo and Magda flirt with each other in the final scene. As in other examples of the subgenre, the psychological explanation feels slight and perfunctory, with little satisfaction to be gained from its surprise resolution. Indeed, in *giallo* the final explanation of the killer's identity and motivation is very often nonsensical, appearing incidental to the real business of the films, which is to provide atmospheric setups and thrilling set pieces. As Ian Olney puts it, the *giallo* should be seen as a kind of '"anti-detective" cinema', in which viewers watch not to see the narrative mystery resolved, but instead to enjoy the films' play with 'disruption, transgression, undecidability, and uncertainty'.[60] Certainly, *Strip Nude for*

Your Killer aligns with Olney's analysis of *Blood and Black Lace*, in which, following a series of reversals, twists and misdirections, 'we are denied any real sense of closure'.[61] Neither the detectives nor the viewers, he observes, are offered any genuine pathway towards deducing the killer's identity.[62] Similarly, L. Andrew Cooper observes that the titular creature in Argento's *Bird with the Crystal Plumage* is merely a minor plot detail that leads the police closer to the killer but bears no further significance in its own right,[63] while the painting that is supposed to provide an insight into the killer's motivation provides a 'psychoanalytic thread' that ultimately 'leads nowhere'.[64] Rather than psychoanalysis as the final word, we are offered 'an assertion of aesthetic engagement with spectacle as film's most important source of interest—its most *meaningful* element, if "meaningful" can be divorced from the clarity or truth commonly associated with "meaning"'.[65] Psychoanalytical explanations are thus disarmed by a kind of hypertrophic parody. Meaning itself is placed in suspension, while aesthetics takes over as the primary system of ordering.

Ultimately, then, the serial patterning of *Strip Nude for Your Killer* involves a series of aestheticised subtractions that fail to 'add up' to a definitive meaning. Its array of fatal incisions recalls Karla Oeler's argument that the act of killing is always also an assertion of meaning (or the lack thereof): 'the murderer violently asserts that the victim's life has but limited and disposable significance'.[66] In the cinematic context, the narrative itself may assist in this act of disposal, by moving on from the character in question, signalling that they are dispensable.[67] The murder scene can present the victim as 'someone real' but also as 'information that has importance for the plot, but not in itself'.[68] In *Strip Nude for Your Killer*, this dynamic is particularly evident: the narrative guides us through an episodic series of deaths, with each victim given little thought following their elimination. This serial element is emphasised towards the end of the film, when one of the models, Doris, witnesses a television news report in which the film's catalogue of murder victims is enumerated. Minutes later, Doris and her abusive boyfriend Stefano have been slaughtered, and thus tendered as further additions to the list. There is relatively little narrative investment in these characters, who tend overall to be vapid, oafish or sadistic. They are there primarily to be eliminated. In its narrative patterning no less than its visual design, *giallo* is defined by fatal edges.

The Matter of the Cut

These aesthetically-motivated incisions cut across matter in two senses: matter understood as meaningful content, 'the matter at hand'; and matter understood as stuff, thingness, materiality (whether of bodies or of media). The 'matter of the cut' is thus double-edged. For if the editorial cut raises the matter of signification, inscribing and articulating meanings, then in the case of the *giallo* it also leads, conspicuously, towards the dissection of material forms. Here, we feel in a visceral way how the imposition of aesthetic patterning inflicts itself on physical matter, even as we also observe how *giallo*'s aesthetic motivations distort and fragment the other kind of matter – the matter of narrative, sense and logic. The *giallo*'s signature tactic is to put both forms of matter under the sign and force of the cut. The violence of aesthetics thus menaces both bodies and meaning. *Giallo* is *about* aesthetic form – and about form as dislocation, rearticulation, bricolage, separation and flattening.

This editorial logic occupies every level of the work, providing a conception of matter and media that implicitly challenges phenomenological accounts of human experience. For phenomenologist Merleau-Ponty, 'the body is not an object', since conceiving of it as a collection of 'third person processes' cannot capture how these processes are 'all obscurely drawn together and mutually implied in a unique drama'.[69] The *giallo*, by contrast, teases apart the body, rendering it as an object. In this sense it is aligned with Jean-Luc Nancy's post-phenomenological perspective. Nancy insists on exteriority: '[t]he body is always outside, on the outside. It is from the outside'.[70] In Nancy's framing, the body is alien: 'corpus *is never properly me* . . . It's always an "object", a body objected precisely *against the claim of being a body-subject*, or a subject-in-a-body'.[71] As illustrated by the *giallo*, cinematic editing threatens always to bring out the body's objecthood, undermining phenomenological perspectives on the body. A similar response to phenomenology emerges via montage theory. Referring to Merleau-Ponty's argument that we experience our body not as a collection of discrete objects but as elements that are mutually enveloped, Karla Oeler asserts that silent era montage 'systematically destroyed this integrity'.[72] As conceived by film theorists like Balázs and Eisenstein, montage renders bodily fragments as things, on the same plane as inanimate objects.[73] Editing demonstrates its power to remake the body as an assembly of signifying parts, which can be presented not only as 'something real' (a three-dimensional form viewed from different perspectives) but also as 'abstracted signification'.[74] Any guarantee of experiential or semiotic integrity is thus revoked.

The implications of this argument extend to questions of meaning. For Merleau-Ponty, the subject's body itself serves as 'a meaningful core',[75] which actively 'interprets itself'.[76] This perspective on the body requires, according to Merleau-Ponty, 'a new meaning of the word "meaning"', based organically in lived experience.[77] Through its intensified engagements with physical experience, the *giallo* offers a potential means for articulating this kind of embodied meaning. And, indeed, it does so, conveying bodily expressions of terror, dread and desire in ways that 'speak' to the spectator's body. However, although Merleau-Ponty's conception makes room for an 'element of senselessness',[78] the desubjectified bodies of *giallo* incorporate a more radical evacuation of meaning, which aligns with Nancy's emphasis on objecthood. For Nancy, the body's fundamental exteriority presents us always with a threshold of 'non-sense', where the corporeal is not coterminous with the self/subject, but instead, 'infinitely other'.[79] Rather than a 'meaningful core', we are faced with the body as a disarticulated 'corpus'.

Accordingly, the *giallo*'s aestheticised dissection of bodies and spaces works to neutralise and undermine meaning. Nowhere is this more evident than in the 'art-horror' film *Amer* (Hélène Cattet and Bruno Forzani, 2009), which draws extensively on tropes from *giallo* cinema, including stylised imagery, lurid psycho-sexual scenarios, intense colours and contrasts, and the ubiquitous black-gloved killer. Amplifying the stylistic quirks of an already stylised subgenre, Cattet and Forzani push the logic of fragmentation still further, combining a fractured and dreamlike narrative with a disorienting, kaleidoscopic visual aesthetic. Whereas in classic *gialli* it is primarily the murder sequences that are disjointed and elliptical, here it is the entire film. *Amer* presents three loosely articulated tales that show a woman, Ana, at three stages of life (childhood, adolescence and adulthood) grappling with scenarios involving desire and death. This tripartite structure implies a narrative of progression, but the sense of a unified subjectivity threading together the three episodes is almost entirely lacking. Indeed, as Donato Totaro points out, the film's structure recalls Mario Bava's portmanteau film *Black Sabbath* (1963), which presents three entirely unrelated tales.[80] In *Amer*, despite the notional throughline, the three segments are shaped by sharply differing aesthetic approaches, which help to dissever rather than connect the plot.

Both structurally and visually, *Amer* demonstrates the logic of the cut. Reviewers of the film commonly remark on its fragmentary aesthetic. Anton Bitel describes it as 'a mosaic of hints and suggestions for a narrative that remains elliptical and ambiguous to the end'.[81] For Martin Conterio, both *Amer* and the directors' subsequent work *The Strange Colour of Your Body's Tears* present dreamlike narratives where 'crucial moments, shots and images resemble shards of stained glass, and the viewer is invited to pick up the pieces and put them back together'.[82] This aesthetic approach is signalled in the opening sequence, which makes

extensive use of split-screen effects to juxtapose an array of images simultaneously: eyes in extreme close-up, sweat-drops on skin, a gear-stick, a
steering wheel, sunlight on water, sunlight through trees. At one point,
three pairs of eyes are presented in distinct horizontal bands, one above
the next. These eyes would appear to belong to Ana at the three different
ages depicted in the film, although that connection is not signalled clearly
by the sequence itself. Instead, this juxtaposition gestures more emphatically towards the film's intensive concern with visuality and looking, and
points towards the kaleidoscopic aesthetic that will shape the film's editing
and narrative structure.

Like many *gialli*, *Amer* plays with the signifiers of psychoanalytic depth,
only to frustrate their meaningful articulation. Here, the tendency towards
irresolution is magnified by the sheer excess of aesthetic gestures. The
first narrative segment follows Ana as a young girl, as she witnesses both
her parents' sexual congress and her grandfather's dead body. Although
this segment can be read as a kind of coming-of-age story, the editing is
extremely elliptical, offering a chain of disjunctive impressions rather than
a cohesive narrative. The commitment to aesthetics slices across matter
in two senses, cleaving both meaning and materiality. At one point, Ana
sits at the dinner table preparing to eat some meat off her knife, when she
spies a pair of eyes reflected in the blade. The shock of this sudden splice
(eyes-knife) is answered by a reverse shot revealing that the eyes belong,
not to another participant in the scene, but to a face depicted in a painting
hanging on the wall behind Ana. The editing thus juxtaposes a series of
discrete elements: knife, meat, eyes, art. In so doing, it gives rise both to
an affective frisson and an abstract relation. It connects vision and violence
as well as art and the body, restating key themes of the classic *giallo* but
concentrating them via an excessive foregrounding of aesthetics and of
the cut. In another scene, as Ana spies on her parents through a keyhole,
Cattet and Forzani find further ways to break up the image. A close-up
of Ana's eye is duplicated kaleidoscopically. The reverse shot shows her
father arched backwards in pleasure, replicated in three adjacent frames,
each one tinted a different colour. Close-ups of body parts are also rendered in red, blue and green, thus disarticulating the body into discrete
forms. The accompanying sounds (sighs, breaths, water drops) are also
distinct and separate, underlining this effect of disarticulation. Later, as
Ana steals a fob watch from her grandfather's dead body, different areas
and objects within the frame are lit in contrasting colours. A blue face is
set against a red backdrop. The keyhole is green. Later, she opens the fob
watch to find a green-lit eye inside, staring out at her. Channelling themes
of sex and death, innocence and guilt, these images nonetheless fail to

resolve into clear-cut narrative forms and are subordinated instead to the film's intensely fragmentary aesthetic.

Subsequent narrative segments extend the exploration of perspectives and optics. The second segment shows Ana as a teenager, ogled by men on the street as she walks by with her mother. There is heavy use of slow motion, and once again sensual details are presented via a series of cuts: a face, a breast, hands, an ant crawling across the skin, a strand of hair in Ana's mouth, her legs, her eyes. At one point, the two women are reflected in the glasses of a man who is staring at them; at another, they are viewed through windows; later, Ana's cleavage and body are illuminated by a patch of light cast by a motorbike mirror, before her reflection appears in the same mirror, distorted. This array of glassy surfaces highlights the mediation of the body. In the third segment, Ana (now an adult) returns from the city to the country, and is picked up at the station by a mysterious driver, who stares at her in the rear-view mirror as he drives her to a large empty house, in which she is soon menaced by a gloved, knife-wielding assailant. The look is powerfully emphasised: from the stare of the driver behind his shades, to the eyes in the paintings in the house (later torn out) that seem somehow to be watching Ana. Indeed, Donato Totaro suggests that each section of *Amer* presents a different kind of looking: from the pleasure of looking in the first section ('Ana-the-voyeur looks at others') to the pleasure of being looked at in the second ('Ana-the-exhibitionist is looked at') to, ultimately, the third section in which 'the act of looking is taken to its twisted logical conclusion' (Ana looks at herself and fantasises that a killer is pursuing her).[83] However, each of these sections contains within itself a corresponding counter-look: from the fob-watch that 'looks' back at the young Ana, to teenage Ana's return of the voyeurs' gaze, to

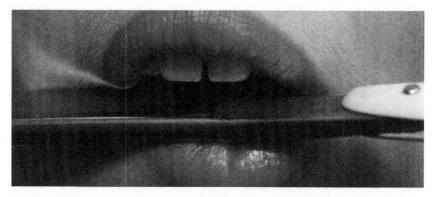

Figure 4.3 The blade becomes an object of sensual play in the neo-*giallo Amer* (Hélène Cattet and Bruno Forzani, 2009).

adult Ana's movement between contradictory roles in a violent game of cat-and-mouse. This fragmentation of perspectives provides a disorienting refraction of the *giallo*'s characteristic tropes.

This prismatic rendering of the *giallo* is perhaps most pronounced in the concluding section, in which Ana oscillates between the positions of victim and black-gloved killer. In a sequence that concentrates perspectival fragmentation and editorial violence, Ana uses a razor blade on her erstwhile attacker. Her sadistic ministrations are depicted in a chain of close-ups: her gloved finger probing the wound on his hand, then his panicked eyes, then his mouth. She cuts his face, his lips, his face again; her blade hovers over his eye. She catches his tears gently with the razor, then slashes him again. Her arm is raised. Again, the blade menaces his eye. And now she presses his own switchblade against his throat, until, with a gristly crunch, it penetrates. After a further series of violent edits, there is a cut to black. Ana subsequently finds herself lying on the floor next to a pool of blood. She looks up and suddenly, confusingly, she finds herself outside the house, with a dark figure looming above her. This series of abrupt editorial gestures parallels the slashing of the razor, pursuing a dislocation that starts from the body before moving out to cut apart space, time, perspective and narrative logic. Instead of unified subjectivity, editing in *Amer* articulates a confusion of bodies. Ultimately, after Ana has once again stabbed her assailant, she appears supine on a mortuary table. She is not dead, however: her eyes open just before the film ends with a cut to black. This movement between perspectives and ontological states confronts us, in Nancy's terms, with the body as corpus, which is '*never properly me*'.[84] Bodies in *Amer* are presented in their exteriority, as objects. This disarticulated array fails to assemble itself into a unified sign; it is, rather, 'infinitely other'.[85]

The cutting of matter, the matter of the cut. Cattet and Forzani push the narrative beyond breaking point, as Ana oscillates between murderer and victim. In doing so, they amplify and reflect on *giallo*'s aesthetic strategy, producing a kind of 'anti-suture' through which the film is reflexively dismembered. Rather than working to produce subjective coherence, this anti-suture entails a process of becoming-object, which is enacted within the film itself as, more specifically, a process of becoming-media: the becoming-media of the victim, who is cut up and re-edited, as it were, and the becoming-media of the killer, who disappears into the text as a spatiotemporal cut-out. If the film is stitched back together, it is not by convincing us that we inhabit a seamless world, but by reflexively foregrounding the mediating role of aesthetics. In the process, Cattet and Forzani present a meta-theorisation of *giallo*'s sensual engagement with material surfaces (from steel to skin to fabric to glass), tracing their potential for fragmentation or aesthetic unity. In this push and pull between order and chaos, *Amer* presents 'meaning' itself as a fraught property: the spectacle of the victimised body suspends corporeal signification between extreme disorder and aestheticisation, disarticulated forms and empty signs.

Notes

1. Here, I will not be delving into debates about the definitional boundaries of the *giallo*, which is sufficiently varied that some have questioned whether it can be approached as a coherent generic category. For example, Gary Needham argues that the *giallo*, spanning 'gothic horror . . . police procedurals . . . crime melodrama . . . and conspiracy films', may be best considered not as a genre but framed instead via the Italian word *filone*, since it is 'used to refer to both genres and cycles as well as to currents and trends'. Needham, 'Playing with genre: an introduction to the Italian "giallo"'.

2. In addition to *Deep Red* (discussed here), see *Four Flies on Grey Velvet* (1971), *Tenebrae* (1982) and *Phenomena* (1985) as well as the *giallo*-adjacent *Suspiria* (1977) and *Inferno* (1980).

3. Beyond producing doubt about the killer's whereabouts, these shots recall the 'emptied' spaces of Michelangelo Antonioni's modernist cinema, a resonance further amplified by the casting of David Hemmings, star of Antonioni's *Blow Up* (1966) in the role of Marcus.

4. Koven, *La Dolce Morte: Vernacular Cinema and the Italian Giallo Film*, p. 150.

5. Ibid. p. 148.

6. Oeler, *A Grammar of Murder: Violent Scenes and Film Form*, p. 4.

7. The notion of killer as textual artefact is also picked up, in a less generally stylised way, by the American slasher film, in particular via the use of POV cinematography and the mechanism of the shot-reverse shot, which occasionally seems to allow the killer to appear and disappear at will.

8. Indeed, the agency of objects is reflected in the fact that so many of these films are named for ornaments, animals, dolls or aesthetic objects. Examples include: *The Bird with the Crystal Plumage, The Short Night of Glass Dolls* (Aldo Lado, 1971), *Four Flies on Grey Velvet, Blood and Black Lace* and *A Lizard in a Woman's Skin* (Lucio Fulci, 1971).

9. Some suture theorists, like Jean-Pierre Oudart, concentrate on the shot-reverse shot, with its structuring absences, as the key locus of cinematic suture. See Oudart, 'Cinema and suture', p. 36. In 'Notes on suture', by contrast, Heath argues that suture is not bound by the shot/reverse shot exchange, but instead functions across the whole discursive system of the film. Heath, 'Notes on suture', p. 68.

10. Heath, 'Narrative space', p. 99.

11. Ibid. p. 101.

12. Silverman, *The Subject of Semiotics*, p. 204.
13. Ibid. p. 205.
14. Oeler, *A Grammar of Murder*, p. 51.
15. Ibid. p. 51.
16. Olney, *Euro Horror: Classic European Horror Cinema in Contemporary American Culture*, p. 111.
17. Ibid. p. 112.
18. Diffrient, 'A film is being beaten: notes on the shock cut and the material violence of horror', p. 53.
19. Ibid. p. 53.
20. Ibid. p. 54.
21. Ibid. p. 55.
22. Ibid. p. 59.
23. Ibid. p. 75.
24. Ibid. p. 56.
25. Koven, *La Dolce Morte*, p. 16.
26. Ibid. p. 16.
27. Ibid. p. 156.
28. Ibid. p. 146.
29. Schneider, 'Murder as art/the art of murder: aestheticizing violence in modern cinematic horror', p. 177.
30. Ibid. p. 177.
31. Ibid. p. 191.
32. Oeler, 'Eisenstein and horror', p. 317.
33. Ibid. p. 318.
34. Schneider, 'Murder as art/the art of murder: aestheticizing violence in modern cinematic horror', p. 177.
35. Ibid. p. 178.
36. Cooper, *Dario Argento*, p. 30.
37. Hunt, 'A (sadistic) night at the opera: notes on the Italian horror film', p. 330.
38. Kannas, 'All the colours of the dark: film genre and the Italian giallo', p. 174.
39. Ibid.
40. Black, *The Aesthetics of Murder: A Study in Romantic Literature and Contemporary Culture*, p. 190.
41. Ibid. p. 66.
42. Ibid. p. 63.
43. Ibid. p. 66.
44. Ibid. p. 67.
45. Needham, 'Playing with genre: an introduction to the Italian "giallo"'.
46. Nancy, *The Ground of the Image*, p. 2.
47. Ibid. p. 7.
48. Ibid. p. 7.
49. Ibid. p. 7.
50. Ibid. p. 22.

51. Ibid. p. 22.
52. Ibid. p. 10.
53. Ibid. p. 10.
54. Branigan, *Projecting a Camera: Language-Games in Film Theory*, p. 143.
55. Ibid. p. 143.
56. Kannas, 'All the colours of the dark: film genre and the Italian *giallo*', p. 175.
57. Lowenstein, 'The giallo/slasher landscape *Ecologia Del Delitto, Friday the 13th* and subtractive spectatorship', p. 133.
58. Ibid. p. 136.
59. Ibid. p. 136.
60. Olney, *Euro Horror*, p. xiii. Olney draws the term 'anti-detective fiction' from Stefano Tani, who uses it to describe post-war Italian *giallo* novels, in which an avant-garde sensibility emerges, leading to narratives that shun resolution and downplay the centrality of the detective's rational perspective (p. 106). Olney finds this to be a decisive influence on *giallo* cinema, as well as Italian art films including Bernardo Bertolucci's *La commare secca* (1962) and Michelangelo Antonioni's *Blow-Up*, which were themselves 'partly inspired by the anti-detective novel' (p. 107).
61. Ibid. p. 108.
62. Ibid. p. 109.
63. Cooper, *Dario Argento*, p. 29.
64. Ibid. p. 37.
65. Ibid. p. 60–61.
66. Oeler, *A Grammar of Murder*, p. 5.
67. Ibid. p. 6.
68. Ibid. p. 14.
69. Merleau-Ponty, *Phenomenology of Perception*, pp. 230–1.
70. Nancy, *Corpus*, p. 129.
71. Ibid. p. 29.
72. Oeler, *A Grammar of Murder*, p. 52.
73. Ibid. p. 53.
74. Ibid. p. 13.
75. Merleau-Ponty, *Phenomenology of Perception*, p. 170.
76. Ibid. pp. 173–74.
77. Ibid. p. 170.
78. Ibid. p. 170.
79. Nancy, *Corpus*, p. 13.
80. Totaro, '*Amer*: the three faces of Ana'.
81. Bitel, '*Amer* (movie review)', p. 47.
82. Conterio, 'Doors and their secrets: the legacy of 1940s Hollywood in *The Strange Colour of Your Body's Tears* (2013)'.
83. Totaro, '*Amer*: the three faces of Ana'.
84. Nancy, *Corpus*, p. 29.
85. Ibid. p. 13.

CHAPTER 5

Chromatic Transfusions:
Colour, Genre and Embodiment

As a fundamental material property, colour provides a rich field for horror's engagement with bodies and media. The manipulation of colour can be used to emphasise the distinctness of forms but it can also serve to blur physical and environmental boundaries, moving across bodies, objects and spaces. By extension, it can blur other boundaries as well, such as those relating to genre, gender and meaning. Colour is unstable and volatile; it invokes cultural codes and conventions but also overflows them. In the horror genre, imaginative use of colour can produce complex interplays between interpretation and affect. In spite of this, many contemporary filmmakers fall back on more predictable choices. Since the turn of the millennium, a certain gritty, desaturated look has arguably become something of a template. This trend can be seen in early 2000s horror remakes like *The Texas Chain Saw Massacre* (Marcus Nispel, 2003) and *The Last House on the Left* (Dennis Iliadis, 2009), in the long-running *Saw* franchise (2004–2017), and in recent examples including *The Conjuring 2* (James Wan, 2016) and *The Silence* (John R. Leonetti, 2019).[1] Although it is perhaps too easy to criticise filmmakers for failing to engage with the expressive possibilities of colour, I will be concentrating on works that explore its boundary-crossing potential. These examples are not restricted to a particular horror subgenre, although it is worth noting that some of the most chromatically inventive films display a common concern with issues of ontology and embodiment.

Colour is at once a fruitful and a fraught object of analysis, traversing physical experience and signification: it is possible to regard it both as an affective, embodied phenomenon and as a semiotic, conceptual system. A key source of horror's bodily address to spectators, colour also speaks to the occult codes and symbols that underpin many horror narratives. Indeed, the intensity of this dual address to the senses and to sense-making is one reason why colour often resists description and analysis. Colour, it might be argued, always challenges the boundaries between the affective and the semiotic. As Steve Neale argues, drawing upon the work of Julia Kristeva, colour 'is neither purely subjective not purely objective. Nor are its meanings simply a matter of cultural convention'; instead, it simultaneously calls upon objective, subjective and cultural dimensions.[2] In what follows, I do not attempt a definitive untangling of these various threads. Instead, I wish to point out that the characteristic effects of colour are closely bound up with generic codes and expectations, without being wholly determined by them. The meanings that we attach to colour in the horror film are thus the result of both cultural traditions and raw sensations. With this in mind, I will turn first of all to the chromatic conventions of the horror film before analysing the sophisticated use of colour cues in *High Tension* (Alexandre Aja, 2003), *A Tale of Two Sisters* (Kim Ji-woon, 2003) and *The Neon Demon* (Nicolas Winding Refn, 2016), focusing in particular on the way such cues are used to modulate shifts between embodied and atmospheric horror.

The Colour of Fear

Familiar colour templates in genre cinema have included the use of burnished tones for the western, cold blues and intense reds for sci-fi, and warm pastels for romantic comedy. In each case, the logic of colour is determined by a combination of semiotic and affective associations. Thus, the western's colour template evokes the spare, dusty landscapes of the American West, while also recalling sepia photographs as a visual reference point. Although individual films often assert their own chromatic identities, such templates nonetheless establish generic norms that, when ignored or modified, draw our attention to the conceptual and affective structure underpinning the film in question. What, then, are the colours of horror? Is there an established template that dictates and shapes creative choices? Despite the contemporary trend towards desaturated colours, it is difficult to identify a uniform colour schema that spans the genre. Nonetheless, it does seem that certain cycles and subgeneric groupings display a recurrent colour aesthetic, as Brigid Cherry has observed regarding the rich and sensual colours of the Hammer horrors of the late 1950s and 1960s.[3]

Indeed, Hammer arguably revitalised Gothic screen narratives by imbuing them with a heightened sexual charge which was amplified via the use of colour. Thus, the powerful sensuality of Christopher Lee's performance in Hammer's *Horror of Dracula* (Terence Fisher, 1959) is embellished by the chromatic decadence of the décor and the costumes. From this point on, horror became more and more a colour genre, moving away from the restrained Gothic black-and-white atmospherics typified during the 1930s and 1940s by Universal Studios' *Dracula* (Tod Browning, 1931), *Frankenstein* (James Whale, 1931) and *The Wolf Man* (George Waggner, 1941), and by Val Lewton's eerie productions *Cat People* (Jacques Tourneur, 1942) and *I Walked with a Zombie* (Jacques Tourneur, 1943).[4] The shift to colour heralded a more embodied aesthetic, as audiences were granted access to a new spectrum of sensual and visceral connotations. Although Alfred Hitchcock's *Psycho* (1960) and George Romero's *Night of the Living Dead* (1968), arguably the two most influential films in the genre's move from Gothic to graphic horror, were both black-and-white productions, it was colour that would enable the full deployment of embodied horror effects. It is impossible to imagine the development of the splatter film, from Herschell Gordon Lewis's *Blood Feast* (1963) to Sam Raimi's *The Evil Dead* (1981) and Peter Jackson's *Braindead* (1992), without visualising it in colour. Colour thus facilitated an altogether more visceral invocation of bodily materiality.

Horror's slow shift towards colour did not bring with it a standardised chromatic aesthetic, notwithstanding the relative consistency of Hammer's lurid palette. Certain tendencies are evident across the genre, however. Red is certainly an important colour to horror, for reasons that are likely obvious. While Jean-Luc Godard famously declared 'not blood, red' when asked about the sanguinary excess of *Pierrot le Fou* (1965), the horror genre works in reverse, saturating the *mise-en-scène* with signifiers of the visceral.[5] In Stanley Kubrick's largely gore-free film *The Shining* (1980), a conversation between hotel caretaker Jack Torrance and the ghost of his predecessor takes place in a bathroom with a striking red and white colour scheme. Here, the scarlet paint extending halfway up the walls suggests a vessel filling with blood, as well as Jack's escalating rage as he loses control of his family and his sanity. Furthermore, this scene rhymes graphically with a disturbing vision experienced by Jack's son earlier in the film, in which blood cascades out of an elevator shaft. The redness of the bathroom walls is thus not simply red, but also blood. Similarly, the climactic scene of Brian De Palma's *Carrie* (1976), in which a telekinetic teenager unleashes her powers at a high school prom, makes heavy use of red lighting in order to emphasise both the intensity of Carrie's anger and the fact that she has been doused with pig's blood. In *Mandy* (Panos Cosmatos, 2018), washes of red tint the entire image: these serve initially as a premonition of the titular character's murder; later, they index the vengeful rage of her partner, Red Miller, and the bloody excess of his killing spree. Ultimately, Red's chromatic moniker is matched both by the gore sprayed across his face and by the ambient crimson light that floods the latter stages of his quest.

A less obvious but perhaps no less significant colour is green. Indeed, an all-pervasive desaturated green seems characteristic of the colour grading in many contemporary horror films, including *The Eye* (Oxide Pang Chun and Danny Pang, 2002), *The Ring* (Gore Verbinski, 2002), *The Texas Chain Saw Massacre* (Marcus Nispel, 2003), *Saw* (James Wan, 2004), *Insidious* (James Wan, 2010), *Green Room* (Jeremy Saulnier, 2015), *A Cure for Wellness* (Gore Verbinski, 2016) and *Rings* (F. Javier Gutiérrez, 2017). Green is certainly not the only keynote colour in contemporary horror (muddy browns and icy blues are also quite common), but it is arguably the most distinctive. The prominence of green in contemporary horror, however, is not unprecedented. As I will go on to suggest, green has performed an important role in many of horror's most memorable and influential films. Its significance even appears to predate the genre's wholesale migration to colour: selected release prints of James Whale's 1931 version of *Frankenstein* were tinted green, and screenings of these prints were promoted as offering audiences 'the colour of fear'.[6] Why green and not red? Or, indeed, blue? The answer is far from straightforward, but an exploration of green's cultural connotations will go some way towards explaining its prominence.

Sergei Eisenstein noted that green is 'directly associated with the symbols of life – young leaf-shoots, foliage and "greenery" itself – just as firmly as it is with the symbols of death and decay – leaf-mould, slime, and the shadows on a dead face'.[7] Importantly, Eisenstein warns against trying to tie colours to fixed values and meanings. 'In art', he argues, 'it is not the *absolute* relationships that are decisive, but those *arbitrary* relationships within a system of images dictated by the particular work of art'.[8] As Edward Branigan puts it, 'the psychophysics of colour perception as well as the function of colour in a textual system depend exclusively on context and relation'.[9] Nonetheless, these contingent relationships can be traced beyond the boundaries of a single work and out into larger cultural practices and phenomena. Green, I would suggest, is important to the horror genre because of its affective and semiotic connection with the organic, and because it seems to mediate between the living (young leaf-shoots) and the dead (the shadows on a dead face).

Green can evoke cleanliness and freshness; it can also evoke decomposition. It is the colour of snot and (under the right conditions) slime, bile and vomit. Importantly, green also marks the liminal area where humans encounter the organic environment. Here, green is at once of the body and not of the body. To put it bluntly, green is an appropriate colour for plants.

When a person is green, something is wrong. Green is thus a colour that highlights the culturally inflected relationship between 'natural' and 'unnatural'. This understanding of green's mediating role recalls, on the one hand, Freud's notion of the 'uncanny', since the uncanny arises precisely at the point where the alien becomes confused with the familiar, or the living with the dead.[10] On the other, it recalls anthropologist Mary Douglas's exploration of the way that cultural categories determine the social meaning of purity and dirt.[11] As Noël Carroll puts it, 'Douglas correlates reactions of impurity with the transgression or violation of schemes of cultural categorisation'.[12] For Carroll, the powerful fascination associated with the figure of the monster in horror fictions can be explained by its transgression of such schemes of categorisation. Colour itself, I argue, can also take on this transgressive role by moving across spaces, bodies and cultural categories, evoking both fear and fascination.

A number of horror films play on the categorical uncertainty of green. In *The Shining*, Jack Torrance visits a room in the Overlook Hotel and is greeted by the vision of a naked young woman climbing out of a bathtub. His expression changes from fear to lust as she approaches. A sense of dread is evoked through the use of slow motion, but also through the precise shade of green on the bathroom walls. Should we associate it with growth and youthfulness or with decay and death? The film answers our apprehension by having the woman transform suddenly into the decaying corpse of an old woman. Green has migrated from the physical environment and onto the human body. Similarly, in Dario Argento's chromatically inventive *Suspiria* (1977), the impending death of a young woman is signalled through the use of lurid green backlighting. The character in question eventually makes her way along a red hallway, and ultimately into a blue-lit room filled with coils of wire where she meets her demise, but it is green that most markedly signals her fate. This is undoubtedly because it is outside of narrative film's conventional colour dialectic, which, according to the demands of cinematic realism, alternates between the blue of daylight and the orange of tungsten lights. The red and blue illumination in this scene, although far from the ideal of realistic colour design, can nonetheless be rationalised in relation to this conventional dialectic. Green, however, stands apart as unnatural: it belongs in the background and not on the body.

Here, one might be reminded too of the famous green-lit scene in *Vertigo* (Alfred Hitchcock 1958), where the protagonist Scotty remakes Judy as the object of his obsession, the 'dead' Madeleine. Richard Allen, reflecting on the 'pale jade' of this scene's eerie neon lighting, connects it with Hitchcock's memories of London stage shows, in which green lighting was associated with spectral or villainous characters. 'Perhaps pale jade', Allen speculates, 'is associated with ghostliness because it is close to the colour of mould and hence evokes the presence of death'.[13] Similarly, in *Mandy*, when Red experiences a posthumous vision of his murdered partner, a cool emerald light illuminates her face, offsetting the violent crimson that dominates the preceding scenes. Alongside these examples of ghostly green in lighting and production design and the ambient green colour grading of much contemporary horror, one might also include films that associate green directly with substances that enter, issue from or threaten the human body, including pea-green vomit in *The Exorcist* (William Friedkin, 1973), fluorescent green serum in *Re-Animator* (Stuart Gordon, 1985) and the titular threat from the 1968 monster movie *The Green Slime* (Kinji Fukasaku).

In all of these examples, it is the mobility of colour that evokes emotions of dread or disgust: the sense that colour can come untethered, moving in uncanny ways among bodies and the environments they inhabit. This mobility is certainly not confined to green or to red. For example, in *Rosemary's Baby* (Roman Polanski, 1968), canary yellow is the keynote colour, appearing consistently in the decor and in Rosemary's costumes. Here, yellow's connotations of brightness and optimism eventually give way to associations with nausea and illness, as Rosemary's body becomes overtaken by a mysterious (and diabolical) pregnancy. Furthermore, the ubiquity of yellow helps to evoke Rosemary's loss of autonomy, matching her clothing with her surroundings and thus enmeshing her in the physical setting. As a general tendency, green remains the horror genre's most popular colour for signifying the alienation of bodies from their vital spirit. Yet this tendency has never resolved itself into a uniform chromatic schema. If there is any consistently applied convention, it has to do instead with the way that colour in horror apparently refuses to be bound to its object. The films I will now go on to discuss are particularly strong examples of this phenomenon.

Chromatic Bodies

In the first two film examples I discuss here, *High Tension* and *A Tale of Two Sisters*, categorical uncertainty regarding colour is associated with two other layers of categorical uncertainty. The first is ontological: events that we assumed to be real are revealed as occurring within the disturbed imagination of a central character. As a result, we cannot take for granted the material status of the bodies that we see onscreen, even as they undergo extremes of physical violence and suffering. The second area of categorical uncertainty is generic: these films do not sit neatly within the horror genre, and display characteristics in common with what Thomas Elsaesser has called the 'mind-game' film. According to Elsaesser, the key feature of the mind-game film is 'a delight in disorienting or misleading spectators (besides carefully hidden or altogether withheld information, there are the frequent plot twists and trick endings)'.[14] The antecedents of this category include mid-century 'art cinema' and the 'Victorian Gothic tale'.[15] However, the mind-game film arguably goes a step further by highlighting the textual operations through which such fictions are generically constituted: viewers are prompted to make sense of mind-game narratives via a process of 'pattern recognition' and to approach cinematic images 'as picture puzzles, data-archives, or "rebus-pictures" (rather than as indexical, realistic representations)'.[16] *High Tension* and *A Tale of Two Sisters* both call attention to such decoding processes by foregrounding the point at which their own generic 'rules' are rendered obscure or illegible. These films are readily identifiable as horror movies, but both also draw substantially upon the overt twists and tricks of the mind-game film, requiring their viewers to solve the psychological 'puzzles' that structure their respective narratives.

In *High Tension*, two female friends, Marie and Alex, are visiting Alex's family at their countryside home when it is invaded by a murderous psychopath wearing a boiler suit. The murderer slaughters Alex's mother, father and brother before kidnapping her and driving off in his van. Marie becomes the hero of the piece, following the killer, concealing herself inside his van and preparing to confront him in the woods. So far, the dynamic of the film has closely resembled that of the classic slasher film. Yet the end of the film offers a monumental (and contentious) twist. It is revealed that Marie herself is the killer: driven by a fascination with Alex, she has destroyed Alex's family and kidnapped her. The man in a boiler suit is merely a projection of Marie's troubled psyche. This twist thus shifts the film abruptly from the linearity of the slasher film to a non-linear dynamic, subject to revisions and reversals. In this case, many reviewers and horror fans were indignant that the filmmakers had chosen to exchange the physical thrills of classic body horror for the convoluted psychology and alternate worlds of the mind-game film. *High Tension* thus formulates generic identity as a particular type of mind–body problem.

Colour is central to the articulation of this problem. In particular, the heavy use of green in production design and colour grading contributes to the narrational and generic ambiguity of the film. In terms introduced by Noël Carroll and developed by Cynthia Freeland, it mediates between the emotions of dread and horror. Freeland suggests that dread is an emotion particular to a certain type of atmospheric horror film. Unlike horror, which attaches itself to a specific object (a monster, for example), dread is 'a vague sense of impending doom and disaster'.[17] Freeland finds a re-emergence of the aesthetics of dread in films including *The Sixth Sense* (M. Night Shyamalan, 1999), *The Blair Witch Project* (Daniel Myrick and Eduardo Sánchez, 1999), *The Others* (Alejandro Amenábar, 2001) and *Signs* (M. Night Shyamalan, 2002). In these films, 'the horror is subtle and lingering, a matter of mood more than monsters'.[18] This is in contrast both to parodic horror and to the violent slasher films of the 1970s and 1980s. It is closer, in fact, to the Gothic mood pieces produced by Val Lewton in the 1940s. 'Instead of ever more developed gore and special effects', writes Freeland, 'we see only fog and shadows'.[19]

Freeland's account of these 'atmospheric' horror films implies, in turn, a certain colour aesthetic. One can easily imagine the subdued palette associated with such films and their deployment of 'fog and shadows'. It is telling that the Lewton films are all black and white, while the contemporary films named by Freeland are generally characterised by cool greens and blues, muted browns or murky greys. Yet desaturation alone does not seem sufficient to communicate the sense of dread that Freeland describes. After all, an exaggerated monochromatic aesthetic has become *de rigueur* in contemporary horror films of all stripes, including those that rely upon explicit violence, torture and gore. By contrast, the films I discuss here are notable not merely for the predominance of sombre tones, but also for the careful modulation of colour effects. In each case, colour's affective and semiotic charge derives from its mobility and its mutability.

High Tension's second scene introduces a rich, all-pervasive green that helps to capture the sense of vague unease that Freeland describes. Here, a Steadicam shot follows the main character, Marie, as she stumbles along through a forest. We see that she has been wounded and may surmise that she is being chased. At the same time, however, the threat is never made specific, and the foggy, verdurous imagery suggests a more free-floating sense of unease. In short, it is a scene evoking dread. Freeland notes that dread is often associated with natural phenomena; it corresponds to eighteenth-century philosopher Edmund Burke's notion of the sublime, which Freeland describes 'as a feeling of terror in response to an object or force with vast power, danger, scope, and/or obscurity'.[20] This discussion of the sublime recalls the longstanding distinction, in Gothic literature and criticism, between terror and horror. Notably, Gothic novelist Ann Radcliffe used the sublime as the basis for articulating her preference for 'terror' (which is characterised by obscurity, mystery and suspense) over 'horror' (which is characterised by physical disgust and viscerality).[21] As

Marie stumbles through the forest in *High Tension*, the murky greenness of the natural setting lends it an overwhelming but undefined sense of menace that gestures strongly towards this sense of terror and the sublime. Indeed, Edmund Burke explicitly associated the sublime with gloomy colours, arguing that 'soft or cheerful' tones are 'unfit to produce grand images'. For Burke, 'the cloudy sky is more grand than the blue; and night more sublime and solemn than day'.[22] The rich yet sombre green of the forest in *High Tension* is, I suggest, consistent with this aesthetic.

Furthermore, the line of questioning this scene provokes is not simply physical (who is chasing Marie?); it is also overwhelmingly psychological (whose perspective is this?). At this point in the film, we are unable to crystallise a specific threat, but the aesthetic of the scene offers a clue that the source of the horror is not simply an embodied one. Indeed, we soon discover that the scene is a dream sequence (it is also, importantly, a flashforward). In the following scene, Marie confides to her friend Alex that she had a dream in which she could not tell if she were the hunter or the hunted (it was 'like I was chasing myself', she says). Here, there is a clue to the film's ultimate twist, in which it is revealed that the initial images are really showing us Marie as the attacker. No one is chasing her; she is in fact chasing Alex.

After the dream sequence, *High Tension* resolves itself into something much closer to a conventional slasher film, in which Marie must evade and finally outsmart the relentless killer. At this point, the film's colour scheme acquires earthier connotations. The muddy green of the forest appears on the killer's boiler suit and his van, and the dirt that accumulates on Marie's clothes carries a greenish cast too. Meanwhile, the film blossoms with rich, dark reds as the killer claims his victims. By the end of the film, we realise that Marie was the killer all along, and that the man in the boiler suit was merely a projection of her murderous desires. This creates a narrational problem – many viewers felt cheated by the use of the 'mind-game' ending in what had appeared to be a satisfyingly visceral horror film. It also creates an identificatory problem for the audience. In effect, the film literalises the mobile sense of gender that Carol Clover detects in earlier slasher films – the sense that the so-called 'final girl' and the psychopath himself oscillate between feminine and masculine attributes, depending on the affective and symbolic requirements of the story.[23] Here, however, there is no liberatory dimension to the final girl's victory. Instead, it appears that her lesbianism and her psychosis are one and the same thing (tellingly, the killer's arrival is immediately preceded by a scene in which Marie masturbates). The film thus appears based on the reactionary conceit that female and/or lesbian desire, not male aggression, is the drama's central problem and animating cause.

In revealing its fluid structure of identification, in which the audience finds itself aligned with the villain, *High Tension* returns us to a state closely resembling the dread described by Freeland. For Freeland, 'dread is itself a more abstract or intellectual emotion than horror or fear, because its object is something vague that requires conceptualisation'.[24] This is indeed the case with the psychological puzzle that culminates the film. It creates a dimension of ontological uncertainty in the world depicted onscreen that recalls the twist at the end of another green-hued film, *The Sixth Sense* (in which the protagonist discovers that he is already dead). In this context, neither mind nor body serves as a reliable index of reality. Our sense of threat is displaced from the relentless physicality of the killer and becomes something more free-floating and psychological. Bodies are not simply given to vision; they become a product of the main character's psychological projections. At the same time, however, Marie's violent pursuit of Alex continues in extravagantly visceral fashion: at the film's conclusion, she menaces Alex with a concrete saw before the creative use of a crowbar defeats her. Disembodiment thus alternates with embodiment in *High Tension*. Bodies are at once visually foregrounded (bleeding, twitching, traumatised) and dematerialised (the man in the boiler suit is not really there).

Green is central to this oscillation between the embodied and the disembodied, between horror and dread. The film makes heavy use of digital colour grading in order to compress different shades of green into a fairly narrow range of hues. Through this technique, various elements of the *mise-en-scène* are chromatically connected: the forest, the killer's boiler suit, the wallpaper in Alex's bedroom, the gag placed in her mouth. The green colour grading inflects the world with a sense of the immaterial. Much like the use of green in *The Matrix* (Larry and Andy Wachowski, 1999), it signals that the main character's world is really a projection of virtual or psychological origin.[25] At the same time, green comes to be associated with the body. Here, the muddy green of *High Tension*'s colour scheme suggests a body in decay, and also reminds us of the dull green of the killer's boiler suit – as if the bodily presence of the killer has somehow been displaced into the body of the film itself. The film's distinctive green tone is also blended with vivid, visceral reds, notably during the bloody murder of Alex's mother and in the climactic scene, in which the red of Alex's bloodied face is juxtaposed strikingly with the green of Marie's concrete saw. By mediating between the material and the intangible, green in *High Tension* thus offers the sign that the psychological and the physical have contaminated one another. Bodies are corrupt because the psychologically projected world that animates them is corrupt, and vice versa.

Figure 5.1 Marie's blood-spattered face contrasts with the uncanny green of Alex's saw in *High Tension* (Alexandre Aja, 2003).

In this way, the state of bodies (missing, wounded, corrupted) and of minds (frightened, paranoid, psychotic) is made manifest in the 'body' of the text itself. Similarly, the slasher film and the mind-game film have contaminated one another here. Colour mediates between the two, as the restrained green of dread reveals itself as interchangeable with the abject visceral green of body-horror.

Orchestrating Colour

The South Korean film *A Tale of Two Sisters* also focuses on the breakdown of the family. Like *High Tension*, it oscillates between dread and horror, and offers a plot twist hinging on ontological confusion: at least one of the characters is not really there and is an artefact of the protagonist's troubled psychology. In this film, the titular sisters Su-mi and Su-yeon move into a country house with their recently widowed father and his new wife. The girls suspect that their stepmother is trying to attack them, and the appearance of a cadaverous, long-haired figure, familiar from J-horror films such as *Ring* (Hideo Nakata, 1998), further raises the tension. Gradually, it is revealed that there is a malevolent force at work in the house, although it is hard to tell whether it is a supernatural element or derives instead from the stepmother's machinations. The plot becomes more and more confused (and more bloody) until we discover that the horrifying secret underlying the narrative is the suicide of Su-mi's mother and the accidental death of her sister. Su-yeon has not really been present. Instead, Su-mi's sister is in fact her own hallucinatory projection, and we may surmise that Su-mi has also imagined many of the events involving her stepmother.

As with *High Tension*, there is a sense that this film has diverged from its generic track. The film is based on a Korean folk tale and is immediately reminiscent of contemporary 'J-horror' films, in which disturbing supernatural events are traced to an originating act of neglect or cruelty. Examples include *Ring* as well as *Pulse* (Kiyoshi Kurosawa, 2001), *Dark Water* (Hideo Nakata, 2002), *Ju-on: The Grudge* (Takashi Shimizu, 2002) and *One Missed Call* (Takashi Miike, 2004). Like many of these films, *A Tale of Two Sisters* features a pale, long-haired female ghost, and evokes a strong atmosphere of dread around its central mystery. However, the plot proceeds via a decidedly non-linear itinerary, and often appears deliberately confusing. It becomes increasingly difficult to sort out imagined events from actual events, as we begin to suspect that much of what we see is taking place in Su-mi's mind. *A Tale of Two Sisters* is, unlike the most prominent examples of J-horror, a 'mind-game' film. Furthermore, the film moves at a particularly slow and deliberate pace and could be mistaken for a 'festival' film, particularly during its first twenty minutes. A great deal of time is spent setting up the hostile relationship between the two sisters and their stepmother before disturbing supernatural elements are introduced.

Colour mediates among these generic equivocations. As in *High Tension*, colour is associated both with free-floating dread and with raw visceral horror. The visceral is suggested most of all by the bright red floor in the kitchen, which anticipates the bloody trail left by Su-yeon's body as it is dragged through the house in a cloth sack. It is also suggested by the trail of red blood that runs down the leg of the ghost that appears one night in Su-mi's room. Beyond these very direct physical associations, however, colour in *A Tale of Two Sisters* is also an index of the troubled psychology of its characters, offering clues about the shifting relationship between the material and the virtual worlds.

Although colours in the film are not organised into an overarching semiotic system, they are used as a way of triggering and modulating affects, and also act as leitmotifs. Each of the main characters is loosely associated with particular colours. For a start, Su-mi's father is emphatically colourless. His drab clothes and grey hair foreshadow his ineffectual role in what turns out to be a story of warring female characters. Su-mi herself is often seen wearing red, which may associate her with bodily presence and vitality. Indeed, Su-mi is the only female character who emphatically occupies the physical world, since Su-yeon and the stepmother, Eun-ju, are often merely phantasmal projections. Su-yeon herself appears frequently in off-white but is most strongly linked with green (the dress she is wearing when she dies is bright emerald). The stepmother, Eun-ju, is often seen wearing or surrounded by a combination of champagne and indigo. This is not a

rigid or static system of signification. One scene, for example, connects the
stepmother with green reflected light from outside the house, underlining
the idea that she is a hostile external force. However, colour associations
in the film are gradually reconfigured to hint at the idea that both Su-yeon
and Eun-ju are projections of Su-mi's troubled mind. As Eun-ju begins
to take on aspects of Su-mi's paranoid worldview, she becomes increasingly linked with red (hitherto Su-mi's leitmotif). A series of jump-cuts
showing Eun-ju pacing distractedly in front of a wall covered first with
champagne and indigo wallpaper and then in front of one covered in red
wallpaper economically illustrates this sense of ontological mobility.

An earlier scene in which Eun-ju hallucinates that someone is hiding
under the kitchen sink also underlines the use of colour to mediate between
the real and the virtual. In a drawn-out suspense sequence saturated with
dread, Eun-ju leans down to look under the sink. Suddenly, her arm is
grabbed by a blackened hand, and she turns to find herself confronted by
a girl in a bright green dress. The turquoise of the cupboard doors and the
emerald of the girl's dress contrast with the red of the floor and of Eun-ju's
top. These contrasts draw attention to key dramatic elements, thus amplifying the mood of suspense, but also invite us to consider the orchestration
of colour across the film. For example, although it lacks a straightforward
semiotic correlation, the colour green in this film mediates between living
and dead, and is frequently counterposed against the vitality and force
of red. Notably, this colour is associated not only with Su-yeon but also
with the girls' dead mother, as illustrated in a flashback scene showing
her attired in a rich green. Meanwhile, the deep, oversaturated reds in
the kitchen scene foreshadow the film's movement from dread to horror,
anticipating the shocking violence of later scenes.

Colours in the kitchen scene also help to orchestrate the relationships
(both real and virtual) between the characters. Here, Eun-ju, dressed in
red, is confronted by her guilt about Su-yeon's death, embodied in the
mysterious, green-clad figure of Su-yeon herself. Concluding the scene, a
sudden dissolve takes us from Eun-ju's startled face to a close-up of a hand
offering two white pills. This appears to indicate the tenuous ontological
status of the scene, as it was in fact Su-mi's imagined construction of
her stepmother's guilt (terminated by the arrival of Su-mi's medication).
The red top is a clue that Su-mi has projected herself imaginatively into
her stepmother's place, and that she may herself be dealing with guilt as
a result of Su-yeon's death. The redness of Su-mi's projected guilt thus
comes face to face with the greenness of Su-yeon's mortal fate. Such psychologically based signification does not supply fixed and final meanings
for the film's complex colour system, however, for these meanings coexist

Figure 5.2 Eun-ju, wearing red, faces the ghostly apparition of Su-yeon in her emerald dress in *A Tale of Two Sisters* (Kim Jee-woon, 2003).

with other, more visceral connotations: red is associated with blood, and green with the decomposing hand that seizes Eun-ju by the wrist. The mobility of colour across environments and bodies in *A Tale of Two Sisters* thus acts as an expressionistic device; it is an index of the unstable state of bodies and minds and the relationship between them.

High Tension and *A Tale of Two Sisters* belong with the mind–game films that Thomas Elsaesser describes, as well as the films of art-dread discussed by Cynthia Freeland (indeed, with their narrative reversals and uncertain ontologies, these are really two overlapping groups). In particular, both films display 'plot twists and trick endings'[26] that are related to two of the common motifs listed by Elsaesser: 'a protagonist has a friend, mentor, or companion who turns out to be imagined' and may be 'unable to distinguish between different worlds'.[27] They also, like many mind–game films, depend heavily upon schizophrenia as an ontological and epistemological base for the narrative: 'usually the frame of "normality" against which a character's behaviour can be measured is absent, and even the revelation of his or her condition does not provide a stable external reference point'.[28] At the same time, they stage another game, which involves exchanging these conceptual tricks and psychological effects of the mind–game film for the visceral shocks of body horror. As I have argued, the colour green is central to this game, because it mediates between the foggy obscurity of dread and the abject messiness of the human body. The unstable semiotic and affective associations of colour in these two films suggest that in the horror film at least, it is not easy being (or reading) green.

Chromophobia

Meanwhile, both films resonate with broader cultural patterns that involve both colour and gender. Steve Neale comments that the female body has tended to provide a focus for the 'scopophilic pleasures involved in and engaged by the use of colour in film'.[29] In the context of horror cinema's more ambivalent pleasures, it is not surprising to find that so many of its most striking colour 'events' are associated with the female body.[30] These include examples already discussed in this article, from the young girl vomiting green in *The Exorcist*, to the old woman's perambulating corpse in *The Shining*, to the backlit victim-to-be in *Suspiria*. In *Carrie*, the red lighting in the climactic scene corresponds to the pig's blood with which the main character has been doused, but also recalls the arrival of Carrie's first period, which occurs in the film's opening scene and heralds the escalation of her supernatural powers. A sense of threat is thus associated both with the female form and with colour itself.

These parallel tendencies are intimately connected in cinematic discourse, but also within the culture at large. Specifically, David Batchelor has identified in western culture a pervasive 'chromophobia', which he defines as follows:

> Chromophobia manifests itself in the many and varied attempts to purge colour from culture, to devalue colour, to diminish its significance, to deny its complexity. More specifically: this purging of colour is usually accomplished in one of two ways. In the first, colour is made out to be the property of some 'foreign' body – usually the feminine, the oriental, the primitive, the infantile, the vulgar, the queer or the pathological. In the second, colour is relegated to the realm of the superficial, the supplementary, the inessential or the cosmetic [. . .] Colour is dangerous, or it is trivial, or it is both.[31]

Although chromophobia is found in a host of cultural contexts, it may be that the horror film provides us with one of its most emphatic manifestations, by linking colour, danger and the female body.

Certainly, it is tempting to see both *High Tension* and *A Tale of Two Sisters* as straightforward examples of chromophobia. Such an argument would be supported by the reactionary conceit at the heart of *High Tension*, in which the mobility of identity and colour is attached to unchecked (and pathological) female desire. In the case of the Korean film, however, the applicability of Batchelor's concept is less clear since he frames it specifically as a western cultural discourse extending back at least as far as Aristotle. Moreover, as the above quotation suggests, chromophobic discourse has typically presented 'oriental' cultures as the polychromatic 'Other'. Yet as art historian John Gage notes, a 'disdain for colour' is evident in both European and Asian cultures.[32] Chromophobia, as Batchelor describes it, may be a distinctly western phenomenon, but at least some of its background conditions can also be found in other cultural contexts. Furthermore, both *A Tale of Two Sisters* and *High Tension* (like other chromophobic texts) establish parallels between 'female pathology' and the prominence and mobility of colour. The significant links in this instance may therefore be generic rather than national, as aspects of the horror genre are recycled and repurposed across different cultural contexts.[33] Within the context of the horror film at least, the discourse of chromophobia appears capable of traversing national borders. Moreover, it resonates particularly strongly with the pairing of colour and psychosis in the two films under discussion here.

Treating *A Tale of Two Sisters* as a 'chromophobic' text would also seem to support K. K. Seet's argument that 'the current Asian horror film', as exemplified by *Dark Water* and *A Tale of Two Sisters*, 'is ultimately conservative and functions as a form of narrative containment, the modern purification ritual that emphasises the need for recuperation into the male order of things'.[34] In this film, it is the women who are both the victims and vivid embodiments of horror, while the father is altogether colourless in both his attire and his actions. It is therefore possible to see both of these films as representatives of a parallel pathologisation of both colour and femininity that extends across the horror genre and beyond it into the culture at large.

However, while acknowledging the usefulness and relevance of Batchelor's concept to horror cinema, I argue that the story of colour's importance to the genre cannot be summed up completely in terms of its 'othering' or rejection, just as female characters in the slasher film are not merely figures of otherness to male viewers but may also offer points of identification.[35] In *A Tale of Two Sisters*, it does not appear that the neutralisation of colour is the film's narrative goal, nor that the father, the film's key representative of colourlessness, is the ultimate bearer of moral authority or sympathetic identification. Thus, although I certainly make no claim for the film as politically progressive, it seems to me much less narrow and conservative than K. K. Seet's analysis allows. A closer look at both films' deployment of whiteness will help to develop this point.

Again, an acknowledgement of cultural context is in order, since whiteness holds specific connotations within Korean culture, which include death (it is the traditional colour of mourning) as well as purity and morality. Yet the *specific* role of whiteness in the opening scene of both films is strikingly similar. Both *High Tension* and *A Tale of Two Sisters* begin in white rooms, with Marie and Su-mi wearing white gowns. Each has been incarcerated in a mental institution, and it seems that colour, too, has been somehow confined. In contrast to the mobility of colour that generally characterises both films, the whiteness of the outfits and the rooms in these opening scenes represents chromatic neutralisation. Yet this whiteness is associated not simply with purity and abstraction but, more importantly, with a sense of oppressiveness. This whiteness frames, in turn, the negotiation of identity.

In *A Tale of Two Sisters*, the first image is a close-up of hands being washed in a white bowl filled with water. In *High Tension*, we see a woman's feet rubbing together, as Marie whispers to herself: 'I'll never let anyone come between us anymore'. The first line in *A Tale of Two Sisters* is delivered by a doctor, who asks the silent and withdrawn Su-mi: 'who do you think you are?'. These strikingly similar elements work together in each case to raise questions of identity and bodily integrity. The paired hands and feet, for example, imply both unity and separation, pointing towards the psychological split that afflicts the protagonist in each film, while the opening lines of dialogue emphasise the fragility of identity (the 'us' referred to by Marie might be her and Alex, or her and the killer). The incarceration of the body and of colour is thus also a way of corralling and controlling the various identities that will run loose later in the film. However, although the protagonists' psychosis is associated with colour, neither film seems to suggest whiteness as a desirable 'way out' of the problem. In these colourless settings, the protagonists are alienated from their bodies and their subjectivities.

Yet in each case, there are indications that this neutralisation of colour is partial and incomplete. Shadowy areas of the frame betray a coloured cast (green in *A Tale of Two Sisters*, blue-green in *High Tension*). The white room is thus not really white, revealing instead the impossibility of excluding colour. The conclusion of *High Tension* returns us to this provisional whiteness, as Alex peers through one-way glass at Marie, who is now locked in a cell. At the last minute, despite official assurances to the contrary, Marie senses Alex's presence and stares right back through the glass at her, as if to suggest that the white room will never be enough to contain her. Although this resolution has a chromophobic cast, it would be a mistake to identify colour in the film purely with anarchic femininity. Instead, the film's muddy green colour scheme suggests another type of chromatic confinement, rather than the free play of colours across a spectrum. Moreover, this particular shade of green is imbued with masculine, military connotations, an interpretation that is reinforced by its presence on the male psychopath's boiler suit (by contrast, Marie wears a white

T-shirt throughout the film, which becomes increasingly discoloured as she attempts to thwart and finally confront the killer). *High Tension*'s chromophobia is thus complicated by colour's movement across gender boundaries as well as its oscillation between the dreadful and the visceral.

A Tale of Two Sisters also returns to whiteness, first by revisiting the mental institution, but later in more absolute terms by desaturating the images themselves. The film's final scene is a flashback that shows Su-mi walking away from the house, unaware that her sister lies dying inside. A freeze-frame stalls the image before it turns to black and white. Finally, we see Su-mi sitting alone on a pier where she and Su-yeon used to spend their time. Again, the image is in black and white, but Su-mi herself gradually regains her colour, so that her red top contrasts with the monochrome backdrop. This ending marks the film out as less clearly chromophobic than *High Tension*. Here, whiteness is associated with order but also with death (an association that may reflect white's funereal connotations within Korean culture). While the desaturation of the image marks Su-yeon's demise, the resaturation of Su-mi's red top is a sign of the vital energy that still inhabits her, in spite of her recurrent visions of cruelty and death. The earlier scene in which Su-mi's father tells her that Su-yeon is dead reinforces this link between death and colourlessness. Here, the image is slightly desaturated, and both girls are dressed in white. In *A Tale of Two Sisters*, colour is connected both with dread and with visceral horror, yet the absence of colour (and the associated negation of form, shape, weight, depth and the body) is also disturbing. While based on a chromophobic premise, the film does not depend on the wholesale rejection of colour.

'God, I Love This Colour On Me'

Nicolas Winding Refn's *The Neon Demon* invokes chromophobia in a more direct manner than my previous two examples. Like the other two, it concerns itself with the excessive mobility of colour, and attaches this to notions of danger and ontological instability. It is even more insistent, however, on the connection between colour and gender. The film follows aspiring 16-year-old model Jesse as she tries to gain a foothold in the cut-throat and predatory world of the Los Angeles fashion industry. Jesse finds herself in an ambiguous friendship with fellow models Sarah and Gigi, who become increasingly jealous of the neophyte's rapid ascent, and with makeup artist Ruby, who makes little secret of her sexual desire for Jesse. When Jesse spurns Ruby's aggressive sexual advances, the trio murder and cannibalise her. This not only serves as a clumsy indictment of the fashion industry's tendency to 'consume' its victims, but also presents this violence as a female problem. As in *High Tension*, the eruption of psychosis is connected, via a regressive stereotype, to the expression of lesbian desire. It is also associated with the depiction of colour itself as both dangerous and alluring.

One early scene works to link the female characters with chromatic excess. Invited to a glamorous party, Jesse finds herself in the bathroom with Ruby, Gigi and Sarah. 'God, I love this colour on me', declares Gigi, looking at herself in the mirror as she paints on lip gloss, her face illuminated with a turquoise key light that contrasts sharply with the magenta backlight and fill. The subsequent conversation revolves around the names of lipsticks, beginning with Ruby's application of 'Redrum' (an obvious reference to *The Shining*, where the same word, viewed in a mirror, serves as a fatal foreshadowing), before moving on to a catalogue of food- and sex-related monikers. 'Black honey, plum passion, peachy keen', recites Ruby, prompting Gigi to chime in with 'pink pussy'. After Jesse has entered the room, Ruby directs this discussion of colour and sensuality at her, demanding: 'are you food or are you sex'? As we will later discover, these are indeed Jesse's two choices, since turning down sex with Ruby lends quite directly to being eaten. 'Is this your natural colour?' Gigi asks Jesse, as her face and Ruby's both shine an uncanny green. The air of artificiality and menace is heightened further still, as a magenta Ruby occupies the foreground of a mirror shot, while the cadaverously hued Gigi touches Jesse's face in the background, asking 'is that your real nose?' After the others have left, Jesse gazes at herself in the mirror, tinted by a slight turquoise cast as if the encounter with Gigi, Sarah and Ruby has sapped her of life.

This scene thus engages with colour on multiple levels, dealing with

Figure 5.3 Ruby applies colour to Jesse's lips as Sarah looks on in *The Neon Demon* (Nicolas Winding Refn, 2016).

it as a surface layer (the lipstick), an optical property (the lighting), and a linguistic signifier (carrying ideas of sexuality and consumption). The sophisticated staging, which takes full advantage of the spatial complexity produced by mirror images, helps to produce a constantly shifting colour dynamic, within which magenta and turquoise negotiate for dominance and significance within the darkened space of the bathroom. The associations shift dynamically. Ruby is associated with an exaggerated magenta that mirrors her barely veiled erotic fervour, while Gigi's turquoise key light renders her corpselike and sinister. Jesse, meanwhile, is shunted around within this bichromatic space, subjected to eerie colour combinations that are not 'natural'. Here, the 'threat' presented is both visceral and symbolic: it produces uncanny affects through its transformation of human skin tones, and it is connected symbolically with sex, embodiment and murder ('redrum'). Moreover, the ongoing chromatic shifts in this scene emphasise colour's ephemerality and surface qualities. Colour in *The Neon Demon* thus aligns strongly with David Batchelor's argument that, in Western culture, 'colour is dangerous, or it is trivial, or it is both'.[36]

As in *High Tension* and *A Tale of Two Sisters*, ontological questions come to the fore. Does colour 'belong' to the body, or should we read it as an extrinsic, nonessential property? What *kind* of body is implied by these chromatic games? By counterposing colour as a surface property of objects and colour as light, the film invites us to see bodies both as material forms occupying physical space and as phantasmal projections, as corporeal presence and as optical abstraction. The application of surface colour to the body features in a number of crucial scenes. For example, Ruby is shown applying lipstick not only to Jesse, but also, in her other role as embalmer, to a dead body. The erotic, vital aspect of colour is thus imbued with necrotic connotations, a connection that is further heightened when Ruby begins to kiss the corpse. Dead bodies and living ones become equivalent. Sex becomes food and 'redrum' becomes murder. Perhaps the most striking instance of applied surface colour is the extended sequence in which Jesse is left alone with the menacing professional photographer, Jack. Commanding Jesse to strip naked against a pure white backdrop, he proceeds to coat her neck and arms with gold paint. Sexual threat is commuted into sublime fulfilment, as colour outlines the body but also abstracts it from the mortal world.

Elsewhere, however, applied colour tends to be tainted with more abject connotations. At the beginning of the film, following a photoshoot in which she sports a simulated neck wound, Jesse attempts to wipe away the fake blood in front of the dressing room mirror, an effort that seems only to smear it along her arm. Whereas the photographer's gold paint elevates Jesse beyond the earthly realm, this red fluid marks her out as a mortal body. It also prefigures the cut on Jesse's hand, caused by a shattered bathroom mirror, that arouses Sarah's vampiric attentions, as well as the shocking spectacle of Ruby, Gigi and Sarah bathing in Jesse's blood at the end of the film. Following Jesse's murder, a dark sanguinary flood courses from Ruby's body as she lies on the bare floor, illuminated by a beam of moonlight that underlines the menstrual associations. In each of these cases we see colour as a material substance linked with feminine adornment (lipstick and gold paint) or physiology (menstruation). In these orchestrations of surface colour, the film thus recalls not only Batchelor's argument regarding chromophobia but also Barbara Creed's claim that horror films link the feminine body with images of abjection.[37]

As its title indicates, *The Neon Demon* is also concerned directly with optical colour, an element that it associates with both ontological and semiotic instability. This is evident in the bathroom scene, in which magenta and turquoise light sources imbue the various characters dynamically with qualities of passion or morbidity. Following this scene, Jesse ventures into the main room of the party, which is totally dark until illuminated by an intermittent pink strobe. As Jesse and the others look on, a woman's figure becomes visible. Suddenly, the flash of the strobe reveals that the woman is now suspended horizontally from the ceiling, appearing like an abstract form against the black background. As the scene goes on, the hue of the strobe becomes harder and bluer. The fleeting images of Jesse, Ruby, Gigi and Sarah lose their vital warmth and become cold and deathly. These luminous bodies seem prone to abrupt appearance and disappearance: they are images rather than fleshly forms. Whereas surface colour in *The Neon Demon* tends to pull the body down to earth, grounding it in mortal corporeality, optical colour dematerialises it. As in *High Tension* and *A Tale of Two Sisters*, colour is associated with an oscillation between the material and the spectral, producing both fleshly and evanescent bodies.

Furthermore, the blending of the corporeal and the optical is reflected at the level of metaphor, as Jesse herself is compared with a luminous celestial body. Expressing her jealousy of Jesse's popularity, Sarah asks: 'What's it like? To walk into a room, and it's like in the middle of winter, you're the sun?' This solar metaphor is reproduced visually by the shining gold paint that Jack spreads across Jesse's body, a transformation that seems to elevate her sense of power and agency. By contrast, the moon seems associated with the dispassionate gaze of the fashion industry itself. Standing at a lookout above the city and illuminated by a full moon, Jesse tells her friend Dean that she often feels the moon is watching her. The metaphor is implicit: just as the moon borrows its 'pale fire' from the sun, both the camera lens and the industry at large appropriate Jesse's projected light. This appropriation will find its highest expression in the actions of Ruby, Sarah and Gigi, as their blank, predatory stares are translated into real violence. Ultimately, as the moon itself bears witness to Ruby's bloody flow, its gendered connotations are not only menstrual but also mythical, recalling Diana, the Roman goddess of both the hunt and the moon.

The metaphorical ascendancy of the moon over the sun is also reflected in some of the film's chromatic progressions, which appear to be based on the transition from warm 'solar' light to cold 'lunar' light: the magenta glow on Jesse's face is replaced by turquoise, the pink strobe turns blue, and the climactic scenes of violence play out under a pervasive sapphire cast. In the lead-up to this climax, the film cuts between Jesse, who tries on a magenta gown and dusts her cheeks with pink sparkly makeup, and Ruby, who is applying purplish lipstick to a corpse within the chilly blue-lit space of the mortuary. Ultimately, flanked by golden interior design elements (curtains, mirror frame, lamp and bedspread), Jesse chooses blue, replacing her gown with a gauzy ice blue dress. Wearing this dress and standing on the diving board above an empty swimming pool, watched from below by Ruby, she reflects on the beauty industry and declares pride in her own appearance, saying 'women would kill to look like this'. Soon after, however, she lies dead on the blue concrete below, cast down from her quasi-celestial position and robbed of her vital glow by her three tormentors.

Colour in *The Neon Demon* does not simply spill across boundaries, however: it is also shaped by a countervailing geometric aesthetic, in which sharp lines predominate. This encounter between line and colour is directly linked to the film's orchestration of Eros and Thanatos, through which characters can transform all too easily from sex to food. As Brian Price outlines, the question of line and colour has a long art-historical heritage. Price describes the way that the conventional privileging of line (as 'mimetic accuracy') over colour (as 'decorative charm') was challenged around the time of the Renaissance.[38] Whereas line is associated with structure, form and mastery, colour is 'fleeting and subjective', connoting impurity and desire.[39] Describing Matisse's bold use of colours freed from clearly delineated forms, Price finds an articulation of 'erotic desire as an experience of formlessness'.[40] This chromatic intimacy compresses distance, producing 'a space more haptic than optic', and rendering colour as 'an erotic surface that solicits our sense of touch visually'.[41] Price finds a similar erotic ambiguity in sequences of visual abstraction in films like *Punch-Drunk Love* (Paul Thomas Anderson, 2002), *Millennium Mambo* (Hou Hsiao-hsien, 2001) and *Beau travail* (Claire Denis, 1999). The visual abstraction of *The Neon Demon* points towards a similar invocation of sensual intimacy.

However, colour in *The Neon Demon* also confronts line, in configurations that are not only erotic but also violent. Following the other models out onto the catwalk, Jesse finds herself alone against a dark backdrop, facing three upended triangles, delineated as blue outlines: a flat abstract form floating in space. Walking along the empty catwalk towards the three suspended triangles, Jesse enters a further triangular space, the interior of which is mirrored. After the blue light within this enclosure turns to red, she exchanges kisses with the reflected versions of herself on either side. As she begins to back away, the reverse shot shows that the inverted triangles are now outlined in pink. She returns to the entrance, which is now flooded with reddish light, and is enveloped in a shimmering field of magenta. These intense colours are associated with Jesse's erotic sense of self, and in moving from blue to red they highlight a moment of ascendancy for her. At the same time, however, the schematic triangular outlines suggest (as in the *gialli* of the previous chapter) a cutting edge, a break, a separation. Although she does not cut herself on this particular mirror (unlike the earlier scene in which Sarah tastes Jesse's blood), the geometrical arrangement of reflective surfaces nonetheless produces an array of virtual cutting edges, fragmenting the image and identity itself. Colour's capacity to overlap these edges is erotic, but these symmetrical lines suggest violence and menace. Eros turns to Thanatos. In a similar way, the ominous presence of the three suspended triangular outlines seems to anticipate the deadly triumvirate of Ruby, Sarah and Gigi.

The film's conclusion, in which Gigi and Sarah travel to Malibu for an outdoor photo shoot, also brings together colour and line. Gigi's visceral discomfort is amplified by the red inflexible top she is wearing and the intense red backlights behind her. Overcome by nausea, she rushes inside the house and enters a small angular alcove, where a triangular white corner couch is flanked by walls patterned with cold blue swastika-like geometrical patterns. As Gigi coughs up Jesse's eyeball and then stabs herself in the belly with scissors, Sarah looks on, the geometrical layout of the scene reflected in her shades. Gigi's death is defined by the schematic lines of the space and punctuated by a sudden cutaway to the red backlight that coincides with her stabbing action. This moment presents a violent confluence of colour and line, chromatic formlessness and geometric structure, desire and death. It also returns us, in the crudest way, to the film's oscillation between the optical and the haptic: reaching down, Sarah picks up Jesse's eyeball off the blood-stained blue carpet and swallows it. The organ of vision, addressed by the film's panoply of chromatic gestures, is here rendered as a mere piece of bodily tissue. The alternation between spectral and physical forms ends with an insistence on raw matter. At the same time, however, this final scene's movement between red illumination and blue geometry presents colour as an open-ended puzzle, which subjects bodies and spaces to the visceral and the schematic in equal measure.

Ultimately, colour in horror cinema refuses to be bound to its object. It is both ontologically and semiotically volatile, and thus lends itself to the genre's fascination with categorical uncertainty (between living and dead, human and animal, culture and nature). Moreover, colour can be an agent of categorical uncertainty in relation to genre itself. In *High Tension* and *A Tale of Two Sisters*, horror blends with the 'mind-game' film, while *The Neon Demon*'s spare, non-psychologised narrative partakes of 'art' cinema as well as the Italian *giallo* in its focus on fashion, modernity and aesthetic excess. In each of these films, colour mediates a series of shifts between the restrained atmospherics of what Cynthia Freeland refers to as 'art-dread', and the raw power of graphic horror, between psychological anxiety and visceral embodiment. Characters in this context can be phantasmatic projections, already dead, or marked for death. And as in many Gothic stories, the state of bodies (missing, wounded, corrupted) and of minds (frightened, paranoid, psychotic) is made manifest in the 'body' of the text itself. Just as cinematic bodies behave like media, gaining or shedding chromatic values, media, in their chromatic variability, resemble something that bleeds and rots. In this context, colour is an agent of instability, capable of defining bodily forms but also, in its transgressive migrations across figures and settings, causing them to blur, break down or disappear.

Notes

1. Richard Misek comments that the 'most prominent visual cliché' associated with digital colour grading since its advent at the turn of the millennium has been 'colour monochrome', which is 'achieved by partially desaturating a full colour image and then adding a single coloured tint to it'. See Richard Misek, *Chromatic Cinema: A History of Screen Colour*, p. 164.
2. Neale, *Cinema and Technology: Image, Sound, Colour*, pp. 156–7.
3. Cherry, *Horror*, p. 75.
4. There are earlier examples of horror films in colour, notably *Doctor X* (Michael Curtiz, 1932) and *Mystery of the Wax Museum* (Michael Curtiz, 1933), both of which were shot in two-strip Technicolor. Nonetheless, horror remained, for the most part, a monochrome genre until the 1960s.
5. Godard, *Godard on Godard: Critical Writings*, p. 217.

6. Clarens, *An Illustrated History of the Horror Film*, p. 80. Also see Glut, *The Frankenstein Catalog*, p. 201.
7. Eisenstein, *Film Form: Essays in Film Theory, and, The Film Sense*, p. 124.
8. Ibid. p. 150.
9. Branigan, 'The articulation of color in a filmic system: two or three things I know about her', p. 179.
10. Freud, 'The uncanny', pp. 219–52.
11. Douglas, *Purity and Danger: An Analysis of Concepts of Pollution and Taboo*.
12. Carroll, *The Philosophy of Horror, or Paradoxes of the Heart*, p. 31.
13. Allen, 'Hitchcock's color designs', p. 137.
14. Elsaesser, 'The mind-game film', p. 15.
15. Ibid. p. 16, 25.
16. Ibid. p. 39.
17. Freeland, 'Horror and art-dread', p. 189.
18. Ibid. p. 189.
19. Ibid. p. 189.
20. Ibid. p. 192.
21. Radcliffe, 'On the supernatural in poetry', pp. 145–52.
22. Burke, *A Philosophical Enquiry into the Sublime and Beautiful*, p. 81.
23. Clover, *Men, Women, and Chain Saws: Gender in the Modern Horror Film*.
24. Freeland, 'Horror and Art-Dread', p. 195.
25. Emerald City in *The Wizard of Oz* (Victor Fleming, 1939) performs a similar function: its excessive greenness is an index of its unreality (in contrast with the black-and-white matter-of-factness of Kansas).
26. Elsaesser, 'The mind-game film', p. 15.
27. Ibid. p. 17.
28. Ibid. p. 26–27.
29. Neale, *Cinema and Technology*, p. 152.
30. As Linda Williams argues, horror belongs, with porn and melodrama, in a triumvirate of 'body genres' in which 'the bodies of women figured on the screen have functioned traditionally as the primary *embodiments* of pleasure, fear and pain'. See Williams, 'Film bodies: genre, gender and excess', p. 143.
31. Batchelor, *Chromophobia*, pp. 22–3.
32. Gage, *Color and Meaning: Art, Science, and Symbolism*, p. 136. See also Izutsu, 'The elimination of color in far eastern art and philosophy', pp. 167–95.
33. Transcultural exchanges within the horror genre are not at all uncommon. For example, the western-style decor inside the family's house in *A Tale of Two Sisters* evokes the spaces of European Gothic fiction, while the distinctive figure of the long-haired female ghost has rapidly migrated in recent years from eastern to western cinema screens.
34. Seet, 'Mothers and daughters: abjection and the monstrous-feminine in Japan's *Dark Water* and South Korea's *A Tale of Two Sisters*', p. 243.
35. Clover, *Men, Women, and Chain Saws*.
36. Batchelor, *Chromophobia*, p. 23.

37. Creed, *The Monstrous-Feminine: Film, Feminism, Psychoanalysis.*
38. Price, 'Color, the formless, and cinematic eros', p. 25.
39. Ibid. p. 25.
40. Ibid. p. 28.
41. Ibid. p. 28.

CHAPTER 6

Sensory Disjunctures:
From Audiovisual Rupture to
Violent Synchrony

In horror, both bodies and media are haunted by the possibility of sensory misalignment. Indeed, cinema itself is underpinned by the technical separation of sound and vision, a separation that horror films have addressed with varying degrees of self-reflexivity. In *The Exorcist* (William Friedkin, 1973), for example, a young girl's body plays host to the ghastly, multi-layered growl of an ancient demon. This audiovisual mismatch between body and voice is further underlined when Father Karras, who is assisting with the exorcism, listens closely to an audio recording of these inhuman vocalisations. Here, the underlying media metaphor frames the victim's possession as a kind of diabolical 'overdubbing'. A similar idea animates *The Evil Dead* (Sam Raimi, 1981), in which a tape recording of occult incantations triggers a series of demonic possessions, rendering the characters' bodies and voices hilariously incongruous. More frequently, however, horror's decoupling of sound and image is accomplished without overt reflexivity, most obviously through the provision of limited or contradictory sensory information. This is exemplified by a range of conventional horror tropes, from disembodied noises and spectral apparitions to occluded views and uncanny silences. In paranormal tales from *The Haunting* (Robert Wise, 1963) to *The Conjuring* (James Wan, 2013), the occupants of ill-fated dwellings are menaced by mysterious sounds that lack a visible source. Conversely, the masked figure of Michael Myers, from *Halloween* (John Carpenter, 1978) to *Halloween* (David Gordon Green, 2018), presents a striking visual form made all the more uncanny by his lack of vocal presence. Accordingly, the credits of the original film grant Myers a purely visual dimension by referring to him simply as 'The Shape'. Intentionally or otherwise, horror films attempt to unsettle the viewer/auditor in ways that recall cinema's underlying split between sound and vision.

In recent years, a renewed exploration of sound–image relations has occurred in the emergent category of 'sensory horror' films, in which characters are prevented in various ways from seeing, hearing or speaking.[1] Key examples include *Don't Breathe* (Fede Álvarez, 2016), *Hush* (Mike Flanagan, 2016), *Bird Box* (Susanne Bier, 2018), *A Quiet Place* (John Krasinski, 2018), *The Silence* (John R. Leonetti, 2019) and *The Invisible Man* (Leigh Whannell, 2020). Although some of these films include aspects of technological reflexivity, as a group they are most directly concerned with characters who are placed at a sensory disadvantage in relation to a menacing adversary or environment, a situation which often entails misalignments between vision and hearing. *Hush*, for example, centres on a deaf woman who is terrorised in her home by a sadistic attacker, with much of the suspense deriving from her inability to hear impending threats. In *A Quiet Place* and *The Silence*, meanwhile, the danger presented by predatory alien creatures is elevated by their uncanny auditory ability, which requires the human characters to conduct their lives in near-silence. Conversely, vision is the problematic sense in *Bird Box*, as characters who fail to cover their eyes witness a mysterious apparition that drives them to suicide.

Such films provide the opportunity to think about mediation as it relates to bodily experience in general, regardless of whether or not they incorporate an explicit reflection on technology. For the phenomenologist Maurice Merleau-Ponty, mediation is implicated in every act of perception: '[t]he body is our general medium for having a world'.[2] In 'The Film and the New Psychology', he goes on to propose that cinema provides an ideal metaphor for this corporeal medium, 'mak[ing] manifest the union of mind and body, mind and world, and the expression of one in the other'.[3] Asserting that 'a film is not a sum total of images but a temporal *gestalt*',[4] he finds particular metaphorical relevance in the cinematic relation between sound and image, arguing that 'the way they are put together makes another new whole, which cannot be reduced to its component parts'.[5] Merleau-Ponty's use of this metaphor allows us to see horror cinema's audiovisual reflexivity as directed not merely towards media technology but also towards subjective experience and embodiment.

However, horror's presentation of bodily mediation and sensory disunity aligns more closely, I argue, with Jean-Luc Nancy's perspective, which draws on phenomenology's foregrounding of sensory experience but also deconstruction's emphasis on discourse (and discursive rupture). This is reflected in Nancy's play on the term 'corpus', which suggests a body, *the* body, but also a compilation or compendium of elements. For Nancy, the body presents a 'corpus of features' that are 'foreign to each other' and are 'coming together *and* being dislocated at one and the same time'.[6] Just as horror cinema's depiction of non-concordant audiovisual experience undermines sensory unity, Nancy ponders: 'aren't senses separate universes? Or else the dislocation of every possible universe?'[7] Horror cinema often plays upon this fragmentary quality, exploiting and amplifying the differences between the senses. In this chapter, I argue that media-reflexive and 'sensory horror' films explore this phenomenon of senses 'coming together *and* being dislocated at one and the same time'. I will start by looking at two films that depict horror cinema's postproduction process, before moving on to discuss three contemporary examples of 'sensory horror', arguing that each film offers a kind of essay on the senses in which mediation plays an important role.

Decoupled Senses

Blow Out (Brian De Palma, 1981) and *Berberian Sound Studio* (Peter Strickland, 2012) both concentrate reflexively on postproduction sound, in each case enmeshing a sound-recordist protagonist in a paranoid plot where close listening takes on a central role for characters and audiences alike. Although the former is not strictly a horror film and the latter an atypical example, the film on which each protagonist is working fits squarely within the genre. Here, horror serves as a generic vehicle for exploring sound–image relations, mediation and embodiment. Moreover, elements of horror seem increasingly to infuse both narratives as they reach their respective conclusions. Ultimately, these two films-about-horror present the decoupling of the senses in ways that recall key academic discussions of film sound in general and horror sound in particular. For example, Mary Ann Doane has argued influentially that film's synchronisation of sound and image helps to 'conceal for a time the fragmentation of a position, the splitting of the senses which characterises the spectator's reception of the spectacle'.[8] It is thus the role of sound designers and editors to mitigate film's tendency towards fragmentation. As Peter Hutchings observes, however, horror often exploits this very tendency, highlighting instead the mismatches between sound and image.[9] Both *Blow Out* and *Berberian Sound Studio* turn this practice into a reflexive game, exposing postproduction processes in ways that produce unsettling resonances for characters and audiences alike.

A certain degree of reflexivity about sound–image relations is inherent to the genre itself. Horror sound designers, argues William Whittington, typically play on the fact that sound effects need not be causally linked with their visual referents, creating 'intellectual uncertainty or cognitive dissonance'.[10] This kind of acoustic uncertainty, Whittington argues, can produce a kind of implicit reflexivity, as horror films undermine the con-

ventional balance between the senses, deprive sound effects of their 'func-
tional and unobtrusive' role, and separate sounds from their sources.[11]
Indeed, Whittington suggests a morbid bodily connection between horror
sound and its subject matter:

> [s]ound designers actively cultivate and construct a cabinet of sonic curiosities—
> scrapes, knocks, screeches, creaking doors, groans, body hits, and falls—for horror
> sound libraries, and during the editorial process, they lay out these effects as if on an
> autopsy table, mixing and matching them against the visuals.[12]

Pursuing a related line of argument, K. J. Donnelly has used horror itself
to illustrate general points about film and synchronisation. Donnelly refers
to the process of sound–image synchronisation as 'occult', firstly because
the process must remain concealed in order to represent coherent audiovisual worlds, and secondly because it involves a kind of magical fusion,
'generating something that is infinitely more than the sum of its parts'.[13]
Drawing on examples from *The Shining* and *Evil Dead 2* to *Ju-on* and *Saw*,
Donnelly suggests that '[h]orror films appear to know more about the
occult of aesthetics than other films: they play around with this lynchpin
of cinema far more than other genres'.[14]

What is it, however, that horror cinema seems to 'know' about mediation and the senses? Taking a phenomenological perspective, Donnelly
refers to the way that sound cinema achieves 'the unifying of image and
sound into a single Gestalt perception', playing upon our inherent desire
for perceptual unity.[15] Horror cinema commonly exploits this desire by
obscuring visual elements and forcing the audience to 'focus on sonic
aspects'.[16] Although Donnelly's emphasis is on the search for perceptual
unity, he suggests that 'there is a residual psychological disturbance to the
divorce of sound and image in cinema'.[17] For Donnelly, while synchronisation 'offers a form of repose' by providing a sense of comfort and order,
'the lack of synchronisation between sound and images has to be characterised as potentially disturbing, perhaps even [as] moments of textual
danger'.[18] Donnelly identifies a number of examples of disturbing asynchrony or misalignment from horror cinema. These include the noiseless
skeletal Knights Templar in *Tombs of the Blind Dead* (Amando de Ossorio,
1972), the extended sequences of dislocated sound design in the vampire
films of Jean Rollin and in Herk Harvey's *Carnival of Souls* (1962), and
the 'striking mismatch of claustrophobic visual space with expansive and
echo-laden sonic space' in *Saw* (James Wan, 2004).[19] What horror films
'know' about 'the occult of aesthetics', then, is manifested in their overt
manipulation of sound–image dynamics, and their challenge to the human
tendency to look for sensory concordance. In this knowing playfulness

with our desire for synchrony, horror cinema introduces a metaphorical disjuncture into our sensory experience, inviting us to think of both the cinematic medium and the bodily medium as fundamentally fractured.

Whereas Donnelly argues that deliberately reflexive films like *Blow Out* 'do not require much analysis as they provide their own within the films themselves', I would suggest there are insights to be gained by elaborating on their metatextual strategies.[20] In *Blow Out*, a sound recordist named Jack is seeking out location sound when he witnesses a car crashing into a river, capturing the event with his shotgun microphone and reel-to-reel Nagra. Rescuing a young woman named Sally from the submerged vehicle, Jack eventually forms a romantic relationship with her as his curiosity leads him to investigate the circumstances around the crash. He soon learns that it was staged as part of a politically-motivated murder plot, and that the culprits are desperate to procure the tape and suppress his testimony. As the title implies, De Palma's film aims to extend the epistemological explorations of Michelangelo Antonioni's *Blow Up* (1966), in which a fashion photographer is led to question the nature of photographic 'truth' after initially believing he has captured visual evidence of a murder. *Blow Out*, however, focuses more intently on the schematic conceptual separation of the visual and the auditory. Sally and Jack's professions are distinguished along sensory lines: she is a makeup artist, while he is a sound designer. In other words, she is image, he is sound. Moreover, Sally's ditsy, simple personality contrasts with Jack's aura of brooding seriousness, thus suggesting a caricature of these two senses, in which the visual is shallow and unreliable while the auditory carries values of depth and authenticity.

Although *Blow Out* is best characterised as a thriller, it is bracketed by signifiers of the horror genre. Indeed, it opens with footage from a stereotypical slasher movie, which turns out to be the film on which Jack is working. A POV camera peers into a college dormitory populated by nubile young women, as heavy breathing dominates the soundtrack. Entering the dorm, the killer seems able to draw improbably close to his prospective victims without being observed, in spite of the noise he is making. In any case, this conventional horror sequence unites sound and image by aligning them both spatially and temporally: sonic and visual perspectives are fused. The sequence concludes with an obvious reference to Alfred Hitchcock's *Psycho* (1960), and perhaps too to De Palma's own *Dressed to Kill* (1980), as the killer brandishes his knife at a young woman in the shower. The prospective murder is interrupted by a cut to a mixing suite, where Jack and the slasher film's director are reviewing the preceding sequence. Discussing the apparent inadequacy of the victim's scream, they mute every other channel on the mixing desk to expose the thin and unconvincing vocalisation. The scream, an archetypal cinematic figure that anchors sound and image in a single body, thus becomes the site of a dramatic audiovisual split, as the filmmakers consider replacing the woman's voice. The separation of sound and image is underlined by the director's crude and callous declaration: 'I didn't hire that girl for her scream, I hired that girl for her tits'. Later in the film, Jack and the director audition other young women to see if one of them can offer a suitable replacement scream, again underlining the genre's grounding in what is presented as a kind of fundamental inauthenticity.

This scene thus adds representational violence to physical violence. For Philip Brophy, the figure of the female scream in horror provides 'an "erosonic" moment', which substitutes for erotic representations of sexual violence.[21] Moreover, this scream announces a threat not only to bodies but also to meaning. It might be intended to communicate (whether desperation or resistance), but in the process it 'short circuits all linguistic operation', and blurs the distinctions 'between delight, terror, fancy, pain'.[22] Similarly, Mladen Dolar argues that while the voice 'raises the expectation of meaning',[23] it is also 'strangely recalcitrant' to it: 'the voice is the material support of bringing about meaning, yet it does not contribute to it itself'.[24] This is the problem confronting the filmmakers in *Blow Out:* the scream all too easily loses its meaning, in this case transmitting comedy rather than horror. Here, the infrastructure of technical mediation serves to amplify this problem by separating the scream from its proper body. At this moment of mortal violence, the synchronic shock of the look and the scream is unmasked as mechanistic, false and manipulated.

As I have already indicated, *Blow Out* is not strictly speaking a horror film. In fact, the opening slasher sequence is intended to provide a point of contrast with the film itself, which soon establishes itself as a political thriller. Accordingly, the narrative builds upon Jack's discovery that Sally was involved in a blackmail plot aimed at crippling the career of potential presidential candidate George McRyan. It soon emerges that Burke, the malevolent fixer hired to orchestrate this plan, had decided instead to shoot out the tyres of McRyan's car, precipitating the accident Jack witnessed. Burke then goes on to murder several women as a pre-emptive cover for his planned elimination of Sally. As the film progresses, however, the details of the political plot seem to become less important, as the narrative reduces to a more basic equation. Indeed, using a garotte concealed in his wristwatch and an ice pick as weapons of choice, Burke increasingly resembles the killer in a *giallo* film, while the serial progression of deaths also connects *Blow Out* to the slasher films it appears to parody in its opening sequence. Ultimately, Burke kidnaps Sally, whom Jack has fitted with a microphone and transmitter. Using audio surveillance in order to track them down, Jack arrives in time to defeat Burke but is unable to save Sally. The film thus comes back to the spectacular death of a beautiful woman, announced by her scream.

In a macabre twist, Jack uses the recorded sound of Sally's scream to replace the inauthentic cry of the shower victim in his film. Jack thus fails to save Sally, while saving her scream instead. This improbable detail might be regarded as a reflection on the superficiality of cinema, or as a misogynistic attempt to link femininity with abjection, disorder and death (in accord with Brophy's formulation of the 'ero-sonic'). Arguably, it is both of these things. However, *Blow Out*'s final twist also serves to provide a generalised reflection on mediation and sensory disarticulation. The film's ultimate separation of sound and image contrasts with an earlier scene in which Jack replays the car accident by matching his own audio recording with contemporaneous still photographs from the scene. Moving his body in the darkened studio, he orients himself towards each microevent as it replays, reperforming the movements of his directional microphone and summoning up the spatiotemporal 'reality' of the location itself. By the end of the film, however, the horror genre's tendency towards fragmentation is in the ascendant, and we are confronted with the dissolution of both the conspiracy narrative and of the notion of a coherent body in space. The recording of Sally's scream provides evidence not of a total spatiotemporal reality, but of the cinematic body as incomplete and internally divided. This dislocated voice is all too easily wrenched from its origin, a signifier to be attached arbitrarily to other signifiers. *Blow Out* thus uses desynchronisation to undermine order, sense and meaning.

The reflexive contemplation of horror production is pushed further in Peter Strickland's *Berberian Sound Studio*. In this film, a shy English sound recordist named Gilderoy is hired to work on an Italian horror film evocatively titled *The Equestrian Vortex*. *Berberian Sound Studio* is evidently set at some point during the 1970s, based on its visual aesthetic and array of vintage media devices. Indeed, the film abounds in details of the studio environment, with endless close-ups of reel-to-reel tape machines, oscilloscopes, microphones and consoles. Even the receptionist's orange telephone is included in this fetishisation of analogue sound technologies. Meanwhile, Gilderoy is disturbed by the violent content of the film he is working on, a narrative about witch-hunting which features intense scenes of torture. Required to produce sound effects to match hair being torn out, flesh hacked and the bodily application of a hot poker, he becomes increasingly upset and eventually begins to hallucinate. He attempts to find solace in the letters he receives from his mother in England, and revisits his field recordings to summon up the bucolic landscape of his home country. Yet these two worlds, domestic and foreign, begin to bleed together, as when one of the Italian actresses begins spontaneously reciting portions of his mother's letters, and when the film strip itself seems to burn through, revealing underneath a rural scene from a documentary that Gilderoy had worked on previously. As Chris Darke puts it in his review, 'the film's narrative space becomes increasingly layered and looped, like a sound composition'.[25] Ultimately, Gilderoy's descent into psychological crisis is represented in sonic terms, specifically as a loss of synchronisation.

To an extreme degree, *Berberian Sound Studio* separates sounds from their sources. With one brief exception, the film that Gilderoy is working on remains offscreen but audible. The viewer does not witness the witches in the film being tortured; instead, they are shown the performers record-ing their dialogue and screams in the recording booth, with the knowledge that these vocalisations are to be reattached to the witches in the finished film. In other scenes, the studio window serves as a barrier to separate sound and vision: we see actions taking place through the glass, but without hearing the corresponding sound. The film is thus an extended riff on what soundscape theorist R. Murray Schafer calls 'schizophonia', in which sounds are separated from their original contexts.[26] K. J. Donnelly argues that horror cinema is often schizophonic, using asynchrony to undermine

Figure 6.1 Silvia rehearses her scream in *Berberian Sound Studio* (Peter Strickland, 2012).

synchronisation's primary role, which is to 'retain an ordered, sensible, and comforting experience from irrational chaos and the psychological terror of meaninglessness and futility'.[27] Accordingly, *Berberian Sound Studio* deploys an excess of schizophonic techniques in its progressive dismantling of spatiotemporal and narrative order.

The film's asynchrony also enables an applied demonstration of what Michel Chion identifies as the three listening modes: causal (which has to do with identifying a sound's source), semantic (which has to do with meaning, and is primarily focused on language) and reduced (which has to do with the specific qualities of the sound, 'independent of its cause and of its meaning').[28] For Chion, reduced listening is important because '[t]he emotional, physical, and aesthetic value of a sound is linked not only to the causal explanation we attribute to it but also to its own qualities of timbre and texture, to its own personal vibration'.[29] In *Berberian Sound Studio*, these affective qualities are brought to the fore as semantic and causal links are weakened. In terms of semantic listening, the studio is a space of indeterminacy for Gilderoy. For one, he is surrounded by conversations he cannot understand, given his lack of fluency in Italian. Moreover, the actors' vocal performances in the recording booth tend towards unintelligibility. These include the Latin incantations and inarticulate screams of the 'witches', as well as the disturbing vocalisations of 'the Goblin', represented sonically by a hired voice actor who gibbers and howls nonsensically into the microphone. As in *Blow Out*, there is a great deal of attention to the female scream, with the producer becoming unhappy with a replacement actress's unsatisfactory cry. The repetition of this scream amplifies its inarticulacy, inviting the listener to experience vocal utterances in terms of the 'personal vibration' of reduced listening rather than the signifying logic of semantic listening.

Berberian Sound Studio undermines causal listening by demonstrating postproduction processes of recording and looping. We see Gilderoy's horror at what he is witnessing on the studio screen, but it is difficult to immerse ourselves entirely in his perspective, given the absence of the corresponding images. The sizzle of water in a pan might evoke a hot poker applied to human flesh, but given that the image we see is still of the pan, the sound resists its designation, becoming tethered instead to this more mundane reference point. Again and again, sound reveals a weak filiation to its intended referent. Imaginative projection is thus central to the film: a sensory input is missing or mismatched, and the viewer/auditor must work cognitively to produce the corresponding field. For Lucy Fife-Donaldson, *Berberian Sound Studio* demonstrates how sound *on its own* 'can conjure the qualities of bodily movement and affect', as illustrated by its capacity to evoke 'the action and visceral horror of traumatised flesh'.[30] She qualifies this assertion by admitting that we are given verbal cues and visual reactions as well. However, it is important to acknowledge that these cues and reactions are not incidental but crucial. As Michel Chion observes, 'the figurative value of a sound in itself is usually quite nonspecific'.[31] Context and convention are both vitally important. Writes Chion, '[t]he same sound can convincingly serve as the sound effect for a crushed watermelon in a comedy or for a head blown to smithereens in a war film'.[32] Indeed, the watermelon itself is the object of choice for the film's Foley artists, comically named Massimo and Massimo, as they set out to soundtrack a scene of unspeakable violence. 'I didn't quite know I'd be working on this sort of film', murmurs Gilderoy as the Massimos hack away with blunt weapons, creating wet and pulpy sounds and high-lighting, in the process, two causal relationships: one with the onscreen violence (which we cannot see) and one with the mutilated plant matter (which we can). In this way, Strickland partially neutralises the causal mode of listening, asking us to hear these sounds as sensory effects in their own right, possessing their own affective qualities that are semi-detached from their source.[33]

Moreover, the relay between causal and reduced listening, as sounds are disconnected and reconnected to various sources, produces an onto-logical flattening of bodies, spaces and matter. For example, we learn only obliquely that the radish stalks Gilderoy is twisting, apparently as prepara-tion for a salad, will ultimately serve as sonic representations of hair being pulled out. This particular scene creates a spatial and ontological shift, transporting us seamlessly from Gilderoy's room to the recording studio, blurring the boundary between the everyday world and the world of the film, and merging vegetable matter and human flesh. Indeed, the ontologi-cal stability of bodies is a recurring issue in the film, since the process of recording and replaying sound is associated with physical disarticulation. Arguing that *Berberian Sound Studio* depicts filmmaking 'as a fragmented and layered process', Lucy Fife Donaldson uses the term 'corporeal mis-matching' to describe the moment when one of the two Massimos walks across the studio in high heels, soundtracking the footsteps of a female character.[34] Such scenes, Fife Donaldson argues, highlight what Mary Ann Doane calls 'the material heterogeneity of the "body" of the film'.[35] If this is the case, then the notion of corporeal mismatching must apply not only to bodies that stand in for others, but also to the relationship between bodies, objects and environments. In *Berberian Sound Studio*, the body of the performer is mapped to other kinds of metaphorical bodies, whether cinematic, organic or inert. The delinking of sounds and their sources thus carries us away from and towards the body at the same time, producing disturbing associations as bodies take on the qualities of vegetable matter or mechanical objects.

Ultimately, the strongest metaphorical connection in Strickland's film is between bodies and audio technologies. In the absence of the bodies that are at stake in the film-within-the-film, *Berberian Sound Studio* dwells fetishistically on analogue audio technologies, lending a bodily, sensual aspect to mechanisms and interfaces. Close-recorded sounds of spindles whirring and switches clicking are often accompanied by shallow-focus close-ups that imbue these devices with an organic, corporeal quality. At one point, a rapid cut from a close-up of an actress's screaming mouth to a close-up of sauce in a blender is accompanied by a sound dissolve, fusing the human and the technological in unsettling fashion. At another point, the camera lingers over dials, spools and meters, as the soundtrack is overtaken by guttural voices, ominous drones and incidental noises, merging the sounds of the occult body and the sounds of media. The displacement of the voice is central to this metaphorical melding of bodies and technologies. Referring to the unified 'fantasmatic body'[36] projected by conventional sound cinema, Mary Ann Doane argues that it is threatened by post-synchronisation and looping, since 'the voice is disengaged from its "proper" space (the space conveyed by the visual image)'.[37] Both summoning up and fracturing this phantasmatic body, *Berberian Sound Studio* turns the voice into an artefact of mediation. This is particularly the case when filters and other effects are applied, as in the scene where Silvia's voice is run through a reverb and delay. Silvia experiments with turning the knob herself, marvelling at the transformation as she modulates the effect. Here, the voice is detached from the body and vested in technology, via the film's fetishisation of the analogue interface, its erotics of knobs and buttons. Through the disarticulation of sound and image, technology acquires a body.

At the same time, both bodies and media reveal themselves as susceptible to the loss of meaning. Isabella Van Elferen has argued that '[s]ound's slippery relation to signification, reference and meaning makes it inherently horrific'.[38] Whether or not this is true as a general principle, *Berberian Sound Studio* would appear to affirm her point. It is no accident that *The Equestrian Vortex*, Strickland's offscreen film-within-a-film, is a horror movie. As Van Elferen argues, the horror genre 'is pervaded by unembodied sounds':[39] filmmakers play upon sound technologies' capacity to 'disconnect . . . "live" sound from its origin, thereby making it un-live while it is also un-dead'.[40] In *Berberian Sound Studio*, the capacity to communicate through sound is presented as fraught and fragile.

The voice is dislocated, and there is a loss of mastery over language, as nonsignifying noise (whether in the form of broken phrases or rending flesh) takes over. Ultimately, the sound-image dislocations of *Berberian Sound Studio* escalate, as Gilderoy's sensory and cognitive world appears to collapse on itself. Spatial and sonic overlaps are multiplied: the transitions between bedroom and studio become more fluid and disorienting, and passages of recorded dialogue infiltrate both spaces as Gilderoy proceeds with his sound looping and mixing. Meanwhile, the other characters have ceased speaking English altogether, and Gilderoy's own dialogue is now inexplicably dubbed into Italian (in a nod to *giallo*'s penchant for dubbing). Violence, disorder and noise seem to have leached out of *The Equestrian Vortex* and into the world of its production. Moving back and forth across media formats, the film ultimately links sound recording and reproduction with psychological and phenomenological rupture. Here, both bodies and technologies act as sonic interfaces, which both speak and are spoken through, fluctuating between subject and object, articulation and non-sense.

Fatal Synchrony

Within the horror genre, overt reflexivity regarding film technologies and processes is less evident than in 'off-genre' films like *Blow Out* and *Berberian Sound Studio*. However, recent years have seen the emergence of horror films focused on the restriction of characters' sensory capacities. These 'sensory horror' films depend primarily not on temporal desynchronisation but on various kinds of sensory occlusion or misalignment. One such film is *Don't Breathe*, a horror-thriller in which sound synchronisation is maintained and causal listening remains central. In *Don't Breathe*, three friends named Money, Rocky and Alex break into the house of a blind Iraq War veteran, hoping to make away with $30,000 they believe is stowed inside. However, they get much more than they bargained for, as it turns out that the blind man is uncannily adept at making use of his remaining senses. The film is replete with clever setups that involve the main characters having to remain as quiet as possible, while the blind man deploys his sensory skills to track them down. In one scene, after killing Money, the veteran prepares to dispose of his body. Rocky and Alex try to stay quiet, but a creaky floorboard alerts him to their presence. They remain frozen in tense silence as he points his gun around the room, unknowingly targeting each of them in turn. The sudden vibration of a cell phone prompts him to fire, and they are lucky to escape unharmed and undetected for the moment. Other senses soon come into play. Catching the aroma of their

Figure 6.2 The blind veteran points his gun into the room as Rocky and Alex try to remain silent in *Don't Breathe* (Fede Álvarez, 2016).

shoes, discarded by the front door, the blind man realises that there are other intruders. Engaging his sense of touch, he goes on to count how many shoes there are, and proceeds to hunt down their owners. Sound, however, is the film's most dramatically foregrounded sense.

Don't Breathe centres on the disparity between the sensory capacities of protagonists and antagonists, thus recalling *Wait Until Dark* (Terence Young, 1967), in which a blind woman must use her resourcefulness to fight off criminal thugs that have infiltrated her apartment. Here, the key difference is that the intruders are the protagonists. In any case, an uneven adversarial relationship is also evident in other recent examples of 'sensory horror' like *Hush* and *Bird Box*, in which the protagonists must operate in the absence of audition and vision, respectively, and also in *The Silence* and *A Quiet Place*, in which the alien antagonists are endowed with enhanced auditory capacity. Such horror has a heightened spatial dimension, playing on characters' and audiences' anxiety regarding the location of the threat, as well as sound's spatially dynamic qualities. Sound itself becomes a source of terror and anxiety in this context. This accords with Michel Chion's observation that sound's mobility and physicality, together with the difficulty of excluding sonic stimuli and 'a lack of any real aural training in our culture', mean that 'sound more than image has the ability to saturate and short-circuit our perception'.[41] Similarly, Isabella Van Elferen has described sound in horror as exemplifying 'dorsality', or 'that which is behind our back: the invisible, sinister, sinister presence that just escapes our peripheral vision when we turn around'.[42] Indeed, Van Elferen argues that sound is inherently dorsal, a fact which horror cinema leverages in order to produce dread and suspense. Sensory horror films play reflexively on this aspect of sound by making the audience acutely aware of the plight of characters who are unable to hear a threat approaching from behind (as in *Hush*) or who can hear the threat but not locate it visually (*Wait Until Dark*, *Bird Box*, *The Invisible Man*).

In *Don't Breathe*, the spatial relation between sound sources and potential threats becomes a central narrative question. This question is made more uncertain by the ambiguous relation between the veteran's compromised vision and his unexpected facility with the remaining senses: which sensory data will he apprehend, and how smoothly can he navigate the spaces of the house? In a particularly suspenseful scene, Alex lies atop the conservatory's glass roof, having fallen out of the window above. We are made painfully aware of the tiny crick, crick noises that the glass makes as he lies on it, but also of the immediate presence of the blind man standing immediately below him. Will Alex fall through the glass or will his adversary detect the sound? The question is answered when the man reappears suddenly in a completely different location, shooting at Alex from the upstairs window and sending him crashing noisily through the glass. The concentration on the veteran's capacity for hearing amplifies the significance of spatial positioning, and reveals the vulnerability of Rocky and Alex, who must reckon with sound's 'dorsal' quality. In short, *Don't Breathe* offers an essay on causal listening. The significance of the sound in each case is vested in its source, as the blind veteran listens for the number and location of the intruders while Rocky and Alex respond to sonic cues in trying to elude him. What is at stake for the characters is the capacity to read space, and to read bodies in space.

However, the dorsality of sound also raises issues of timing. While *Berberian Sound Studio* is characterised by a lack of synchronisation, *Don't Breathe* presents a rhetorical excess. Here, sound and image are aggressively synchronous. There is an impression of sound and image (and, by extension, touch) snapping violently into synch. This is a particularly emphatic example of the phenomenon Michel Chion terms *synchresis*, which refers to the 'spontaneous and irresistible weld' that forms between sound and image when they coincide in time.[43] Chion suggests that the audiovisual point of synchronisation, 'where the audiovisual "arch" meets the ground before taking off again'[44] is seen particularly clearly in the physical blow, which he dubs 'the most immediate audiovisual relationship'.[45] The audiovisual depiction of violence thus takes on a structural function: 'the punch with sound effects is to audiovisual language as the chord is to music, mobilising the vertical dimension'.[46] Similarly, K. J. Donnelly argues that synch points, whether speech, action or musical punctuation, 'might be approached as the crucial pillars of structure in a film'.[47] Again, Donnelly draws on horror as an example: 'in horror films such as *Halloween* (1978), there are regular build-ups in terms of tension that are capped by a moment of violence or an anticlimax, with the former usually accompanied by a loud musical stinger'.[48] *Don't Breathe* observes this convention by supplying such stingers at key moments. For example, as Rocky cowers in the closet, an abrupt metallic noise signifies the presence of the veteran; when she accesses his safe, a series of beeps from the keypad is followed by a deep emphatic rumble that is obviously not produced by the door itself, but is matched with it temporally and underlines the threat. Sound and image collaborate to produce a unified space, in which physical causes and consequences are aligned. In another scene, as the blind man, having realised that Rocky and Alex must be in the basement below him, audibly makes his way towards the basement door, we get a point-of-view shot from their perspective, as the camera pans across the basement ceiling, tracking the movement of the blind man's feet above. Here, we are reassured that sound and image are in lockstep, and that the impending violence will be rendered as immediate and spatially condensed.

As a counterpoint to this fatal synchrony, the film features several moments of exaggerated yet benign audiovisual alignment. At the beginning of the film, riding in a car with her companions, Rocky inhales from her cigarette, and we hear (impossibly close and distinct) the sizzle of the embers at the end. When a ladybird walks along her arm, we hear its footsteps, and when it flies away there is a distinct whirr. All of this can be discerned over the noise of the car. The ladybird is important because it is, for Rocky, a symbol of her wish to leave behind her life of poverty in Detroit. Much later, after Alex has died and Rocky has been dragged back to the house, the ladybird returns as a reminder of this dream. In this case, the whirr of the ladybird as it once more ascends introduces a rack focus that draws attention to the alarm system's remote control, a sonic technology that will ultimately offer Rocky one more chance to claim freedom. In any case, these examples of benign synchrony serve not only as dramatic accents but also as invitations to listen closely and with care, and as counterparts to the more violent synchronic moments that punctuate the narrative.

Although synchronisation can, as Donnelly argues, produce a sense of comfort and order, thus generating 'a form of repose',[49] *Don't Breathe* illustrates horror's potential for articulating fatal synchrony. Whereas the killer's presence may initially take the form of disarticulated shadows, creaks and whispers, the moment of synchrony brings these sensations together into an audiovisual peak that signifies the arrival of the threat. The unity of sound and image is thus deadly. Moreover, in the case of

Don't Breathe and other sensory horrors in which silence equals survival, sound itself acquires an abject dimension, manifesting as an unwanted quality that attaches itself to the body. It is the body that defeats its owner by persistently producing sound, as emphasised by the interdictory titles of *Don't Breathe* and *Hush*. In *Don't Breathe*, the veteran largely remains silent. We do not hear his voice until relatively late in the film, as he explains his twisted rationale for keeping a young woman captive in his basement: he holds her responsible for his daughter's death in a traffic accident, and has impregnated her with a view to producing a compensatory child. There is a scratchiness to his voice that suggests unfamiliarity of use, and after this scene he ceases further speech. The young woman, conversely, is associated with excessive sound: her mouth is taped up, and the veteran has soundproofed the basement walls with cushions in order to muffle any cries for help, in a setup that provides an uncanny analogue to a recording studio. Harking back to Brophy's argument regarding the 'erosonics' of the scream, *Don't Breathe* thus links exclamatory vocalisations with gendered violence. The price of failing to maintain silent is illustrated after the young woman has been freed, when the veteran entraps Rocky in the same space and tries to inseminate her. After Rocky escapes, her struggle is once again to slough off sound, to put sound and image at a distance from each other, delaying the mortal consequences of synchrony.

Yet if *Don't Breathe* seems to centre on the unity of sound and vision, then in another sense it also highlights a fundamental division. In particular, it does this through the figure of the blind man. We are asked to project ourselves imaginatively into his attenuated sensory perspective, one that is, in its dislocation of auditory and visual inputs, curiously aligned with cinema itself. The film thus invites its viewers to inhabit two distinct spaces: the house as experienced by the blind man and the house as experienced by Rocky and Alex. As they cower from his methodical search of the premises, the extent of his sensory and cognitive reach remains the central narrative question. The audience's sensory alignment is thus split between the protagonists and the antagonist. *Don't Breathe* complicates this scenario by imposing a virtual blindness on Rocky and Alex when the veteran shuts off the lights in the basement, leaving them in total darkness. The filmmakers opt not to mimic this imposition of blindness, however, using a washed-out greyscale effect instead to show us what is, to the characters, completely invisible. The images thus fail to correspond either to the protagonists' or the antagonist's sensory experience, evoking instead a kind of abstracted camera-vision. In this grey half-world, we witness Rocky and Alex stumbling desperately about, incapable of matching the veteran's expertise at negotiating sensory limitations. Unaware of his proximity, Rocky almost touches the blind man's shoulder, at which point a noise from Alex prompts him to fire his gun. Here, a high ringing tone takes over the soundtrack. Although the film refuses to show us Rocky's visual perspective, this tinnitus effect nonetheless aligns with her auditory perspective. In placing sound and vision on separate ontological planes, the film thus produces another rupture between represented and imagined experience. This ontological split parallels that of *Berberian Sound Studio,* even though it not expressed through desynchronisation. In *Don't Breathe,* the insistence on temporal alignment highlights the simultaneous misalignments between and within different characters' sensory perspectives.

Moreover, although *Don't Breathe* does not, unlike *Blow Out* and *Berberian Sound Studio,* concern itself with recording technologies, it nonetheless provokes a heightened awareness of all the objects and technologies that produce sound. This includes not only the various sound-producing interfaces that the characters must negotiate, including their mobile phones, the house's alarm system, the safe and the washing machine. It also extends to the everyday objects that are transformed into sound-generating interfaces as the characters attempt to avoid triggering them, including the creaky floorboard, the splintering conservatory roof and the door bolt. As a result of this elevated sensory awareness of the object world, the space of the house becomes mediatised, becomes interfacial. Just as the audio technologies of *Berberian Sound Studio* serve to denaturalise human sensory experience, a less overt process of denaturalisation applies here. Although the characters acquire the codes to the alarm system and the safe, they lack the codes for deciphering this devisualised, sonified space. The various everyday items they encounter are alien objects that illustrate the limitations of the senses and the divisions between them. At the same time, the characters are forced to pay attention to the sound-producing and transmitting qualities of their own bodies. The body itself is thus rendered as a sonic object, a medium for producing sound.

Sensory Alienation

The objectification and alienation of the sensing body is evident in other examples of sensory horror, including *A Quiet Place* and *The Invisible Man.* Like other sensory horrors, and unlike *Blow Out* and *Berberian Sound Studio*, these films do not overtly promise a sustained reflexive exploration of media technology. Nonetheless, technology performs a vital framing function in both films, underlining sensory limits and divisions. *A Quiet Place* depicts a post-apocalyptic scenario in which humans are menaced by predatorial alien beings. The aliens are blind but possess an extremely advanced sense of hearing. In eking out a precarious existence, the main characters Evelyn and Lee Abbott, together with their three children, must live in near silence, avoiding activities and technologies that might alert the aliens to their presence. To an extent, the Abbotts occupy a post-technological world, in which modern-day mechanical devices have been set aside in favour of quieter and more rustic tools. As if to underline this point, the film begins with the death of the youngest child, Beau, who has acquired a battery-powered space shuttle toy in spite of his parents' warnings. His fate is sealed at the moment when the toy, the token of an abandoned hi-tech world of space travel, begins to beep and flash, attracting the deadly, scythe-like aliens within seconds. Following Beau's death, the family awaits the birth of their next child as they strive to maintain a low-decibel lifestyle, living in a rustic farmhouse and observing old-fashioned domestic rituals. For example, Evelyn washes the family's clothes in the laundry tub, eschewing the treacherous vibrations of the electric washing machine.

Electric and electronic technologies are not altogether absent, however. The family has strung up a network of lightbulbs outside the house as a silent warning system, and Lee has assembled a trove of salvaged audio-visual equipment in the basement, including a bank of video monitors connected to exterior surveillance cameras. Lee also spends time sending out SOS signals on different radio frequencies, and experiments with cobbled-together components in an attempt to repair his daughter Regan's cochlear implant. Moreover, the family has access to basic medical equipment, including a stethoscope, oxygen tank and blood pressure kit, which are used to assist with Evelyn's pregnancy and labour. All of these technologies are conspicuously pre-digital, despite the fact that the setting is roughly contemporaneous (the film was released in 2018, and Beau's memorial marker places his death in 2020). It is as if the alien invasion has somehow triggered a return to an earlier era, in which older technologies are pressed back into service and family life has reverted to a normative template. For the Abbotts, foraging, cooking and cleaning duties are divided up along traditional gender lines, dinner takes place under lanternlight and family routines are uninterrupted by handheld screens.

Although the basement's trove of audiovisual technologies will play a significant part in the plot's resolution, the characters' sensory alienation is not caused in the first instance by technological factors. Rather, it involves being subjected to the sensory perspective of a radically unknowable other, in the form of the aliens. The human characters are made painfully aware not only that their own sensory reach is limited but also that the world they occupy is no longer a world for them: it is an alien world, which can only be revealed through alien senses. They are forced to think of themselves as sound sources, as objects of their adversaries' sensory grasp. To make a noise is to single oneself out as a living body and thus as a target. In this way, the film expands upon horror's conventional use of silence as a generic device. William Whittington observes that horror films commonly use auditory representations of 'silence' to suggest danger: '[w]hen the wind stops or the footfalls cease, death is near'.[50] *A Quiet Place* adds to these mortal connotations by having its characters undertake a kind of self-annihilation through silencing. In their hushed subordination to the aliens' sensing capacities, they are forced to 'play dead'.

In this context, sound itself becomes an alien property, as the characters struggle with its excess or absence. *A Quiet Place* deals with this sensory alienation in somewhat regressive ways, by linking it with both disability and femininity in addition to technical mediation. Most overtly, these conceptual links are centred on the Abbotts' eldest child Regan, who is congenitally deaf and whose cochlear implant has ceased functioning. Regan's deafness links her to the aliens at several key moments. First of all, it is Regan that gives her brother the space shuttle toy his father has already denied him, unaware that Beau is also pocketing the batteries that will turn the toy into a deadly beacon, summoning the aliens. When the toy starts beeping, Regan's deafness means that she is the last to realise what has happened, even though she is closest to Beau. Later in the film, however, Regan's deafness takes on more positive associations when it is revealed that the aliens are incapacitated by the audio feedback from her cochlear implant. Placing the device on a microphone and amplifying it, she transforms sonic technology into a weapon, causing an alien's cranial carapace to open up involuntarily, and thus rendering it vulnerable to Evelyn's shotgun. A similar kind of sonic weaponisation occurs in *Don't Breathe*, when Rocky turns on the burglar alarm to overwhelm the blind man's hearing, and in *Hush*, when the protagonist disorients her attacker with a high-volume fire alarm for the deaf. In this case, however, Regan and the aliens share the same experience of auditory overload, a detail that seems to imply some kind of ontological alignment between them, even though her loyalty to the family is never in question. Indeed, one reason why the family has survived to this point is that they are able to communicate using sign language, which they have acquired as a result of Regan's disability. Her deafness is thus given both dangerous and redemptive connotations.

Sonic alienation in *A Quiet Place* is also associated with femininity and reproduction. Given her impending labour, Evelyn seems the character most at risk of advertising her presence to the aliens. By contrast,

Figure 6.3 Regan amplifies the feedback from her hearing aid in order to disable the aliens in *A Quiet Place* (John Krasinski, 2018)

Lee appears to have the greatest control over sound: on the one hand, he confidently suppresses sound by using the noise from a waterfall to cloak his conversation with his son; on the other, he deploys it decisively towards the end of the film by calling out to attract the aliens, thus sacrificing himself and saving his children's lives. Evelyn, however, struggles to manage sound's intimate attachment to the body. Going into labour in an empty bathtub, she must try to stifle her scream in order to avoid alerting the alien that has entered the house. As in the other films I have discussed, the trope of the female scream here evokes abjection, requiring bodily expulsion even as it locates and defines the (female) subject. The bloody smear that Lee later discovers in the bathtub is a visual index of this abjection, raising the question of whether Evelyn's involuntary vocalisation has proved fatal. As it turns out, she has eluded the alien by hiding in the shower. Later in the film, Evelyn takes refuge with her baby in the basement, which is filling with water owing to a leaking pipe. This watery, amniotic space is soon infiltrated by the questing alien, which lowers itself beneath the surface as Evelyn desperately plans her exit. Once again, sound threatens to escape the bounds of bodily discipline, as Evelyn is responsible for managing not only her own sonic imprint but also her baby's. Eventually, the baby is concealed within a bespoke soundproof coffin, as the family reassert their control over sound. Thus, on the one hand, sound is a sign of life: it is what mothers and babies produce. On the other, it is associated here with death, disorder and abjection.

The aliens' physical form extends this gendering of sound. Although there is no direct representation of their reproductive process that would match the uncanny eggs and grotesque 'facehugger' of the *Alien* franchise, these aliens' auditory organs nonetheless connect them to femininity and

reproduction. On several occasions the camera tracks into the moist cavi-
ties of their ear canals, which throb visibly in response to sound inputs.
This imagery conveys obvious vaginal connotations, as well as recalling
the human throat and, by extension, Evelyn's scream as she is giving birth.
A tight metaphorical relationship thus binds together various thematic
terms: vocalising and listening, the auditory canal and the birth canal,
the morbid corporeality of the aliens and the reproductive corporeality of
Evelyn. The aliens' auditory design also appears to blend the organic and
the mechanical. This is highlighted when Evelyn activates a kitchen timer
in order to distract one of the creatures. The ticking of the timer is interpolated with the similar ticking sound made by the alien as it listens, and
the timer's dial is matched graphically with the circular form of the alien's
auditory organ. Sound generation and sound reception are thus merged.
Similarly, Regan's use of her cochlear implant to overload the aliens with
feedback folds together sonic outputs and sonic inputs, mechanical and
organic vibrations, and human and alien audition. *A Quiet Place* thus
builds towards a kind of sensory and thematic feedback loop, in which
bodily experience and technical mediation are both implicated.

Sensory alienation in *A Quiet Place* is therefore not reducible to a representation of technology as threatening. Indeed, technology is linked also
with security, with civilisation and with human ingenuity. Regan's implant
is obviously key to the family's survival, as is their cobbled-together surveillance system. Like other post-apocalyptic narratives, *A Quiet Place*
proposes both technological know-how and human reproduction as vital
to imagining the continued existence of the species. At the same time,
both technological and bodily phenomena in the film are associated with
a loss of sonic control: from the space shuttle toy and the hearing implant
to the organic processes of birth and childrearing. The threat of sensory
alienation can thus be seen as emerging *both* from within technical mediation *and* embodied experience.

Furthermore, technology in *A Quiet Place* arguably works to amplify
experiential dislocations that are already native to the sensing body.
Writing about sonic mediations of cinematic violence, Steven Connor
muses that 'it may be that a certain violence, a violence done to the notion
of a continuous and organised and individuated body, is inseparable from
sound'.[51] From this perspective, Regan's amplification of her hearing aid
does not simply introduce a technological threat (both to the aliens and
herself); rather, it exposes a potential for experiential dislocation that
is already inherent to sound and audition. The senses, from this perspective, are associated in advance not with unity and identity but with
disorder and fragmentation. This account of bodily disarticulation aligns

with Jean-Luc Nancy's post-phenomenological theorisation of the body as a 'corpus of features' that are 'coming together *and* being dislocated at one and the same time'.[52] In *A Quiet Place* this sensory estrangement, this sense of sound as belonging to an alien body, is conveyed not only by the aliens themselves, but also by the various forms of self-alienation that are involved in suppressing sound or losing control over it. The body is therefore always already implicated in processes of mediation and fragmentation. In this context, sound is multi-dimensional and unstable: it is vitality and regeneration but also abjection, violence and disorder; it conveys human expression but also opens into the void of nonmeaning, from the inarticulacy of the scream to the sinister clacking of the aliens.

In *The Invisible Man* (2020), the separation of the senses is achieved via different means, but with a similar dimension of self-alienation. Escaping an abusive relationship, architect Cecilia Kass is tormented by her estranged partner Adrian Griffin, an optical researcher who has designed a suit covered in myriad small lenses that render him invisible. As her friends and family begin to doubt her sanity, Cecilia insists that Griffin, who has ostensibly committed suicide, is in fact very much alive and is stalking her. As in *A Quiet Place*, then, the protagonist is at a sensory disadvantage against a malevolent foe. Griffin's invisibility allows him to intervene in Cecilia's life in ways both small and large; his absent presence thus shapes the organisation of dramatic space. He is also, given his dependence on optical technology, a distinctly cinematic adversary. Whereas H. G. Wells's original novel and James Whale's 1933 film adaptation have the titular character acquire his power through chemical experimentation, in this case Griffin's lens-based suit renders him as a kind of camera-body. However, despite the plot's dependence on it, high technology remains largely concealed, meaning that Cecilia's primary engagements are with the world of everyday objects and appearances.

Griffin's threat is exacerbated by the minimal nature of his sonic presence. In this respect, the film differs from its 1933 counterpart, an early sound film which Michel Chion singles out for its 'discovery of the powers of the invisible voice'.[53] Chion describes the 1933 Griffin as an '*acousmetre*': a concealed vocal presence that is 'neither inside nor outside the image'.[54] He laughs at the authorities as they try to contain him and speaks freely with the other characters even as he remains visually absent. In the 2020 version, however, Griffin eschews verbal utterances for the most part (one notable exception is the 'surprise' that Cecilia hears in hospital as she is sedated following her sister's murder). Sound effects associated with Griffin's presence tend to be subtle, such as the faint sound of breath that accompanies a puff of vapour behind Cecilia's shoulder as she stands nervously outside in the cold. In violent scenes, sounds of bodily contact are fully audible, and later in the film the glitching of Griffin's optical suit produces small digital noises. Beyond that, however, there is an uncanny quietness to Griffin. The faintness of his sonic imprint seems closely aligned with his invisibility.

In this context, the 2020 version of *The Invisible Man* achieves its alienating effects primarily through a disjuncture within vision itself. Wearing his special suit, Griffin manifests only as an indexical presence: the depression in a seat cushion, an uncanny diversion in the earthward course of some raindrops, or the footprint on a bedsheet. As in the 1933 film, in which the police use Griffin's footprints in snow to locate him, Cecilia here sets up indexical clues, sprinkling coffee grounds across the kitchen floor in one scene and, in another, hurling a can of white paint over Griffin, producing a sudden, sinister apparition. Yet whereas the 1933 film has Griffin don bandages and garments, lending him a sense of physical presence in key scenes, here he is almost entirely absent from view. Later in the film, Griffin's suit malfunctions, rendering it as a flickering assemblage of black hexagons, and revealing the uncanny split that has been haunting the visual field throughout the film. In *The Invisible Man*, presence and absence coexist within the frame. In this way, the film provides a fantastical dramatisation of Jean-Luc Nancy's argument that the senses are intrinsically fragmentary, not merely in relation to other sensory modes. Sight, Nancy argues, cannot grasp the body. 'To see *a body* is precisely not to grasp it with *a* vision: sight itself is distended and spaced by this body here, it does not embrace the totality of *aspects*'.[55] The field of the visible is thus always haunted by invisibility. In *The Invisible* Man, the orchestration of dramatic space offers us vantage points from which to 'see' the invisible.

At certain points, this fragmentation of the visual field acquires a haptic dimension, such as when Griffin attacks Cecilia in the kitchen, lifting her up and hurling her around the room. We hear the sound of a metal dustpan hitting his head as she fights him off, but for the most part it is Cecilia's own body that communicates indexical audiovisual signs of Griffin's violent acts. Cecilia thus takes on the role of a medium: she is turned into an object twice over, firstly as a victim of violence and secondly as its sole visible signifier. For Cecilia, these various misaligned sensory cues produce a form of self-alienation that lead her to the point of mental breakdown, since the other characters do not believe her claims about Griffin.

This alienation effect is amplified by the use of film grammar to imply or assert Griffin's presence. Cinematic spatial conventions of framing and camera movement frequently present empty spaces in which one would normally expect to see a figure. The work of the film is thus to convince the viewer of a presence they cannot see. This is anticipated in the film's opening sequence, in which Cecilia escapes Griffin, tiptoeing through the cold, dark spaces of his vast minimalist house. Even though Griffin lies asleep in bed, a strong sense of paranoia is generated by shots implying a point-of-view perspective and lateral tracking movements that seem to 'stalk' Cecilia. As Cecilia carefully deactivates Griffin's security cameras, the film prepares us for the surveillant atmosphere that will pervade the entire narrative. Griffin is already an invisible presence, even before he dons his suit. As in *Don't Breathe*, the aggressor is a textual artefact, a function of the film's grammar that appears able to materialise at will. Later in the film, when Griffin engages in a confrontation with police, his textual agency is expressed through the excessive mobility of the camera, which swivels dynamically around the participants and tilts precipitously to capture the movement of falling bodies. Although the camera's elasticity of motion seems aligned with Griffin's swift and violent actions, his invisibility makes it difficult to distinguish between subjective and objective perspectives. At one point the camera follows the movement of a gun as it appears to float past an astonished officer, turning back to shoot him only after he has exited the frame. We hear the officer's body fall without seeing it. Griffin's invisible body is thus kept in the frame, while the officer's visible body is excluded. Through the use of cinematic devices, vision and bodily presence are broken apart.

Like *A Quiet Place*, *The Invisible Man* ultimately returns to audiovisual technologies in its framing of sensory alienation. At points throughout the film, such technologies present Cecilia with problems of perspective. For example, believing that Griffin has broken into her house, she calls his phone and hears it ringing from the attic; there, she discovers that it contains pictures of her sleeping. The spatial dislocation of images and sound is part of what makes this discovery uncanny. Similarly, when Cecilia infiltrates Griffin's house and explores his workspace, she encounters another type of mediated sensory dislocation, in the form of a video touchscreen through which she can manipulate the perspective of a hidden camera. She identifies herself in the image, viewed from behind, but struggles to find the camera itself. Grappling with this perspectival puzzle, she turns off the camera, at which point the invisibility suit becomes visible and thus reveals itself as the location of the hitherto concealed viewpoint. Similarly, when Cecilia is accused of her sister's murder, the police refer to surveillance video of her leaving the house, asking 'can you confirm the person in this video is you?' In each instance, the body's relationship to vision is defined by alienation.

This thematic thread is picked up and resolved at the end of the film, as Cecilia makes use of audiovisual technologies to turn Griffin's body against itself. Finally acceding to his demands, she goes to his house for dinner. The scene is structured around two types of surveillance, revealed via cutaways: firstly, one of Griffin's security cameras captures high-angle shots of the dining room, and secondly, a concealed microphone smuggled in by Cecilia relays audio to her police officer friend James, who listens from his car outside. Griffin hopes to convince Cecilia to reunite with him, but her mind is set on revenge. After trying and failing to persuade him to confess to his actions, she leaves for the bathroom. In her apparent absence, Griffin takes up a knife and slits his own throat, an event that is registered both via visual and sonic surveillance. Of course, it is not difficult to surmise that Cecilia has donned the suit in the interim and, in invisible form, engineered Griffin's apparent suicide. Strikingly, Griffin's re-entry into visibility in this scene, with the consequent relinking of his body and voice, is what marks him as vulnerable. In this respect, his fate mirrors that of his cinematic precursor: regarding the 1933 Griffin, Michel Chion observes that 'his downfall and death are linked to his return to the common fate of visibility'.[56] Thus, observes Chion, visibility and mortality are linked: 'to leave an impression on film is to be stamped with the seal of death that film places on those it captures'.[57] As in *Don't Breathe* and *A Quiet Place*, audiovisual synchrony bears fatal implications.

However, Cecilia's final triumph also involves a virtual dismantling of the sound–image bond. As she re-enters the room in visible form to 'discover' the fatally wounded Griffin, she performs a shocked reaction for three media channels: for the security camera, for her concealed microphone, and for the emergency responder whom she telephones to report the incident. Her next act remains covert, however: stationing herself out of view of the camera, she whispers 'surprise' to Griffin as his life ebbs away. Using the camera-suit and manipulating monitorial technologies, Cecilia thus escapes surveillance, her act of murder slipping between the gap separating image and sound. Encountering James as she leaves the house, she narrates her own version of Griffin's fate by assigning it to separate media formats, first image ('He cut his own throat. There's security camera video of it') and then sound ('You heard it, right, James? What did it sound like to you?'). In her victory over Griffin, Cecilia has rendered him as media, consigning him to two separate channels. The film concludes with a decisive cut to black as Cecilia closes her eyes: taking control over the senses, she has banished the image of Griffin from her life, making his invisibility final.

Like the other media-reflexive and 'sensory horror' films discussed in this chapter, *The Invisible Man* engages in a metaphorical exchange between bodies and media, inviting us to view each through the lens of the other. Walking away from Griffin's house at the end, Cecilia smuggles his camera-suit out in her bag, its presence revealed by a gentle technical whir. As she enjoys the feeling of having reclaimed her physical autonomy, her retention of this supplementary camera-body leaves open the possibility of further explorations of mediated sensing. As a technological 'skin', which is worn on the exterior of the body, the camera-suit might seem to imply that mediation comes from the outside. At the same time, however, it unveils processes that are internal to perception itself. First of all, it provides an analogue for the 'coming to presence' that Jean-Luc Nancy sees as already inherent to bodies. In this view, the body is not a static, given form, but something that emerges dynamically at the boundary of matter and discourse. Secondly, the camera-suit underlines the sensory estrangement that already inheres within perception, revealing the gaps and misalignments that shape our experience of the world. In the film's tense opening scenes, Cecilia's sensory estrangement is not directly dependent on the presence of the camera-suit's mediatised skin. Rather, this estrangement is already part of the material-discursive assemblage of the body, as a 'corpus of features' that are, writes Nancy, 'coming together *and* being dislocated at one and the same time'.[58] Like other examples of sensory horror, *The Invisible Man* produces an oscillation between unity and disunity, in which the body often seems on the verge of fragmenting into its component sensory worlds. In the process, it articulates a range of disjunctive experiences that emerge from the corporeal no less than the technological. Technology serves not as an alien threat from without, but as the signifier of an alienation that already haunts the body from within.

Notes

1. The term 'sensory horror' has appeared in several popular film review sites and blogs over recent years. See, for example, Kelly, '*Bird Box* and *A Quiet Place*: the trope of disability as a superpower and sensory horror'; 'The sensory themed horror trend has to end'; 'Top 5 sensory horror movies on Netflix'.
2. Merleau-Ponty, *Phenomenology of Perception*, p. 169.
3. Merleau-Ponty, 'The film and the new psychology', p. 58.
4. Ibid. p. 54.
5. Ibid. p. 55.
6. Nancy, *Corpus*, p. 31.
7. Ibid. p. 31.
8. Doane, 'Ideology and the practice of sound editing and mixing', p. 54.

9. Hutchings, *The Horror Film*, p. 134.
10. Whittington, 'Horror sound design', p. 169.
11. Ibid. p. 180–3.
12. Ibid. p. 182.
13. Donnelly, *Occult Aesthetics: Synchronization in Sound Film*, p. 3.
14. Ibid. p. 70.
15. Ibid. p. 22.
16. Ibid. p. 24.
17. Ibid. p. 73.
18. Ibid. p. 8.
19. Ibid. p. 134.
20. Ibid. p. 196.
21. Brophy, 'I scream in silence: cinema, sex and the sound of women dying', p. 53.
22. Ibid. p. 55.
23. Dolar, *A Voice and Nothing More*, p. 14.
24. Ibid. p. 15.
25. Darke, 'Uneasy listening', p. 35.
26. Schafer, *The Soundscape: Our Sonic Environment and the Tuning of the World*, p. 91.
27. Donnelly, *Occult Aesthetics*, p. 208.
28. Chion, *Audio-Vision: Sound on Screen*, pp. 25–6.
29. Ibid. p. 26.
30. Donaldson, 'The work of an invisible body: the contribution of foley artists to onscreen effort', p. 5.
31. Chion, *Audio-Vision*, p. 22.
32. Ibid. p. 23.
33. The act of looping these postproduction sounds also serves to highlight Chion's observation that reduced listening depends upon repeated listening, and therefore upon the recording of sound (p. 26).
34. Donaldson, 'The work of an invisible body: the contribution of foley artists to onscreen effort', p. 5.
35. Doane, 'The voice in the cinema: The articulation of body and space', p. 47.
36. Ibid. p. 34.
37. Ibid. p. 37.
38. Van Elferen, 'Sonic horror', p. 168.
39. Ibid. p. 167.
40. Ibid. p. 168.
41. Chion, *Audio-Vision*, p. 33.
42. Van Elferen, 'Sonic horror', p. 167.
43. Chion, *Audio-Vision*, p. 63.
44. Ibid. p. 59.
45. Ibid. p. 61.
46. Ibid. p. 62.

47. Donnelly, *Occult Aesthetics*, p. 112.
48. Ibid. p. 113.
49. Ibid. p. 8.
50. Whittington, 'Horror sound design', p. 183.
51. Connor, 'Sounding out film', p. 117.
52. Nancy, *Corpus*, p. 31.
53. Chion, *Audio-Vision*, pp. 126–7.
54. Ibid. p. 129. As Chion explains, the acousmetre 'is not inside, because the image of the voice's source—the body, the mouth—is not included. Nor is it outside, since it is not clearly positioned offscreen in an imaginary "wing," like a master of ceremonies or a witness, and it is implicated in the action, constantly about to be part of it' (p. 129).
55. Nancy, *Corpus*, p. 45.
56. Chion, *Audio-Vision*, p. 127.
57. Ibid. p. 128.
58. Nancy, *Corpus*, p. 31.

Bibliography

Abbott, Stacey, *Celluloid Vampires: Life after Death in the Modern World* (Austin: University of Texas Press, 2007).

Allen, Richard, 'Hitchcock's color designs', in Angela Dalle Vacche and Brian Price (eds), *Color: The Film Reader* (New York: Routledge, 2006), pp. 131–44.

Andrew, Dudley, *What Cinema Is!: Bazin's Quest and Its Charge* (Malden, MA and Oxford: Wiley-Blackwell, 2010).

Auerbach, Nina, *Our Vampires, Ourselves* (Chicago: University of Chicago Press, 1995).

Banash, David, '*The Blair Witch Project*: technology, repression, and the eviscera-tion of mimesis'. *Postmodern Culture* September 1999: 10; 1. <http://pmc.iath.virginia.edu/text-only/issue.999/10.1.r_banash.txt>

Barker, Jennifer M., *The Tactile Eye: Touch and the Cinematic Experience* (Berkeley: University of California Press, 2009).

Barthes, Roland, *Camera Lucida: Reflections on Photography*, translated by Richard Howard (New York: Hill and Wang, 1981).

Batchelor, David, *Chromophobia* (London: Reaktion, 2000).

Bazin, André, *What Is Cinema?* Vol. 1, translated by Hugh Gray (ed.) (Berkeley: University of California Press, 2005).

Beard, William, *The Artist as Monster: The Cinema of David Cronenberg* (Toronto: University of Toronto Press, 2001).

Benson-Allott, Caetlin, *Killer Tapes and Shattered Screens: Video Spectatorship from VHS to File Sharing* (Berkeley, CA: University of California Press, 2013).

Beugnet, Martine, *Cinema and Sensation: French Film and the Art of Transgression* (Edinburgh: Edinburgh University Press, 2007).

Bielik, Alain, '*Grindhouse*: pistol-packing VFX', *VFX World*, 27 February 2007. <http://www.awn.com/articles/reviews/igrindhousei-pistol-packing-vfx>

Bitel, Anton, '*Amer* (movie review)', *Sight and Sound*, 2011, 21: 2, p. 46.

Black, Joel, *The Aesthetics of Murder: A Study in Romantic Literature and Contemporary Culture* (Baltimore: Johns Hopkins University Press, 1991).

Blake, Linnie, *The Wounds of Nations: Horror Cinema, Historical Trauma and National Identity* (Manchester and New York: Manchester University Press, 2008).

Blake, Linnie and Xavier Aldana Reyes (eds), *Digital Horror: Haunted Technologies, Network Panic and the Found Footage Phenomenon* (London: IB Tauris, 2016).

Blake, Linnie and Xavier Aldana Reyes, 'Introduction: horror in the digital age', in Linnie Blake and Xavier Aldana Reyes (eds), *Digital Horror: Haunted Technologies, Network Panic and the Found Footage Phenomenon* (London: IB Tauris, 2016), pp. 1–13.

Bogost, Ian, *Alien Phenomenology, or, What It's Like to Be a Thing* (Minneapolis: University of Minnesota Press, 2012).

Bonitzer, Pascal, 'Deframings', in David Wilson (ed.), *Cahiers Du Cinéma: Volume Four, 1973–1978 : History, Ideology, Cultural Struggle* (London and New York: Routledge, 2000), pp. 197–203.

Botting, Fred, *Gothic*, 2nd edition (Abingdon, Oxon and New York: Routledge, 2014).

Botting, Fred, and Catherine Spooner, 'Introduction: monstrous media/ spectral subjects', in Fred Botting and Catherine Spooner (eds), *Monstrous Media/ Spectral Subjects: Imaging Gothic from the Nineteenth Century to the Present* (Manchester: Manchester University Press, 2015), pp. 1–11.

Branigan, Edward, *Projecting a Camera: Language-Games in Film Theory* (London: Routledge, 2006).

Branigan, Edward, 'The articulation of color in a filmic system: *Two or Three Things I Know About Her*', in Angela Dalle Vacche and Brian Price (eds), *Color: The Film Reader* (New York: Routledge, 2006), pp. 170–82.

Briefel, Aviva, and Sam J. Miller (eds), *Horror After 9/11 World of Fear, Cinema of Terror* (Austin: University of Texas Press, 2011).

Brooks, Max, *World War Z* (London: Duckworth, 2006).

Brophy, Philip, 'I scream in silence: cinema, sex and the sound of women dying', in Philip Brophy (ed.), *Cinesonic: Cinema and the Sound of Music* (North Ryde, NSW: Australian Film Television & Radio School, 1999), pp. 51–78.

Burke, Edmund, *A Philosophical Enquiry into the Sublime and Beautiful*. James T. Boulton (ed.), 2nd edn (London and New York: Routledge Classics, 2008).

Cameron, Allan, 'Facing the glitch: abstraction, abjection and the digital image', in Martine Beugnet, Allan Cameron and Arild Fetveit (eds), *Indefinite Visions: Cinema and the Attractions of Uncertainty* (Edinburgh: Edinburgh University Press, 2017), pp. 334–52.

Carroll, Noël, *The Philosophy of Horror, or Paradoxes of the Heart* (New York: Routledge, 1990).

Cavell, Stanley, *The World Viewed: Reflections on the Ontology of Film* (Cambridge: Harvard University Press, 1979).

Cherry, Brigid, *Horror* (London and New York: Routledge, 2009).

Chion, Michel, *Audio-Vision: Sound on Screen*, translated by Claudia Gorbman (New York: Columbia University Press, 1994).

Christensen, Steen, 'Uncanny cameras and network subjects', in Linnie Blake and Xavier Aldana Reyes (eds), *Digital Horror: Haunted Technologies,*

Network Panic and the Found Footage Phenomenon (London: IB Tauris, 2016), pp. 42–53.

Clarens, Carlos, *An Illustrated History of the Horror Film* (New York: Capricorn Books, 1967).

Clover, Carol J., *Men, Women, and Chain Saws: Gender in the Modern Horror Film* (Princeton, NJ: Princeton University Press, 1993).

Colebrook, Claire, 'Jean-Luc Nancy', in Felicity Colman (ed.), *Film, Theory and Philosophy: The Key Thinkers* (Montreal and Kingston: McGill-Queen's University Press, 2009), pp. 154–63.

Connor, Steven, *The Book of Skin* (London: Reaktion Books, 2004).

Connor, Steven, 'Sounding out film', in John Richardson, Claudia Gorbman, and Carol Vernallis (eds), *The Oxford Handbook of New Audiovisual Aesthetics* (Malden, MA: Oxford University Press, 2013), pp. 107–20.

Conterio, Martyn, 'Doors and their secrets: the legacy of 1940s Hollywood in *The Strange Colour of Your Body's Tears* (2013)'. *Senses of Cinema*, no. 87 (June 2018). <http://sensesofcinema.com/2018/split-screen-cattet-forzani/1940s-hollywood-in-the-strange-colour-of-your-bodys-tears/>

Cooper, L. Andrew, *Dario Argento* (Urbana: University of Illinois Press, 2012).

Creed, Barbara, *The Monstrous-Feminine: Film, Feminism, Psychoanalysis* (London and New York: Routledge, 1993).

Cubitt, Sean, *The Practice of Light: A Genealogy of Visual Technologies from Prints to Pixels* (Cambridge, MA: MIT Press, 2014).

Darke, Chris, 'Uneasy listening', *Film Comment*, May–June 2013: 32–5.

Dendle, Peter, *The Zombie Movie Encyclopedia* (Jefferson, NC: McFarland & Co, 2001).

Denson, Shane, *Postnaturalism: Frankenstein, Film, and the Anthropotechnical Interface* (Bielefeld, Germany: Transcript, 2014).

Denson, Shane, 'Crazy cameras, discorrelated images, and the post-perceptual mediation of post-cinematic affect', in Shane Denson and Julia Leyda (eds), *Post-Cinema: Theorizing 21st-Century Film* (Falmer, UK: REFRAME Books, 2016), pp. 193–233. <http://reframe.sussex.ac.uk/post-cinema/>

Diffrient, Scott, 'A film is being beaten: notes on the shock cut and the material violence of horror', in Steffen Hantke (ed.), *Horror Film: Creating and Marketing Fear* (Jackson: University Press of Mississippi, 2004), pp. 52–81.

Doane, Mary Ann, 'Ideology and the practice of sound editing and mixing', in Teresa De Lauretis and Stephen Heath (eds), *The Cinematic Apparatus* (London: Palgrave Macmillan, 1980), pp. 47–56.

Doane, Mary Ann, *The Emergence of Cinematic Time: Modernity, Contingency, the Archive* (Cambridge, MA: Harvard University Press, 2002).

Doane, Mary Ann, 'The indexical and the concept of medium specificity', *Differences*, 2007, 18; 1, 128–52.

Doane, Mary Ann, 'The voice in the cinema: the articulation of body and space', *Yale French Studies*, 1980, 60: 33–50.

Dolar, Mladen, *A Voice and Nothing More.* (Cambridge, MA: MIT Press, 2006).

Donaldson, Lucy Fife, 'The work of an invisible body: the contribution of foley artists to onscreen effort', *Alphaville: Journal of Film and Screen Media*, 2014, 7.

Donnelly, K. J., *Occult Aesthetics: Synchronization in Sound Film* (New York: Oxford University Press, 2014).

Douglas, Mary, *Purity and Danger: An Analysis of Concepts of Pollution and Taboo* (London: Routledge and Kegan Paul, 1966).

Dyer, Richard, *White* (Abingdon, Oxon: Psychology Press, 1997).

Edelstein, David, 'Limp Trysts', *Village Voice*, 11 August 1987, 32: 58.

Eisenstein, Sergei, *Film Form: Essays in Film Theory, and The Film Sense*, translated by Jay Leyda (ed.) (New York: Meridan Books, 1960).

Elsaesser, Thomas, 'Freud and the technical media: the enduring magic of the Wunderblock', in Erkki Huhtamo and Jussi Parikka (eds), *Media Archaeology: Approaches, Applications, and Implications* (Berkeley: University of California Press, 2011), pp. 95–115.

Elsaesser, Thomas, 'The mind-game film', in Warren Buckland (ed.), *Puzzle Films: Complex Storytelling in Contemporary Cinema* (Malden, MA: Wiley-Blackwell, 2009), pp. 13–41.

Freeland, Cynthia, 'Horror and art-dread', in Stephen Prince (ed.), *The Horror Film* (New Brunswick, NJ: Rutgers University Press, 2004), pp. 189–205.

Freeland, Cynthia, *The Naked and the Undead: Evil and the Appeal of Horror* (Boulder, CO: Westview Press, 2000).

Freeman-Mills, Max, 'Mike Booth, the achitect of *Left 4 Dead*'s AI director, explains why it's so bloody good', *Kotaku*, November 20, 2018. <https://www.kotaku.co.uk/2018/11/19/mike-booth-the-architect-of-left-4-deads-ai-director-explains-why-its-so-bloody-good>

Freud, Sigmund, 'The uncanny', in James Strachey (ed. and translator), *The Standard Edition of the Complete Psychological Works of Sigmund Freud* (London: Hogarth Press, 1953), pp. 219–52.

Gage, John, *Color and Meaning: Art, Science, and Symbolism* (Berkeley: University of California Press, 2000).

Gelder, Ken, *Reading the Vampire* (London: Routledge, 1994).

Glut, Donald F., *The Frankenstein Catalog* (Jefferson, NC: McFarland, 1984).

Godard, Jean-Luc, *Godard on Godard: Critical Writings*. Jean Narboni and Tom Milne (eds), translated by Tom Milne (London: Secker and Warburg, 1972).

Grahame-Smith, Seth, and Jane Austen, *Pride and Prejudice and Zombies* (Philadelphia: Quirk Books, 2009).

Grant, Barry Keith, 'Digital anxiety and the new verité horror and SF film', *Science Fiction Film and Television* 2013, 6; 2: 153–75.

Grant, Barry Keith (ed.), *The Dread of Difference: Gender and the Horror Film*, 2nd edn (Austin: University of Texas Press, 2015).

Gunning, Tom, 'Moving away from the index: cinema and the impression of reality'. *Differences*, 2007, 18; 1: 29–52.

Gunning, Tom, 'To scan a ghost: the ontology of mediated vision', *Grey Room*, 2007, 26: 95–127.

Halberstam, Judith, *Skin Shows: Gothic Horror and the Technology of Monsters* (Durham: Duke University Press, 1995).

Hantke, Steffen (ed.), *American Horror Film: The Genre at the Turn of the Millennium* (Jackson: University Press of Mississippi, 2010).

Hantke, Steffen, 'Network anxiety: prefiguring digital anxieties in the American horror film', in Linnie Blake and Xavier Aldana Reyes (eds), *Digital Horror: Haunted Technologies, Network Panic and the Found Footage Phenomenon* (London: IB Tauris, 2016), pp. 17–28.

Heath, Stephen, 'Narrative space', *Screen*, 1976, 17; 3: 68–112.

Heath, Stephen, 'Notes on suture', *Screen*, 1977, 18; 4: 48–76.

Heidegger, Martin, 'The question concerning technology', in *The Question Concerning Technology and Other Essays*, translated by William Lovitt (New York: Harper and Row, 1977), pp. 3–35.

Hervey, Ben, *Night of the Living Dead* (Basingstoke: Palgrave Macmillan, 2008).

Humphries, Reynold, 'Just another fashion victim: Mario Bava's *Sei Donne per l'assassino* (*Blood and Black Lace*, 1964)'. *Kinoeye* November 2001, 1; 7. <http://www.kinoeye.org/01/07/humphries07.php>

Hunt, Leon, 'A (sadistic) night at the opera: notes on the Italian horror film', in Ken Gelder (ed.), *The Horror Reader* (London and New York: Routledge, 2000), pp. 324–35.

Hunt, Leon, Sharon Lockyer, and Milly Williamson (eds.), *Screening the Undead: Vampires and Zombies in Film and Television* (London and New York: IB Tauris, 2014).

Hutchings, Peter, *The Horror Film* (Harlow: Pearson Longman, 2004).

Izutsu, Toshihiko, 'The elimination of color in far eastern art and philosophy', in *Color Symbolism: Six Excerpts from the Eranos Yearbook 1972* (Dallas: Spring Publications, 1977), pp. 167–95.

Jackson, Kimberly, *Technology, Monstrosity, and Reproduction in Twenty-First Century Horror* (New York: Palgrave Macmillan, 2013).

Jay, Martin, *Downcast Eyes: The Denigration of Vision in Twentieth-Century French Thought* (Berkeley: University of California Press, 1993).

Kannas, Alexia, 'All the colours of the dark: film genre and the Italian *giallo*', *Journal of Italian Cinema & Media Studies*, 2017, 5; 2: 173–90.

Karlin, Susan, 'How *The Walking Dead* brings new life to zombies—without CGI', *Fast Company*, 8 October 2010. <http://www.fastcompany.com/1693376/the-walking-dead-amc>

Kelly, Fiona L. F., '*Bird Box* and *A Quiet Place*: the trope of disability as a super-power and sensory horror', *The Mary Sue*, 20 February 2019. <https://www.themarysue.com/bird-box-a-quiet-place-sensory-horror-disability/>

Kermode, Frank, *The Sense of an Ending* (London: Oxford University Press, 1967).

Kim, Jihoon, *Between Film, Video, and the Digital: Hybrid Moving Images in the Post-Media Age* (New York: Bloomsbury, 2016).

Kirk, Neal, 'Networked spectrality: *In Memorium, Pulse* and beyond', in Linnie Blake and Xavier Aldana Reyes (eds), *Digital Horror: Haunted Technologies, Network Panic and the Found Footage Phenomenon* (London: IB Tauris, 2016), pp. 54–65.

Kirkland, Ewan, '*Resident Evil*'s typewriter: survival horror and its remediations', *Games and Culture* 1 April 2009, 4; 2: 115–26.

Kittler, Friedrich A., 'Dracula's legacy', in John Johnston (ed.), *Literature, Media, Information Systems*, translated by William Stephen Davis (Abingdon, Oxon and New York: Routledge, 2012), pp. 50–84.

Koven, Mikel J., *La Dolce Morte: Vernacular Cinema and the Italian Giallo Film* (Lanham, MD: Scarecrow Press, 2006).

Kristeva, Julia, *Powers of Horror: An Essay on Abjection*, translated by Leon S. Roudiez (New York: Columbia University Press, 1982).

Krzywinska, Tanya, 'Zombies in gamespace: form, content, and meaning in zombie-based video games', in Shawn McIntosh and Marc Leverette (eds), *Zombie Culture: Autopsies of the Living Dead* (Lanham, MD: Scarecrow Press, 2008), pp. 153–68.

Lacefield, Kristen (ed.), *The Scary Screen: Media Anxiety in The Ring* (Burlington: Ashgate, 2010).

Leeder, Murray (ed.), *Cinematic Ghosts: Haunting and Spectrality from Silent Cinema to the Digital Era* (New York: Bloomsbury, 2015).

Lowenstein, Adam, *Shocking Representation: Historical Trauma, National Cinema, and the Modern Horror Film* (New York: Columbia University Press, 2005).

Lowenstein, Adam, 'The giallo/slasher landscape: *Ecologia Del Delitto, Friday the 13th* and subtractive spectatorship', in Stefano Baschiera and Russ Hunter (eds), *Italian Horror Cinema* (Edinburgh: Edinburgh University Press, 2016), pp. 127–44.

Luckhurst, Roger, *Zombies: A Cultural History* (London: Reaktion Books, 2016).

MacCormack, Patricia, 'Barbara Steele's ephemeral skin: feminism, fetishism and film', *Senses of Cinema*, 4 October 2002. <http://sensesofcinema.com/2002/feature-articles/steele/>

Marks, Laura U., *The Skin of the Film: Intercultural Cinema, Embodiment, and the Senses* (Durham: Duke University Press, 2000).

McDonagh, Maitland, *Broken Mirrors, Broken Minds: The Dark Dreams of Dario Argento*, Expanded edn (Minneapolis: University of Minnesota Press, 2010).

McIntosh, Shawn, 'The evolution of the zombie: the monster that keeps coming back', in Shawn McIntosh and Marc Leverette (eds), *Zombie Culture: Autopsies of the Living Dead* (Lanham, MD: Scarecrow Press, 2008), pp. 1–17.

Merleau-Ponty, Maurice, *Phenomenology of Perception*, translated by Colin Smith (London: Routledge, 2002).

Merleau-Ponty, Maurice, 'The film and the new psychology', in *Sense and Non-*

Sense, translated by Herbert L. Dreyfus and Patricia Allen Dreyfus (Evanston, IL: Northwestern University Press, 1964), pp. 48–59.

Misek, Richard, *Chromatic Cinema: A History of Screen Color* (Malden, MA: Wiley-Blackwell, 2010).

Monnet, Agnieszka Soltysik, 'Night vision in the contemporary horror film', in Linnie Blake and Xavier Aldana Reyes (eds), *Digital Horror: Haunted Technologies, Network Panic and the Found Footage Phenomenon* (London: IB Taurus, 2016), pp. 123–36.

Mulvey, Laura, *Death 24x a Second: Stillness and the Moving Image* (London: Reaktion Books, 2015).

Nancy, Jean-Luc, *Corpus*, translated by Richard A. Rand (New York: Fordham University Press, 2008).

Nancy, Jean-Luc, *The Ground of the Image*, translated by Jeff Fort (New York: Fordham University Press, 2005).

Neale, Stephen, *Cinema and Technology: Image, Sound, Colour* (London: Macmillan Education, 1985).

Needham, Gary, 'Playing with genre: an introduction to the Italian "giallo"', *Kinoeye* 2002, 2; 11. <https://www.kinoeye.org/02/11/needham11.php>

North, Daniel, 'Evidence of things not quite seen: *Cloverfield*'s obstructed spectacle', *Film & History* 2010, 40; 1: 75–92.

Oeler, Karla, *A Grammar of Murder: Violent Scenes and Film Form* (Chicago: University of Chicago Press, 2009).

Oeler, Karla, 'Eisenstein and horror', *Journal of Visual Culture* 2015, 14; 3: 317–331.

Olivier, Marc, 'Glitch gothic', in Murray Leeder (ed.), *Cinematic Ghosts: Haunting and Spectrality from Silent Cinema to the Digital Era* (New York: Bloomsbury, 2015), pp. 253–70.

Olney, Ian, *Euro Horror: Classic European Horror Cinema in Contemporary American Culture* (Bloomington: Indiana University Press, 2013).

Olney, Ian, *Zombie Cinema* (New Brunswick, NJ: Rutgers University Press, 2017).

Oudart, Jean-Pierre, 'Cinema and suture', *Screen,* 1977, 18; 4: 35–47.

Pagano, David, 'The space of apocalypse in zombie cinema', in Shawn McIntosh and Marc Leverette (eds), *Zombie Culture: Autopsies of the Living Dead* (Lanham, MD: Scarecrow Press, 2008), pp. 71–86.

Pegg, Simon, 'The dead and the quick', *The Guardian*, 4 November 2008. <https://www.theguardian.com/media/2008/nov/04/television-simon-pegg-dead-set>

Pethő, Ágnes, *Cinema and Intermediality: The Passion for the In-Between* (Newcastle upon Tyne: Cambridge Scholars Publishing, 2011).

Price, Brian, 'Color, the formless, and cinematic eros', *Framework,* Spring 2006, 47; 1: 22–35.

Prince, Stephen (ed.), *The Horror Film* (New Brunswick, NJ: Rutgers University Press, 2004).

Radcliffe, Ann, 'On the supernatural in poetry', *New Monthly Magazine*, 1826, 16: 145–52.

Rajewsky, Irina O., 'Intermediality, intertextuality, and remediation: a literary perspective on intermediality', *Intermédialités: Histoire et Théorie Des Arts, Des Lettres et Des Techniques* 2005, 6: 43–64.

Rodowick, D. N., *The Virtual Life of Film* (Cambridge, MA: Harvard University Press, 2007).

Russell, Jamie, *Book of the Dead: The Complete History of Zombie Cinema* (Godalming: FAB Press, 2008).

Sayad, Cecilia, 'Found-footage horror and the frame's undoing', *Cinema Journal* 2016, 55; 2: 43–66.

Schafer, R. Murray, *The Soundscape: Our Sonic Environment and the Tuning of the World* (Rochester, VT: Destiny Books, 1993).

Schneider, Steven Jay, 'Murder as art/the art of murder: aestheticizing violence in modern cinematic horror', in Steven Jay Schneider and Daniel Shaw (eds), *Dark Thoughts: Philosophic Reflections on Cinematic Horror* (Lanham, MD: Scarecrow Press, 2003), pp. 174–97.

Schoonover, Karl, 'Scrap metal, stains, clogged drains: Argento's refuse and its refusals', in Stefano Baschiera and Russ Hunter (eds), *Italian Horror Cinema* (Edinburgh: Edinburgh University Press, 2016), pp. 111–26.

Sconce, Jeffrey, *Haunted Media: Electronic Presence from Telegraphy to Television* (Durham, NC: Duke University Press, 2000).

Seet, K. K., 'Mothers and daughters: abjection and the monstrous-feminine in Japan's *Dark Water* and South Korea's *A Tale of Two Sisters*', *Camera Obscura* 2009, 24; 2: 139–159.

Serres, Michel, *Les cinq sens* (Paris: Hachette Littératures, 1998).

Shaviro, Steven, *The Cinematic Body* (Minneapolis: University of Minnesota Press, 1993).

Shaviro, Steven, *The Universe of Things: On Speculative Realism* (Minneapolis, MN: University of Minnesota Press, 2014).

Shaviro, Steven, 'The glitch dimension: *Paranormal Activity* and the technologies of vision', in Martine Beugnet, Allan Cameron, and Arild Fetveit (eds), *Indefinite Visions: Cinema and the Attractions of Uncertainty* (Edinburgh: Edinburgh University Press, 2017), pp. 316–33.

Silver, Alain, and James Ursini, *The Vampire Film: From Nosferatu to Interview with a Vampire*, 3rd edn (New York: Limelight Editions, 1997).

Silverman, Kaja, *The Subject of Semiotics* (Oxford University Press, 1983).

Sobchack, Vivian, *The Address of the Eye: A Phenomenology of Film Experience* (Princeton, NJ: Princeton University Press, 1992).

Sobchack, Vivian, *Screening Space: The American Science Fiction Film*, 2nd edn (New Brunswick, NJ: Rutgers University Press, 1997).

Sobchack, Vivian, 'The scene of the screen: envisioning photographic, cinematic, and electronic "presence"', in *Carnal Thoughts: Embodiment and Moving Image Culture* (Berkeley: University of California Press, 2004), pp. 135–62.

Sobchack, Vivian, 'What my fingers knew: the cinesthetic subject, or vision in the flesh', in *Carnal Thoughts: Embodiment and Moving Image Culture* (Berkeley: University of California Press, 2004), pp. 53–84.

Spadoni, Robert, *Uncanny Bodies: The Coming of Sound Film and the Origins of the Horror Genre* (Berkeley: University of California Press, 2007).

Stewart, Garrett, *Between Film and Screen: Modernism's Photo Synthesis* (Chicago: University of Chicago Press, 1999).

Stewart, Garrett, 'Body snatching: science fiction's photographic trace', in Annette Kuhn (ed.), *Alien Zone II: The Spaces of Science-Fiction Cinema* (London: Verso, 1999), pp. 226–48.

Stewart, Garrett, *Framed Time: Toward a Postfilmic Cinema* (Chicago: University of Chicago Press, 2007).

Stoker, Bram, *Dracula* (London: Penguin, 2010).

'The sensory themed horror trend has to end', *Filmsane*, 30 March 2019. <https://filmsane.com/the-sensory-themed-horror-trend-has-to-end/>

'Top 5 sensory horror movies on Netflix', *Cinesister*, 5 May 2020. <https://cinesister.com/top-5-sensory-horror-movies-on-netflix/>

Totaro, Donato, 'Amer: the three faces of Ana', *Offscreen* December 2009, 13; 12. <https://offscreen.com/view/amer>

Trigg, Dylan, *The Thing: A Phenomenology of Horror* (Winchester: Zero Books, 2014).

Van Elferen, Isabella, 'Sonic horror', *Horror Studies* 1 October 2016, 7; 2: 165–72.

Vint, Sherryl, 'Abject posthumanism: neoliberalism, biopolitics, and zombies', in Sarah Juliet Lauro (ed.), *Zombie Theory: A Reader* (Minneapolis: University of Minnesota Press, 2017).

Weinstock, Jeffrey, *The Vampire Film: Undead Cinema* (London: Wallflower, 2012).

Wells, Paul, *The Horror Genre: From Beelzebub to Blair Witch* (London: Wallflower, 2000).

Whittington, William, 'Horror sound design', in Harry M. Benshoff (ed.), *A Companion to the Horror Film* (Malden, MA: Wiley Blackwell, 2014), pp. 168–85.

Wicke, Jennifer, 'Vampiric typewriting: *Dracula* and its media', *ELH* 1992, 59; 2: 467–93.

Williams, Linda, 'Film bodies: genre, gender and excess', in Barry Keith Grant (ed.), *Film Genre Reader II* (Austin: University of Texas Press, 1995), pp. 140–58.

Wood, Robin, *Hollywood from Vietnam to Reagan* (New York: Columbia University Press, 1986).

Zani, Steven, and Kevin Meaux, 'Lucio Fulci and the decaying definition of zombie narratives', in Deborah Christie and Sarah Juliet Lauro (eds), *Better off Dead: The Evolution of the Zombie as Post-Human* (New York: Fordham University Press, 2011), pp. 98–115.

Zizek, Slavoj, *Enjoy Your Symptom!: Jacques Lacan in Hollywood and Out* (London: Routledge, 2001).

'Zombies! Run! (TxDOT Is Not Amused)', *NBC Dallas–Fort Worth*, 17 July 2009. <https://www.nbcdfw.com/news/local/Zombies-Run-TxDOT-is-Not-Amused.html>

Index

Illustrations are indicated by page numbers in bold.